LLEWELLYN'S

2015

Magical Almanac

Featuring

Deanna Anderson, Blake Octavian Blair,
Deborah Blake, Boudica, Emily Carlin,
Dallas Jennifer Cobb, Monica Crosson,
Autumn Damiana, Raven Digitalis, Ellen Dugan,
Emyme, Sybil Fogg, Darcy Blue French, Shawna Galvin,
Magenta Griffith, James Kambos, Najah Lightfoot,
Lupa, Melanie Marquis, Lisa Mc Sherry, Mickie Mueller,
Susan Pesznecker, Suzanne Ress, Cassius Sparrow,
Ellen Coutts Waff, Charlynn Walls,
Lunaea Weatherstone, Tess Whitehurst,
Charlie Rainbow Wolf, and Natalie Zaman

Llewellyn's 2015
Magical Almanac

ISBN 978-0-7387-2685-4. Copyright © 2014 by Llewellyn. All rights reserved. Printed in the United States. Llewellyn is a registered trademark of Llewellyn Worldwide Ltd.

Editor/Designer: Ed Day

Cover Illustration: © Tammy Shane

Calendar Pages Design: Michael Fallon

Calendar Pages Illustrations: © Fiona King

Interior Illustrations © Meraylah Allwood: pages 41, 45, 135, 139, 247, 250, 293, 296, 298; © Carol Coogan: pages 27, 31, 72, 75, 121, 124, 225, 228, 281, 283, 329, 331; © Chris Down: pages 35, 37, 79, 83, 85, 127, 237, 241, 266, 270, 286, 288; © Kathleen Edwards: pages 15, 18, 107, 110, 113, 217, 220, 306, 309; © Wen Hsu: pages 13, 20, 23, 59, 61, 62, 77, 89, 90, 115, 118, 215, 253, 279, 317, 319, 323, 326; © Mickie Mueller: pages 46, 48, 50, 65, 68, 93, 96, 141, 144, 147, 231, 234, 274, 277, 303; © Amber Zoellner: pages 53, 54, 56, 101, 104, 257, 261, 263, 313.

Clip Art Illustrations: Dover Publications

Special thanks to Amber Wolfe for the use of daily color and incense correspondences. For more detailed information, please see *Personal Alchemy* by Amber Wolfe.

You can order Llewellyn annuals and books from *New Worlds*, Llewellyn's catalog. To request a free copy of the catalog, call toll-free 1-877-NEW-WRLD or visit our website: www.llewellyn.com

Astrological data compiled and programmed by Rique Pottenger. Based on the earlier work of Neil F. Michelsen.

Llewellyn Worldwide Ltd.
2143 Wooddale Drive
Woodbury, MN 55125

About the Authors

DEANNA ANDERSON is the author of *Magick for the Kitchen Witch* (2009) and *Magick for the Elemental Witch* (2010). A third-degree progressive Pagan with a local coven, she has been practicing for almost ten years. Deanna is a certified freelance writer with Penn Foster (2010) and has been studying tarot for four years. In 2011, she created the study group "STAR: Sumter Tarot and Runes."

BLAKE OCTAVIAN BLAIR is an eclectic Pagan, ordained minister, shamanic practitioner, writer, Usui Reiki Master-Teacher, tarot reader, and musical artist. Blake blends various mystical traditions from the East and West along with a reverence for the natural world into his own brand of modern Neo-Paganism and magick. Blake holds a degree in English and Religion from the University of Florida. An avid reader, crafter, and practicing vegetarian, Blake lives with his beloved husband, an aquarium full of fish, and an indoor jungle of houseplants. Visit www.blakeoctavianblair.com.

DEBORAH BLAKE is a Wiccan High Priestess who has been leading Blue Moon Circle for years. She is the author of *Circle, Coven and Grove, Everyday Witch A to Z, The Goddess is in the Details,* and *The Everyday Witch A to Z Spellbook.* She also runs The Artisans' Guild and works as a jewelry maker, a tarot reader, and an Intuitive Energy Healer. She lives in rural upstate New York with five cats who supervise her activities, both magickal and mundane.

BOUDICA is best known for her professional reviews of books on paganism. She and her husband ran the *Wiccan/Pagan Times* website until retiring it to pursue other ventures. She also ran Zodiac Bistro, a repository of articles, commentaries, and reviews. A supporter of building Pagan community, she has worked in covens and also has a solitary practice. She also presents at events and holds public workshops in the Northeast, and now runs an online

bookstore and reads tarot cards for clients. Boudica lives in Bucks County, Pennsylvania, with her husband of many years and her cats.

EMILY CARLIN is an eclectic witch, mediator, and attorney based in Seattle, Washington. She specializes in shadow work and defensive magick. Emily teaches extensively online at the Grey School and at Pagan events around the Puget Sound area. Her book *Defense Against the Dark*, a guide to all things that go bump in the night and what to do about them, is available online and at major retailers.

DALLAS JENNIFER COBB practices gratitude magic, giving thanks for her magical life, happy and healthy family, meaningful and flexible work, and joyous life. She believes the Goddess will provide time, energy, wisdom, and money to accomplish all her deepest desires. She lives in paradise—a waterfront village in rural Ontario. Contact her at jennifer.cobb@live.com.

MONICA CROSSON is a Master Gardener who lives in the beautiful Pacific Northwest happily digging in the dirt and tending her raspberries with her husband, three kids, two goats, two dogs, three cats, a dozen chickens, and Rosetta the donkey. She has been a practicing witch for twenty years and is a member of Blue Moon Coven. Monica writes fiction for young adults and is the author of *Summer Sage*. Visit her website at www.monicacrosson.com.

AUTUMN DAMIANA is a writer, artist, crafter, and amateur photographer, and has been a mostly solitary eclectic Witch for fourteen years. She is passionate about eco-friendly living and writes about this and her day-to-day walk on the Pagan path in her blog "Sacred Survival in a Mundane World" at http://autumndamiana.blogspot.com/. When not writing or making art, you can find her outside enjoying nature or investigating local history in her hometown of San Jose, California. Contact her at autumndamiana@gmail.com.

RAVEN DIGITALIS is the author of *Planetary Spells & Rituals*, *Shadow Magick Compendium*, and *Goth Craft*, all from Llewellyn.

He is a Neopagan Priest, cofounder of an Eastern Hellenistic Coven and Order called Opus Aima Obscuræ (OAO), and a DJ. Also trained in Georgian Witchcraft and Buddhist philosophy, Raven holds a degree in anthropology and is also an animal rights activist, photographic artist, tarot reader, and co-owner of Twigs & Brews Herbs. www.ravendigitalis.com, www.myspace.com/oakraven, www.facebook.com/ravendigitalisauthor.

ELLEN DUGAN, the "Garden Witch," is an award-winning author and psychic-clairvoyant. A practicing Witch for more than thirty years, she is the author of many Llewellyn books; her newest are *Seasons of Witchery*, *Witches Tarot*, and *Practical Prosperity Magick*. Ellen encourages folks to personalize their spellcraft and to go outside and get their hands dirty so they can discover the wonder and magick of the natural world. Ellen and her family live in Missouri. Visit her at www.ellendugan.blogspot.com or www.ellendugan.com.

EMYME is a solitary practitioner who resides in a multigenerational, multicat household in southern New Jersey. Hobbies that renew her are gardening, sewing and crafts, and home care and repair. Emyme has self-published a children's book about mending families after divorce and remarriage. She is an avid diarist; dabbles in poetry; creates her own blessings, incantations, and spells; and is writing a series of fantasy fiction stories. Her personal mantra is: Curiosity, Objectivity, Quality, Integrity. catsmeow24@verizon.net.

SYBIL FOGG has been a practicing witch for over twenty- five years. Her real name is Sybil Wilen, but she uses her mother's maiden name in Pagan circles to honor her grandparents. She's also a wife, mother, writer, teacher, and belly dancer. Her family shares her passion for magic, dance, and writing. She lives in Saco, Maine, with her husband and children. For more, website: www.sybilwilen.com.

DARCY BLUE FRENCH is a Clinical and Shamanic Herbalist in Tucson, Arizona, where she sees private clients and teaches the Sacred

Earth Medicine Herbal Apprenticeship and offers herbal products and CSA shares. Trained as a clinical herbalist and nutritionist at the North American Institute of Medical Herbalism, she has been using and learning from the plants (both wild and cultivated) since childhood, which fuels her passion for healing and teaching about plants, wilderness, spirit, nourishment, and healing. For more, visit www.shamanaflora.com or www.blueturtlebotanicals.com.

Shawna Galvin has always been drawn to magic and healing, natural elements such as rocks and minerals, and herbal remedies. She has an MFA in fiction and creative writing. Her poetry, reviews, short stories, and flash fiction pieces have appeared in various publications, and her novel *The Ghost in You* was released in 2013. Shawna lives in southern Maine with her husband and son, the most powerful magic in her life. shawnagalvin.com.

Magenta Griffith has been a Witch for more than thirty years and a High Priestess for more than twenty. She is a founding member of the coven Prodea, which has been celebrating rituals since 1980, as well as being a member of various Pagan organizations such as Covenant of the Goddess. She presents classes and workshops at a variety of events around the Midwest. She shares her home with a small black cat and a large collection of books.

James Kambos is a writer and artist living in the beautiful hill country of southern Ohio. His interest in magic began in boyhood watching his Greek grandmother perform spells based on Greek folk magic. An avid gardener, he raises herbs, vegetables, and wildflowers.

Najah Lightfoot is a Priestess of the Goddess. She keeps her faith strong by following the the Pagan Wheel of the Year. She is dedicated to keeping the Old Ways while living in these modern times. Najah has a passion for writing, ritual, magick, movies and martial arts. She can be found online at www.craftandconjure.com, www.facebook.com/priestessnajah and at @priestessnajah/twitter.com.

LUPA is a (neo)shaman, author, artist, and professional mental health counselor living in Portland, Oregon. She earned her master's in counseling psychology and ecopsychology from Lewis and Clark College. She is the author of several books on neoshamanism, including *New Paths to Animal Totems*. When she isn't writing or making ritual tools out of dead things, she hikes, camps, runs, and occasionally sits down long enough to read. www.thegreenwolf.com, www.therioshamanism.com, and www.antlerrunes.com.

MELANIE MARQUIS is the author of *A Witch's World of Magick* and *The Witch's Bag of Tricks* (both from Llewellyn), and *Bugbug and the Ants*, a picture book for children. She's the founder of United Witches global coven, organizer of Denver Pagans, and local coordinator for the Pagan Pride Project. Her work has appeared in national and international Pagan publications including *Pentacle Magazine, Circle*, and *Spellcraft*. A mother, witch, author, artist, and tarot reader, she's all about finding the mystical in the mundane via personalized magick and practical spirituality. www.melaniemarquis.com.

LISA MC SHERRY is a priestess and author living in the Pacific Northwest with her husband and three fur-children. She blogs at www.cybercoven.org, leads the JaguarMoon coven (www.jaguarmoon.org), and is the editor of Facing North (www.FacingNorth.net), which publishes reviews of books, music, and tools of the craft.

MICKIE MUELLER is an award-winning and critically acclaimed artist of fantasy, fairy, and myth. She is an ordained Pagan minister and has studied natural magic, fairy magic, and Celtic tradition. She is also a Reiki healing master/teacher in the Usui Shiki Royoho tradition. She works primarily in a mix of colored pencil and watercolor infused with corresponding magical herbs. Mickie is the illustrator of *The Well Worn Path* and *The Hidden Path* decks, the writer/illustrator of *The Voice of the Trees: A Celtic Divination Oracle*, and the illustrator of *Mystical Cats Tarot*.

SUSAN PESZNECKER is a writer, college English teacher, and hearth Pagan/Druid living in northwest Oregon. Her magickal roots include Pictish Scot and eastern European/Native American traditions. She holds a master's in nonfiction writing and loves to read, stargaze, camp with her wonder poodle, and play in her biodynamic garden. She's cofounder of the Druid Grove of Two Coasts and teaches nature studies and herbology for the online Grey School. Sue has authored *Crafting Magick with Pen and Ink* and *The Magickal Retreat* (both with Llewellyn). www.susanpesznecker.com.

SUZANNE RESS has been writing nonfiction and fiction for many years. She published her first novel, *The Trial of Goody Gilbert*, in 2012, and is currently working on her third. She is an accomplished self-taught gardener, beekeeper, silversmith, and mosaicist. She lives in the woods at the foot of the Alps in northern Italy with her husband, daughter, two dogs, three horses, and an elusive red stag.

CASSIUS SPARROW an Eclectic Pagan Witch, tarot reader, author, and garden enthusiast. He is a devotee of both Hermes and Dionysos, and a practicing Pagan for over ten years. He currently lives on the Gulf Coast of Florida with his darling wife and their cat, Zucca. In his free time, he can be found writing, baking, or working in his herb garden. Contact him at cassiussparrow@gmail.com.

ELLEN COUTTS WAFF is a professed dilettante, enjoying serving as her town treasurer, performing at the Maryland Renaissance Festival, caring for her 1742 home, and writing. She is a founder of the Druid Grove of Two Coasts, and treasurer of the Druid Order of the White Oak. A witch since 1979, she is a founder of Synergy, a celebratory coven, in 1984. She is a fellow of the Society of Antiquaries of Scotland. She owns Laurel Brook Studios, art clothiers.

CHARLYNN WALLS is a member of the St. Louis Pagan Community and serves on the St. Louis Pagan Picnic and Witches Ball committees. She is a member of two covens and has written articles for

Witches and Pagans magazine and recently accepted a post as column editor with the *Pagan World Times*. Visit her blog *Sage Offerings*.

LUNAEA WEATHERSTONE is a priestess, writer, and teacher who has been serving the Pagan community for more than twenty-five years, since her days as owner/editor of *SageWoman* magazine. She offers year-long online programs in goddess spirituality. Lunaea has been working with the tarot for forty years and is the author of *Victorian Fairy Tarot* and *Mystical Cats Tarot*, both from Llewellyn.

TESS WHITEHURST is an advocate of self-love, self-expression, and personal freedom. She's a Llewellyn author, columnist for *newWitch* magazine, intuitive counselor, and feng shui practitioner. Her website and e-newsletter *Good Energy* include simple rituals, meditations, and musings for everyday magical living. Tess lives in Venice Beach, California, with two magical cats, one musical boyfriend, and a constant stream of visiting hummingbirds. www.tesswhitehurst.com.

CHARLIE RAINBOW WOLF is happiest when creating something, especially if it can be made from items others have cast aside. Pottery, writing, knitting, and tarot are her deepest interests, but she happily confesses that she's easily distracted because life offers so many wonderful things to explore. As the Dean of Faculty at the Grey School, she teaches subjects across its sixteen departments. An advocate of organic gardening, she lives in the Midwest with her husband and special-needs Great Danes. www.charlierainbow.com.

NATALIE ZAMAN is the co-author of the *Graven Images Oracle* deck (Galde Press), and the YA novels *Sirenz* and *Sirenz Back in Fashion* (Flux) and *Blonde Ops*. Her work has appeared in *FATE*, *SageWoman*, and *newWitch* magazines, and she writes the feature "Wandering Witch" for *Witches and Pagans*. For more, visit http://nataliezaman .com or http://broomstix.blogspot.com, a collection of crafts, stories, ritual, and art for Pagan families.

Table of Contents

Earth Magic

Backyard Magick

by Melanie Marquis

Often when we turn to spellbooks, we're directed to head to the closest metaphysical supply shop to stock up on fancy herbs, oils, and other suggested tools, which can carry a hefty price tag. Now, I like a good witchy shop as much as anyone, but I don't always have money in the budget for lots of high-end magickal equipment. Luckily for me, I'm a folk witch, and I know how to "make do" with whatever magickal supplies I have on hand. Second only to the kitchen cupboard, the place where I most frequently acquire my magickal ingredients is my own backyard. Wherever you live, most likely your yard or a nearby park will have a ton of great stuff you can use for your magick. If you need to do some spellwork but payday's not till Friday, there's no need to fret. With just a few natural items found outdoors, you can cast an effective spell for nearly any magickal goal. Let's take a look at some of these powerful spellcasting tools and ingredients you can find free of charge any day of the week, right outside your door.

Dirt

Dirt is filled with the power of the earth, and it also absorbs the energies of the surrounding environment, making it a very versatile ingredient for a variety of spellcasting purposes. Dirt has the magickal attributes of strength and wealth, but it can have additional properties depending on where you gather it. Dirt from a riverbank, lakeside, or other area prone to erosion is useful for transformative magick, while dirt gathered from a sunny, grass-covered hill will contain a good dose of solar energy. Graveyard dirt is great for conjuring spirits or communicating with the dead,

and it's also useful in magick intended to cause a termina-
tion or a waning of power. Dirt found near large, old trees
or dirt found in an agricultural field or garden is especially excellent for magick to bring wealth or to increase
fertility. Need something different? Add a bit of water and
make some mud. Depending on the consistency, mud can
be used as paint or as a clay for fashioning magickal dolls,
amulets, and other items.

There are lots of ways to use dirt magickally. You might
empower a pinch of dirt with an energy of strength and then
discreetly dusting a bit of it over your body, your magick
wand, or wherever else it's needed. Alternatively, you could
tie the dirt up in a cloth and make a sort of "grit-grit" bag
intended for personal protection. You might mix up a batch
of magickal mud, concentrating as you stir on bringing out
the dirt's wealth-bringing propensity. You could then paint
a big dollar sign with your magickal mud, perhaps decorat-
ing a dollar bill with the symbol and carrying it with you

as a charm to attract more of the same. You can also use dirt right where it's found—to make use of erosion, simply cast your spell for transformation or reduction into a dirt-covered area with high erosion, and let your worries wash away with the next rain.

Rocks

Rocks are also a great ingredient for magick. They totally rock! We all know that the pretty clear quartz crystals they sell at the stores have amazing magickal properties, but did you know ordinary stones like granite and sandstone can also be powerful spellcasting additions? Rocks are classified into three main categories: igneous, sedimentary, and metamorphic. Igneous rocks are formed from heat and fire, sedimentary rocks are formed from particles being pressed together over time, and metamorphic rocks are formed when a sedimentary rock or an igneous rock changes form due to pressure and/or heat. Igneous rocks contain properties of both fire and earth. One common type of igneous rock is granite, a very hard stone. Magickally, granite can be useful in spells for defense, protection, tenacity, and lasting passion. Sedimentary rocks are great for spells intended to combine energies, as they're comprised themselves of many layers of particles, all united into a single stone. Try sandstone for general combining magick, or limestone (formed from the skeletal remains of sea creatures) if you want to give your spellwork an ocean theme or a dash of underworld flair. Metamorphic rocks are good for metamorphosis, naturally—use quartzite (a common rock formed from pressurized and heated quartz sandstone) for magick intended to cause a change or transformation. Because of the quartz content, quartzite is especially potent for magick intended to boost psychic abilities, magickal power, or creativity.

There are many ways to use rocks for spellcasting. You can fill a rock with the power of a magickal charm and carry it with you as an amulet or talisman or discreetly place it near the place or person the spell is meant to affect. You might draw an image of your magickal intention, then place rocks over or around the image so they can lend their power to the charm. If protection is needed, you might place a large, heavy stone over an image representative of the threatening person or unwanted situation, using the stone to crush and/or contain whatever ails you. Like dirt, rocks pick up the energetic vibrations of the surrounding landscape. Look for rocks in places you find special, sacred, or beautiful, and they're sure to pack a magickal punch.

Sticks

Perhaps even more versatile than dirt and rocks is the mighty stick. With just a twig or a small branch, you can craft and cast spells for movement, swiftness, union, progress, banishing, binding, transformation, and more. While selecting sticks based on type of wood will add an extra layer of power to most any type of magick, virtually any stick will do. Need to join together disparate energies? Empower two or more sticks to represent the forces, people, or resources you'd like to unite, then tie the sticks together into a single bundle. Want to shed the old and welcome the new? Peel the outer layer of bark off a small twig as you think of your intention, then decorate the newly revealed inner layer with symbols to represent the "new you" that has come into being. Need something in your life to get moving a little more quickly? Cast your intention into a small stick, throw it into a river, and think of circumstances quickening as you watch the stick speeding downstream. Need something completely *out* of your

life? Charge a stick to represent the object of banishment, then cast it into a river, bury it, break it, bind it tightly with string, or burn it.

Plants

While more exotic plants like mandrake and belladonna are certainly powerful, everyday plants like grass, dandelions, and clover can be highly useful in magick, too. Grass is a fine ingredient for (nonedible) cheering potions and powders, and it's also great for adding a dash of speedy growth to any spell. Dandelions have a high concentration of solar energy—try using that power for magick focused on success, happiness, friendship, strength, luck, action, or courage. Clovers are perfect for potions and powders designed to bring good luck, prosperity, or creative inspiration.

Other common plants can be used magickally, as well, even unidentified specimens. Just don't ever ingest a plant with which you're not familiar, and avoid plants you suspect might have properties contrary to your spell goal. For instance, if you're trying to attract peace and harmony, you wouldn't use a thorny briar. Use your intuition when choosing plants. What does the plant's appearance suggest? For example, plants with thorns or spiky leaves can be useful in defensive magick—just place a few sprigs around the perimeter of the place in need of protection. Likewise, roots can be used to bring a grounding energy, or to help you connect with underworld deities or even with your own ancestral "roots." Green leaves can be useful in attracting and magnifying energies, or causing growth. You might make a sachet of leaves, empowered to draw to you what you seek, or you can write your wish directly on a living leaf, letting photosynthesis further magnify the charm.

In Your Own Backyard

Lots of other everyday natural objects can also be used for magick. Take a walk around your own backyard and see what sort of ingredients you find. Might a pinecone be useful in a fertility spell? Could a feather be used to add air energies to your magickal blends? How about that maple branch that just broke off the tree—might it actually be your new magick wand? Start exploring, research the ingredients you find, and have fun with your backyard magick. It's economical and practical, and it honors the traditions of folk witches everywhere who use their everyday environment to craft extraordinary magick.

Digging Deeper:
Connecting with a Plant Ally
by Darcy Blue French

Many people have allies, spirit guides, or helpers that come from the animal and stone kingdoms. These allies give us messages, lessons, and support in various aspects of our mundane and spiritual lives. The botanical world is a powerful place to find allies, teachers, and helpers as well. The realm of the plant spirits contains the ancient wisdom of our earth—the plants have been here longer than the animals—and they colonized bare rock, built the soil with their bodies, rejuvenated atmosphere with their respiration, and developed ways to feed themselves and feed all of life. Our culture has believed that because plants did not move or vocalize that they were not sentient, that they did not communicate or feel pain. But this is now known to be untrue—plants have complex nervous systems that can feel pleasure, hear music, and feel your love. They can also communicate with other plants near and far. For millions of years, humans have relied upon plants for food and medicine. Before we hunted, we gathered plants. We have co-evolved with the intelligence of the plants within our own bodies. But plants have far more to teach us—they are more than food or physical medicine for our bodies. The spirits of the plants communicate with us every day through our emotions and electromagnetic and energetic bodies. As beings with a deep understanding of community, adaptation, and resilience, plants can teach us how to walk upon the earth with respect and honor for ourselves and our communities for all of life. They can also teach us how to heal and learn from our emotional wounds with ease and grace, and help alleviate our physical pains and illnesses. They can offer us protection and deep, healing spiritual lessons. We can connect with the plants in our immediate surroundings by walking outside and communing with the tree or shrub that waits every day. And we can take their medicine into our bodies in a very real way to receive and learn from their medicine.

How to Find a Plant Ally

So, how do you find a plant ally to learn from and work with? For some, it can be as simple as choosing a plant that is growing in your yard or for which you have a special liking. If there is a plant you would like to know better, this is a fine way to choose an ally. You can also peruse books with photographs or medicinal uses of plants and find one that speaks to you. But I have found that oftentimes plant allies will choose YOU! When you begin looking for a plant ally—make your intention clear and then start to notice. Perhaps you will have a vivid dream about a plant, or you will begin to see images or hear the name of a plant everywhere you go. Perhaps a plant that you have never seen before suddenly shows up in your yard or along your daily route. It will seem to shine a bit brighter, or it may wave its leaves at you while the wind isn't blowing. You might find a leaf or a flower that falls out of

21

a book or lands on your lap as you sit outside. Most people find they have a strong pull and attraction to a particular plant when they start paying attention with intention. Once a plant begins to call you, it is often insistent and may not leave your mind alone until you acknowledge it.

A few years ago, I moved to a dramatically different bioregion in the middle of winter. There were no plants growing green and lush around me, but as I walked in the winter woods, I kept hearing the name of a tree—birch—incessantly in my mind. I would pick up every shred of papery birch bark I found until I had a giant pile of it in my home. It quickly became clear I was to focus my energy on building a relationship with this tree, which I had just met in my new home.

How to Begin to Work with Your Plant Ally

So now you have a plant whom you would like to ally with or that has made itself known to you as an ally. How do you begin to work with your ally?

Plant Ally Altar

I always suggest starting by building an altar for your plant ally—include pictures, seedpods, live plants/flowers, or dried pieces of your plant ally. You can include teas, tinctures, essential oils, or flower essences of your ally as well. I find it helpful to include an offering bowl or plate where you can leave gifts, intentions, or talismans. The most important piece of a plant altar is that you spend time with it. You can use it for journey work, meditation, daily offerings, or just a few moments of quiet repose contemplating the relationship you have with your ally.

You should find a living representative of your plant ally (or plant one in your garden), with which you can sit, visit, and spend time. I recommend that you sit in meditation with your plant at for at least twenty minutes at least one day a week. You should leave offerings and gifts. (In time, you may find in time your plant friend will ask for specific gifts—they have asked me for songs, art, drumming, fruit, or ceremony.) I also suggest that to begin your work with this individual ally, you do not harvest anything from that plant you are sitting with. I find the relationship deepens on a very emotional/spiritual level—the gifts and lessons received come more clearly when the gifts are offered by the plant in this way, rather than in harvesting medicine physically. This isn't to say you should not harvest from other individual plants, but reserve one as a sacred teacher you sit with and offer gifts to, rather than taking from it.

Journey with Your Ally

I have found some of the most meaningful teachings and wisdom from my plant allies have come during meditation or shamanic journey. You should endeavor to journey to the spirit of the plant in the spirit realms on a semiregular basis. Just like building a relationship with a human, animal, or any other being, it takes time to build trust and understanding. One way to do that is visit with the plant in these realms and listen to what it has to share, and always follow through with any agreements, tasks, or requests an ally makes of you.

Work with the Physical Medicine Every Day

Many plants have medicinal or edible uses and can be used on a daily basis as a tea, infusion, oil/salve, essential oil, or tincture. You can brew a strong tea of your plant ally and place the tea

in your bath. I often take a piece of the plant to my bedroom in a pouch or place it in my pillow at night and invite it to work with me in the dream world. However, before taking *any* plant internally, you *must* research its uses, safety and dosage. If you are unfamiliar with working with herbs in teas or tinctures, it would be wise to consult with an herbalist to get you started. If you have chosen a plant which is not safe to take internally (and there are many plants that are considered toxic but are deep and powerful teachers) you should *not* consume it or put it in your body. You may be able to find a flower essence of your plant ally, which is a safe, nontoxic, energetic medicine that will give you deep teachings and healing on an emotional/spiritual level. In shamanic cultures of the Amazon, many shamans who work with plant medicines undergo what is called *la dieta* or "the diet." They limit their food and drink to very bland foods and consume the medicine of the plant every day. This can be as a tea, as a food, or in other ways. You will find if you work with an ally in this way, by taking it into your body every day, either as a tea, tincture, or flower essence, you will learn the medicine of the plant in a very deep way.

What Can You Learn from Your Ally?

As you begin to develop a relationship and build trust, you will begin to receive gifts and teachings from your plant ally. Plants speak to us through our emotions, our senses, and our memories/imagination. Always pay attention to these aspects of communication when working with your plant ally. Often plants will instruct you in how best to use its medicine. It may suggest ways you can use it to heal yourself or another person. Plant allies may give you songs or other artistic inspiration. The shamans of the Amazon believe that the potency of a plant's healing spirit and power is in its song, and once you have been given the song of a plant, you have received its knowledge and power. At this point, even just singing the song can invoke the healing power of the plant. They often also find ways to represent the song of the plant spirit in artistic ways—embroidery, painting, or weaving. Plant allies may instruct you on particular ways to interact with others in your life or suggest specific practices that enhance your own spiritual growth and healing. Eventually, you may find that the scent of your plant friend leads you somewhere unexpected and powerful on a hike one day—even if your plant doesn't grow in that area.

In return, plant allies often ask of us favors and tasks that they will benefit from in turn. For example, you may be asked to save seeds or teach others about protecting your plant or its habitat, and it may share with you the best methods and timing for harvesting its medicine. It is of utmost importance, as in any loving and lasting relationship, that you honor your plant teacher by respecting its wishes and following through on any teachings, wisdom, or requests it makes of you.

~

You may choose to ally with your plant teacher for life, or for a period of time. I have found that once I have allied with a plant, it tends to stick around. This is true even if you lose the connection in the physical world. If you move away from where a plant ally grows or if one of your allies is an old tree that eventually dies, these allies are with us in the spirit realms and can teach us from that place always. You can tune in to their song, their vibration, and their medicine teachings any time, any place—for yourself or another. The beauty of the plant medicine is that it is accessible in many forms, and you can turn to your plant ally medicines—tinctures, teas, flower essences, plant spirit bundles, journey, or altars anytime—and call upon your ally to help you from any place.

The Lure and Lore of the Graveyard

by Susan Pesznecker

One of the most entertaining moments in my recent Pagan travels came during a private "ghost tour" in Seattle, Washington. At one point late in the tour, the guide launched into a description of an old cemetery that had partially been torn up for a housing development, not an uncommon practice, but in this case, the graves had not been relocated—they were simply paved over. Surprisingly, she said, the site had remained peaceful, albeit, she emphasized, with a change in her voice, *very active*.

This caught our attention, so we were excited when moments later when the van stopped at that very cemetery, and our guide told us we'd be free to check it out. Presumably, most of her usual customers were reticent about walking into a cemetery where the spirits were known to be alive and well, for before opening the van doors, she suggested we gather at the roadside and enter the graveyard together, carefully. Imagine her surprise when we more or less bolted from the van and scampered into the cemetery grounds—not in disrespect but in excitement over the chance to experience a site still alive with spirit. Our guide was entranced. "This has never happened before," she told us.

It turned out to be a wonderful experience. The cemetery indeed felt active, and we sensed a number of individual presences as we walked among the stones. We were excited but respectful, walking carefully between the plots, tracing the lettering on the markers, talking quietly to the people there, and leaving pebbles on the headstones in tribute. The lure of the cemetery had captured us all.

We all know that graveyards are places where the dead are buried. The term "graveyard" is most often associated with a burial site adjacent to a church; as early as the eighth-century BCE, most churches and cathedrals had their own graveyards out behind the church buildings. In those times, burial in the graveyard was reserved for those who could not afford burial "within" the church itself. The famous, wealthy, or socially important were buried in crypts in or beneath the church and the sites marked with elaborately carved stones. A crypt, according to Greek origins, is a concealed, private stone chamber that is typically located underneath a larger structure or building. The very nature of a crypt is its privacy and its permanence; one who is interred in a crypt is expected to remain there—in perpetual rest—forever. A wonderful example of this is in England's Westminster Abbey, where even today one can visit the burial tombs of Charles Darwin, Isaac Newton, Edmund Spenser, and others within the Abbey itself.

For those relegated to the outdoor, less personal graveyard, it became customary to engage stonemasons to carve

headstones for the deceased. The simplest stones might have only a name and date, while more expensive ones were of precious stone—such as marble—and featured tribute sayings, symbols, and scrollwork. Wood and iron markers were sometimes used, too. In general, the more elaborate and the larger the marker, the more status the dearly departed typically enjoyed. When it came to headstones, size mattered.

Today's graveyards are more often called cemeteries—derived from the Greek *koimētērion*, "dormitory," to "put to sleep" or "a place to sleep." Cemeteries are typically not connected to a specific church and in today's times are often sited in beautiful locations with lush natural settings or extraordinary views. Cemeteries came into vogue around the eighteenth century when the rapidly increasing population overwhelmed available space in church graveyards and when graveyards were feared to be associated with outbreaks of communicable diseases. Today's cities and townships invariably have a carefully written set of rules and regulations governing the location, layout, and capacity of cemeteries.

In the past, when graveyards gave way to cemeteries and were closed to further occupancy, graves were sometimes exhumed—dug up—and the bones moved to crypts or catacombs. A catacomb is an underground cemetery characterized by a tunnel network with recesses for burial—either full-body tombs or collections of bones, ashes, or other remains. Catacombs are named for the *catacumbas,* the original subterranean cemetery of St. Sebastian near Rome. One of the best-known examples are the Catacombs of Paris in Paris, France, where the artfully arranged skulls and bones of some six million people can be viewed and visited. The Paris catacombs are an example of an ossuary, a room or container in which bones of one or more dead people are stored and sometimes displayed. A reliquary is a special type of ossuary that holds relics—typically bones, teeth, ashes, body parts, or personal belongings of saints or other once-holy people.

When a monument is built around or over one or more interred bodies, it is called a mausoleum—named for *Mausōlos,* the name of a king of Caria (fourth century BCE) who was entombed in Halicarnassus. The Mausoleum of Halicarnassus, built between 353 and 350 BCE as a tomb for the king and his wife, is one of the Seven Wonders of the Ancient World. In contrast, a cenotaph is, literally, an empty tomb—a monument enacted to one or more dead but in which case no bodies or burials are present. War memorials are excellent modern examples of the cenotaph.

The Draw of the Dead

Details aside, we humans seem to be inexorably drawn to places of the dead. Those who have lost loved ones visit their burial places in order to feel an enduring connection or closeness. We visit memorials—cenotaphs—to commemorate events and honor the heroic dead. We tour old graveyards and trace the headstones as a means of studying the history and lore of a place. And, in some cases, we visit out of pure fascination—out of the idea that spirits may linger and that we may have a conversation with the dearly departed. This is where the *lure* of the graveyard comes in.

Death, of course, has its own folklore and its own traditions. Before the body is buried, cremated, or otherwise dealt with, it rests in a morgue or mortuary, words linked to the old Latin *mortem*, "death." Mortuaries and morgues are typically set aside behind two or more series of closed doors, with the intention that the dead be left in peace and that the living not accidentally stumble in. The morgue sometimes is often as place for identifying bodies and for this purpose may include a "room of rest" in which the dearly departed can be arranged in a bed to make the experience less jarring for his or her survivors.

One of the most interesting bits of death-lore has to do with burial roads, the roads that connected remote towns and communities with places of legally licensed burial. The dead were carried along these roads from their death-place to their burials. Also called corpse roads, church roads, church-ways, or coffin routes, the paths often had colorful names and were well-known to the locals. Puck's words in Shakespeare's *A Midsummer Night's Dream* reference the church roads:

> Now it is the time of night,
> That the graves all gaping wide,
> Every one lets forth his sprite,
> In the church-way paths to glide.

According to historical novelist Deborah Swift, coffins were often carried along the corpse roads by hand, for most remote heath-dwellers lacked the money to provide for a horse and carriage. However they were transported, their bodies were always carried with feet pointing away from their homes; otherwise, the superstitious feared the dead might remember the way home. Mary Ellen Stubb adds that carrying the corpse feet-first also kept him from looking back and inviting another family member to follow. Corpse roads often crossed a bridge over moving water, which it was believed the dead spirits could not re-cross. The roads likewise avoided fields, for carrying a dead body across a field could render it infertile.

Church-ways were often associated with the vigorous movement of sprites, faeries, wraiths, and ghosts, and legends tell of strange lights—usually described as globes of blue or white—along the roads. Sometimes these were referred to as will-o'-the-wisps, mischievous spirits that attempted to startle or frighten travelers in hopes of seeing them lose their way. Nigel Pennick describes the concept of "hungry grass" growing along the corpse roads. If a coffin was set down temporarily, grass would spring up overnight, and anyone standing on the grassy patch thereafter would become instantly and ferociously hungry.

Most corpse roads were rather straight—following a plain path rather than a circuitous one—and some believe that what we know as ley lines or "rose lines" may, in some cases, mark ancient corpse roads (Bord and Bord). Upon reaching the graveyard, coffins were often carried around the property three times in hopes of confusing any wandering spirits—or the dearly departed himself. Stubb notes that funeral processions never left a graveyard along the same route they'd

approached in hopes of obfuscating any spirits that might tag along. The curves of ancient stone, hedge, and turf labyrinths may have been built near townships in an effort to confuse and impede wandering spirits. Today's modern funeral processions—and the typical winding roads that wend through cemeteries—may be remnants of these arcane practices.

Another road-related legend is that of the crossroad, a place where two or more roads intersect or cross one another. The crossroad is felt to be a place of potent magick, of confusion, of transitions and thresholds, and of spirit visitation—even by the devil himself. Death is often described as a type of human crossroad, and the corpse-roads invariably avoided creating or following crossroads at any point along their paths. Even today, cemeteries will add side roads or create branching "Ys" so as to avoid creating a crossroad, and funeral processions are mapped out to avoid crossroads.

Customs Continue Today

And of course, there are any number of smaller customs, rituals, and folkloric expressions in terms of graveyards and cemeteries. According to Stubb, one must hold her breath when passing a graveyard or cemetery; otherwise, a wandering spirit is liable to enter with the next inhalation. Weeds growing on a grave are a testament to the dead one having lived an evil life, while flowers on the grave mean just the opposite. Speaking ill of the dead is always felt to be a bad idea, but doing so in a graveyard or cemetery is almost guaranteed to invite wandering or malevolent spirits. Headstones were felt in the past to help weigh down spirits and prevent their emergence, and placing "visitor stones" on the headstone added to this effect. Today, placing pebbles or small stones on a headstone pays tribute to the departed and notes that a loved one visited.

Although these arcane traditions seem unusual, many remain in practice. Even today, people are generally buried with heads to the west and feet to the east. This was originally believed to echo the Pagan practice of following the Sun's movements; Christians would later claim this practice by stating the final judgment day would come from the east. And when driving past a cemetery, people still fall silent and cross their fingers, hoping to avoid attracting the attention of the local spirits.

While some try to avoid any spiritual connection with the dead, others seek it out. Dirt gathered from crossroads, graveyards, or cemeteries is useful in sympathetic magicks, creating a close connection with the dead. Graveyard and crossroad dirt may also be used in shamanic or astral journeying, both to access the spirit world and to create an anchor for return. Graveyards and cemeteries are also powerful places for any type of divination. It's widely believed that midnight—the so-called witching hour—is the most potent magickal time within a graveyard or cemetery, and Samhain, the time when the veils between living and dead go thin, is probably peak time. But don't fool yourself. If you feel stronger working in the high dark or on certain dates, so be it. Just know that the dead are there 24/7, as are the spirits and energies of the place.

～

If you visit a graveyard today, show respect to those who sleep beneath you as well as to the roaming spirits. Walk between—not over—the graves. Speak quietly, and don't run. Listen for voices. Be aware of those who share the space, whether above or below the ground. Pull weeds from the plots, and leave tribute stones on the grave markers. And be certain to walk in a circular path, leaving the cemetery via a different route than the way you entered. After all, you wouldn't want anyone to follow you home....

For Further Study:

Definitions and etymologies were taken from the *Oxford English Dictionary*, third edition.

Bord, Janet, and Colin Bord. *The Secret Country*. London: Paul Leek. 1976.

"Legendary Dartmoor." No date. http://www.legendary dartmoor.co.uk/coffin_stone.htm.

Les Catacombes. No date. http://www.catacombes.paris .fr/en/catacombs.

"Mausoleum of Halikarnassos (Room 21)." *The British Museum*. No date. http://www.britishmuseum. org/explore/galleries/ancient_greece_and_rome /room_21_halikarnassos.aspx.

Pennick, Nigel. *Celtic Sacred Landscapes*. London: Thames & Hudson, 1996.

Stubb, Mary Ellen. "Cemetery Folklore. The Lighter Side of the Grave." No date. http://www.ci.missoula .mt.us/DocumentCenter/Home/View/8206.

Magickal, Mystical Salt

by Najah Lightfoot

Salt is ancient, timeless, and essential. Without salt we simply could not exist. Our bodies need salt to function, as salt provides the electrical currents necessary for cellular function. In our magickal practices, we feel the power and sacredness of salt. We *instinctively* know salt is a powerful, magickal tool.

Humans first found salt in the form of salt licks by following the trails of our animal kin. We found salt in the sea, dried and waiting to be used, when the sun evaporated the water and left us sea salt. We found salt deep underground in the dark caverns of the earth.

Salt has been highly valued since ancient times. Salt has been used as currency and trade, a practice that continues to this day in some parts of the world. Roman soldiers were paid in salt, hence the word "salary," which is a derivative of the word "salt." Roman slaves were traded for salt, giving us the phrase "not worth his salt."

The Many Uses of Salt

Our first practical use of salt was as a food preservative, which allowed us to travel to far and distant places. Preserving food also helped us get throught scarce times and harsh winters.

You would be surprised to know that most of the salt mined from the earth is not used for food. Only 4 percent of the salt mined in the United States is of food-grade level. The rest goes to the chemical industry for manufacturing purposes. And most mined salt is used for de-icing roads in winter!

In Poland exists one of the most mystical and wondrous salt mines in the world. The Wieliczka Salt Mine is located in the city of Wieliczka, Poland. Deep within its caverns lies one of the most beautiful chapels in the world, completely

carved from salt! It took miners sixty-seven years to construct the chapel. The chapel is dedicated to their patroness of salt, St. Kinga. Legend has it that Hungarian Princess Kinga, upon receiving a marriage proposal from a young Polish prince, wanted to give a gift to the people of Poland. Instead of asking for gold and jewels for her dowry, she asked her father, the king, for salt. Upon visiting the salt mine of her country, she knelt at the entrance, prayed, and threw her engagement ring into the mine—as a symbol of faith. When Princess Kinga left Hungary and began her journey to Poland, she felt led to stop and dig for salt. When the miners traveling with her began to dig, they found her ring. It was buried in a piece of rock salt! On that spot the Wieliczka mine was dug. So revered was the salt mine and so arduous was the work, miners carved the Wieliczka Chapel in honor of St. Kinga. Daily they prayed at her altar for blessings and protection.[1]

---

1 *History Channel; Modern Marvels: Salt*

As Pagans we recognize in St. Kinga the living manifestation of our Divine Mother Goddess. Unto the people of Wieliczka, Poland, she gave blessed salt for their industry and use in their daily lives.

Magickal Uses of Salt

Salt is used as an element of protection. It is also used as a cleansing tool and conductor of energy. But is salt truly an element? Scientifically speaking, salt is a compound sodium chloride, but for our purposes we refer to it as an essential element of our magickal practice.

In show business, it is said one is a triple threat if one can sing, act, and dance. Salt is a triple threat of the magickal world, crossing over all three areas of culinary, medicinal, and magickal realms.

Mix salt with water and you have a created an elixir. In essence you have created holy water, which is water mixed with a pinch of salt, then blessed by a priest. We are all priests and priestesses in our own right. When we mix salt and water and pray over it, followed by using it for the intention of casting a circle, or cleansing or protecting an object, we are performing priestly acts. Therefore, our salt water *is* holy water, infused with our higher thoughts of wellness, divine love, and prayers of intention. Use your holy water to consecrate your circle, crystals, and talismans.

Add some essential oils, herbs, and your intentions to salt and you've made a magickal salt scrub. Use your intuition and your nose to guide you to the oils that work best for you. Some essential oils and herbs that work well with salt are lavender, eucalyptus, rosemary, lemon, and hyssop, just to name a few. Grab a copy of *Scott Cunningham's Encyclopedia of Herbs* to cross reference herbs and their properties.

Cleansing Ritual with Salt

Here is a wonderful salt cleansing ritual, best performed during the cycle of the waning moon:

In the tradition of Conjure, we carry our troubles to the Crossroads. A crossroads is any place where two roads meet forming a T. Plan to perform this ritual in the early hour before sunrise. Gather these materials before you begin:

Salt
Olive oil
Two tealight candles
Eucalyptus oil
Warm water
Clean clothes
Bowl or basin to catch the water

Add a few drops of eucalyptus oil to the salt. Eucalyptus is a powerful essential oil for cleansing. On the tealights, inscribe your name and any symbols of power that are meaningful to you. Anoint the tealights with olive oil. Take the salt in your power hand and say:

Salt of old, salt of new, perform this task I have for you.
Melt away, wash away,
Carry away these troubles I now lay before you.

Add the salt to the water. Light the tealights and place them so you will step between them when you exit your bath.

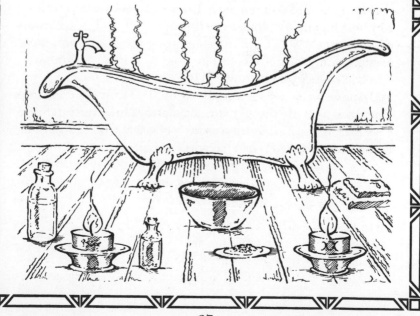

Step into your shower or bath. If taking a shower, stand in a basin so you can catch some of the water. If in a bathtub, plug the tub.

Now as you stand, call upon the Goddess to assist you in your "working." Pour the salt water over your head, thanking it and envisioning it washing away your troubles. Feel the relief as the water cascades down your body. Wash yourself down from head to toe with the salt water.

Next, gather some of your bath water. Step out of the bath, stepping between the two tealights. Allow yourself to air-dry. Put on your clean clothes. You are now going to go to the Crossroads. Don't worry about being seen. You are now in the realm of Spirit, and no one is going to pay any attention to you!

Step into the Crossroads, with your back facing the rising Sun. You are going to throw the water over your left shoulder. Bring up all your energy and cast that water over your shoulder, letting all your worries go! Return home by a different route than whence you came. You will feel refreshed and exhilarated!

Tribute to a Sorcerer

In 2011 I fulfilled a lifelong dream, which was to visit London, England. I hadn't made up my mind if I would visit the Tower of London, knowing its brutal history. Being an empathic witch, I wasn't sure if I would be able to keep my boundaries up, in such an overwhelming place.

However, on a bright and sunny day, from the Thames River taxi we saw the Tower of London and the infamous "Traitors Gate." I knew without a doubt that I had to visit the Tower. In my pocket, I carried some sage. As I walked through the Tower, I used the sage to bless the walkways and holds where people had been imprisoned and tortured—and where some died. One can imagine my surprise when we came upon the infamous "Salt Tower."

Upon entering the Salt Tower, I saw on a plaque on a stone wall. Next to the plaque, carved into the stone, was an astrological sphere. The plaque read:

Hew Draper of Brystow made thys spheere the 30 day of Maye anno 1561.

Draper had been imprisoned in the Tower for just over fourteen months—accused of sorcery—when he made the inscription. He was also reportedly very sick.

The signs of the zodiac surround the sphere. On its left is a grid showing the planetary influence over every hour of the day of the week.

My mouth hung open and goosebumps covered my skin. I knew I had been Goddess-led to the Salt Tower.

What happened to the sorcerer Hew Draper? His death or execution were never recorded in the Tower records. But we do know he was there and that he suffered. But even in his suffering, he left a stone record of knowledge that remains 'til this day.

Before leaving the tower, I placed my hand upon the stone and whispered "we are still here." In my heart, I believe Hew felt my presence and I hope his spirit smiled.

Blessed be, Hew Draper, and blessed be thy element of salt.

Kitchen Witchery: All the Magic That's Fit to Eat

by Cassius Sparrow

A pinch of this, a splash of that, give it a few stirs and it's done. Is it a magical brew or is it dinner? To a Kitchen Witch, it could be both.

The hearth is where the magic happens in a Kitchen Witch's home. Every ingredient is a spell component, and every spoon and spatula is a magical tool. Athames come in different shapes and sizes depending on the meat or vegetable, and something always seems to be boiling away on the stovetop.

Kitchen Witchery is an art and a science. It requires that a witch know the properties of every ingredient to cast the perfect spell. A Kitchen Witch must know how long to bake, boil, braise, or saute, and when to do so. Kitchen Witchery also demands a creative mind to concoct such magical recipes and to arrange the final product artfully on a plate, in a bowl, or even in a glass or mug.

Though it seems demanding, Kitchen Witchery can be fun and intensely rewarding.

Tools of the Trade

Before you go out and invest in a brand-new set of cookware, take a good look around your kitchen. Chances are you're already well-stocked with everything you need to cook up some magic. If you have the essentials to make a home-cooked meal, you have the essentials to begin your Kitchen Witchery.

Besides your hearth—or stove—your most commonly used item will be your cauldron. For the modern Kitchen

Witch, this translates to a saucepan, stockpot, or skillet, depending on the spell. Add in a whisk, spatula, and a ladle, and you have the basics. Expand your toolkit with mixing bowls, measuring cups and spoons, various baking dishes, and of course, more cookware.

There has been some debate in the Kitchen Witch community regarding electric mixers and food processors versus doing it by hand, using whisks and mortars and pestles. It all comes down to taste and preference. If you consider yourself a more old-fashioned, traditional witch, hand-mixing and grinding would be a better fit. However, if technology factors largely into your craft, then by all means use modern kitchen conveniences. As societies and technologies advance, so does witchcraft. So long as the intent and energies are there, the results will be the same.

The Kitchen Witch's Garden

A Kitchen Witch with a green thumb might consider planting a garden box with fresh herbs. Choose herbs that you will use often in your spellwork, as well as herbs with similar soil, moisture, and light requirements. An herb garden is sure to brighten up any kitchen, and the herbs can be dried for later use—and witchy gifts.

If an herb garden is an impractical idea in your kitchen—or if you've had bad luck with houseplants—a well-stocked spice rack makes a great alternative. If you're able, label the spice jars with attributes related to the herbs within them. For example, basil is associated with love, money, and health; sage is associated with purification and protection; and mint with luck, healing, and travel.

Building Your Cookbook of Shadows

The Cookbook of Shadows is a Kitchen Witch's most important tool. The most basic should include a list of common recipe ingredients such as herbs, fruits, vegetables, and other staples, and the attributes associated with them. As every witch is different, every Cookbook of Shadows is different. It can be organized by spell type, ingredients, cooking method, or a variety of other ways. Include a section for notes and for writing your own spells. From these guidelines, create a Cookbook that is practical to your path. Make it as eye-catching or as secretive as you wish, but most importantly, make it yours.

Turning Recipes into Spellwork

When crafting spells into recipes, it's important to identify exactly what effect you want to achieve. Select ingredients that correspond to the type of spell you are casting, and look for ways to incorporate symbolism into your recipe. If you are casting a money spell, try for a recipe that allows you to present a dish that is boldly green, with large, leafy greens. Recipes that use whole basil leaves, spinach, or dark, crisp lettuce are ideal. If you are casting a spell for healing, whether physical or emotional, look for heartier dishes such as stews or casseroles with ingredients that include onions, garlic, peppers, and herbs such as thyme or sage.

The presentation of your spell is limited only by your imagination. You can charm a pie, a batch of cookies, or an entire pot of soup. Brew a pitcher of tea that doubles as a personal cleansing spell. A homemade batch of granola bars can serve as a protection charm placed in your child's lunch. For a Kitchen Witch, the options are limitless.

Kitchen Witchery also provides for discretion. Because the spell ingredients would not look too out of place in any normal kitchen, it allows a Kitchen Witch to be more private with their spellcasting. When you are cooking up some magic in your kitchen, you can embellish the spell as dramatically or as subtly as you choose. If you prefer to speak your intentions over your spells, feel free to whisper, chant, sing, or even shout them. If you prefer a more quiet casting, charge your meal with your intentions, letting the energy flow from you, down your arm and into the food or brew. Give it a good stir, visualizing the end result—the successful casting of your spell. You can even combine the two methods.

Spells, and the recipes that contain them, can be as simple or as complex as you'd like. They can contain a large list of ingredients or just a handful. Here are a couple of simple, easy-to-make spells to get your Cookbook of Shadows started and help you get the feel of Kitchen Witchery.

Charm with Lavender Lemonade

Having trouble with your neighbors? Perhaps you've had a disagreement recently, and you'd like to repair the relationship. Brew up this lavender-lemon potion to help things along.

Bring 5 cups of water to boil in a large pot. Add ¾ cup of fresh-squeezed lemon juice and the juice of half a lime. Reduce heat to simmer, and visualize the disagreements or problems between you and your neighbors. Stir in ¾ cup of sugar, charging the brew with your intentions of sweetening the relationship. When the sugar is fully dissolved, add four fresh sprigs of lavender. Allow the scent of the lavender lemonade fill you with peace and feelings of friendship and harmony. Visualize your relationship with your neighbors healed. Remove the potion from heat and allow to cool to room temperature. Take out the lavender, and chill the lemonade brew in the refrigerator until you are ready to cast your spell. Invite your neighbors over to talk about the situation, and offer them a glass. For an impressive presentation, freeze lavender in ice cubes and serve the lemonade with the lavender ice and garnish with lemon wedges.

When You Wish Upon a Peach Bar

This is a versatile spell that you can customize depending on your wish. Peaches are associated with wishes (especially love and health), and when combined with other ingredients, they can become a deliciously magical shortbread bar.

Preheat your oven to 375 F/190 C/Gas Mark 5, and lightly grease a 9 × 13 pan. Stir together 1 cup of sugar, 3 cups of flour, 1 teaspoon of baking powder, and ¼ teaspoon of salt. If you're wishing for a raise at work, a promotion, or for some quick cash, add 1 tablespoon of freshly grated ginger at this point. Stir in 1 teaspoon of cinnamon. Dice 1 cup (or 2 sticks) of cold, unsalted butter and add to mix, along with 1 large egg. Using your fingers, blend the butter and egg into the dry ingredients, charging the batter with your wish. If you want, speak your wish aloud, visualizing it coming true. The mixture is ready when it is well mixed and crumbly. Pat ¾ of the crumbs into the bottom of the greased pan, pressing firmly.

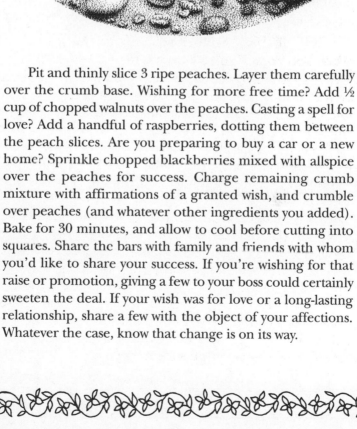

Pit and thinly slice 3 ripe peaches. Layer them carefully over the crumb base. Wishing for more free time? Add ½ cup of chopped walnuts over the peaches. Casting a spell for love? Add a handful of raspberries, dotting them between the peach slices. Are you preparing to buy a car or a new home? Sprinkle chopped blackberries mixed with allspice over the peaches for success. Charge remaining crumb mixture with affirmations of a granted wish, and crumble over peaches (and whatever other ingredients you added). Bake for 30 minutes, and allow to cool before cutting into squares. Share the bars with family and friends with whom you'd like to share your success. If you're wishing for that raise or promotion, giving a few to your boss could certainly sweeten the deal. If your wish was for love or a long-lasting relationship, share a few with the object of your affections. Whatever the case, know that change is on its way.

Natural Magical Tools

by Autumn Damiana

Witches, Wiccans, and other Pagans all love their magical tools. Most of us collect them and will own more than one of each type—some of which cost a small fortune. And while it is inspiring to work with an ornate crystal wand or sparkly silver chalice, sometimes it can be just as rewarding to use the tools that nature provides us. Natural tools are sometimes the only ones necessary if you would like to do impromptu rituals, instant magic, or require items that are environmentally friendly. Working with natural magical tools is also an effective way to grow spiritually and become more magically adept by breaking out of your routine and comfort zone—and spell or ritual components that you use once and then return to the Earth are an excellent way to let go of the energy raised and send it into the cosmos.

Witches know that any stick can become a wand and that seashells are good to use as bowls for holding salt, incense, or offerings. And yet, "natural" should not limit you to "naturally formed" or "naturally occurring" tools such as these, but can encompass anything that is constructed from materials that are biodegradable or will not harm the environment. Some paper and wood products, food and other compostables, and mineral items (like salt or crystals) all fall into this category. Ecofriendly crafting supplies, like white glue, plant-based paints/dyes, and hemp or raffia can also lend themselves to the creation or adornment of natural magical tools. Here are some more ideas.

Around to Be Found (and Adapted)

If you have an open mind and a little ingenuity, you'll be surprised how many ordinary materials can be used as natural magical tools with minimal effort. Here is a short list to get you started. (**Note:** never ingest or apply anything to the skin out of a container that is not food safe! If in doubt, don't do it.)

Bowls/Vessels: Seashells, nut hulls, acorn caps, hollowed out vegetables and peels (peppers, tomatoes, squash, avocados, etc.), fruit and peels (see Picnic section), coconut shells, lettuce leaves, unglazed clay pots, and deep, naturally cup-shaped rocks or stones

Wands/Athames: Sticks; fallen branches; driftwood; long, thin, or jagged crystals/stones; arrowheads; wand-shaped edibles (bananas, celery stalks, vanilla beans, scallions, etc.); woody stems or stalks (roses, pussy willows, rosemary, etc.); disposable chopsticks; reeds; lavender wands, agate or other stone "slices"; and naturally shed animal parts (feathers, antlers, bones, porcupine or sea urchin spines, etc. USE CAUTION when collecting these items, as they can harbor parasites and disease, and in some cases are illegal to pick up. Only handle if you are knowledgeable!)

Other Tools: Grass, reed, or twig bouquets (broom); evergreen boughs (broom); wide, flat stone slabs (altar surface or trivet); rocks with a natural indentation (cone incense burner); flat river rocks (pentacle); herbal or vine wreaths (pentacle); flat pieces of wood (pentacle); and long grasses or vines (can be twisted/braided/knotted into cords, wands, crowns, necklaces, etc.).

Origami Altar Tools

This is a "think outside the box" altar composition. Some may feel that the ephemeral quality of the altar tools or the humble origins of the materials you will use to make them might be unacceptable. That's okay—if this idea doesn't resonate with you, then using these tools will feel strange and empty. However, if you want to give it a try, I feel that the best time is during the fall and winter months, when people are confined inside and the hearth fires are burning, as it provides a project to do and the tools themselves

can be offered to the fire after your ritual. Folding the origami can also be a meditative exercise or a fun way to safely and inexpensively familiarize children with the purpose and use of magical tools.

Decide which tools you want to make. There are myriad patterns and tutorials online for almost anything you might use as an altar tool. Try YouTube or children's craft sites for simple instructions on an origami knife or dagger, cup, bowl, or box. Tightly roll up a piece of paper to use as a wand, rolling it diagonally to get that tapered look. A pentacle can simply be drawn on a piece of paper, or a four-pointed origami star can be used to represent the elements. Fold a fan to wave incense around, or to replace it altogether. And if you want to challenge yourself, try folding your totem animal(s), as many animal patterns exist.

In addition, you can experiment with the type of paper used. Expensive, store-bought origami paper is not necessary—reuse what you have, such as wrapping paper, printer paper, colorful junk mail, brown paper bags, or even aluminum foil or waxed paper (good if you want to fill your origami cup with liquid!). By doing this, you are also honoring the Earth by recycling.

Ritual Picnic Fruit Salad

How about an edible altar setup? Consuming spell-charged food and drink has been a common practice for centuries and is an innovative way to work some magic outdoors under the guise of having a picnic! This is a working best suited to the spring and summer months when fruit is plentiful and can be used as a spell of prosperity, abundance, luck, self-blessing, or sabbat celebration. Create and use this edible tool arrangement on its own or as part of a full meal or larger outing or event.

Decide which fruit you would like in your salad, both in terms of taste and magical properties. Grapes and berries are good choices because they add color and most do not need to be cut up (although you will be able to prepare some of your fruit before the picnic). Also decide what type of dressing, herbs/spices, nuts/seeds, or other garnishes you will use. Part of the fun in planning this fruit salad is in being creative on how you will use your food components in ritual. For example:

Stone fruits (apricots, plums, peaches, nectarines, etc.) cut in half make wonderful little bowls when their pits are removed, as do the rinds of halved citruses (oranges, lemons, limes, etc.) after the fruit has been extracted. Apples and pears, partially cored with the bottom left intact, can also become vessels and make adequate chalices. Hollowed-out melon rinds (watermelon, cantaloupe, honeydew, etc.) are useful as larger bowls or cauldrons, as they hold liquid particularly well and can even be used to serve the fruit salad. A cinnamon stick or mint sprig, before becoming a garnish, can be empowered to use as a wand. Even portable sugar and honey packets make convenient substitutes for salt and anointing oil, and mixed with a little citrus juice can be drizzled over the fruit salad as a dressing afterward. And pentacles are easy to carve into almost any kind of fruit.

With a little imagination, it is possible to adapt many of your picnic items into the magical tools that will be broken down and eaten as part of the ritual, with the exception of the knife used to cut the fruit. For this you can use any kitchen knife or a sharp athame, depending on whether or not you will further use the tool in your working, such as to cast the circle. You might also want to pack a cutting board, a small grater (for the cinnamon), or wooden skewers if you prefer fruit kabobs to salad (and the skewers can double as wands—very handy for groups or covens!). However you do your ritual and prepare your fruit salad, make sure that you leave a tiny bit on the ground as an offering, and dispose of all garbage responsibly when you are finished.

～

Because the natural world around us is the source of magical current, it makes sense for all magical practitioners to work with the raw materials that nature provides in our workings. After all, we already do this to represent the elements on the altar, frequently using soil or salt for earth, feathers for air, lava or pyrite for fire, shells for water, etc. Why not take it a step further, and structure entire rituals that use nothing but natural magical tools? Remember, a tool is only a symbol and a device through which to tap into and direct energy. And while it is true that magical tools can build up energy through repeated use, a tool itself is powerless. Nature, the Divine, and the divine spark within you are the source of all magical power. That makes YOU yourself the most magical tool you will ever have.

The Majesty and Magic of the Horse

by Suzanne Ress

Some mornings, rather than hitting the forest trails, I ride my horse through town. He's an easygoing, friendly gray Arabian with a long white tail and mane and kind, dark eyes. Little girls run up to us saying, "My favorite animal is a horse! Can I touch him?" Parents with kids in their cars drive by slowly with the windows down. "Look, kids! A horse!" Old men out for a stroll stroke his nose and tell me their personal horse stories.

One time, an older lady we encountered on the sidewalk said, "I'm terribly afraid of horses—they are so big and strong—but I've always wanted to touch one. May I?" I led her trembling hand to my horse's smooth white neck. She let it linger there a while, her palm pressed against him, absorbing some of his gentle strength.

When she took her hand away, she was smiling.

"Thank you," she said. "He's beautiful."

When I am walking or running in the woods and unexpectedly encounter a horse and rider, the beauty and power of the animal still never fails to take my breath away.

From the beginning of civilization, we have had a magical relationship with horses. No one knows exactly when horses quit being considered another kind of meat and became transportation, although the most recent estimates suggest that horses were first ridden around 6,000 years ago. Likewise, no one really knows why horses are so willing to carry our weight and work for us. Other animals—donkeys, camels, elephants—can be ridden, but none are as swift, as handy, as reliable, and as trainable as horses. Together, horse and human took the first steps toward globalization.

A human on horseback can cover far more ground than a human on foot, making it much easier for isolated groups of people to meet and trade knowledge and goods with others.

For millennia, war was not possible without horses—a war without horses would have been a mobbing or a riot. With chariots, and, later, war cavalry, came the conquest of territory, which led to the formation of nations, leaders, and governments. Greater mobility created trade, markets, and economies as well as increased knowledge and learning, arts, science. The horse transformed human life.

And horses continue to give us even more than greater mobility and work power. Interacting with horses expands one's physical awareness and ability to communicate with others, both equine and human, nonverbally. In our electronically swamped modern

world, we tend to rely heavily on written or spoken words for communication—instant messaging, emails, social networking, online dating, telephone and Skype calls. It is easy to forget that, according to psychologists, only about 10 percent of human communication is verbal. The rest relies on subtle energetic exchanges, behavior, facial expression, gestures and body language, vocal tones, body odors, breathing patterns, intuition, and many other nuances we are usually not consciously aware of. Relating regularly with any nonhuman animal, but particularly with the sensitive horse, raises your awareness of the nonverbal messages you are expressing and helps you understand others. For this reason, therapists, psychologists, and educators have had very high success rates using hippotherapy (physical, occupational, and speech therapies aided by a horse, which can include incorporating a horse's gait and other movements to influence a patient's response) to treat emotionally or mentally disturbed children and adults.

Because our long-ago ancestors could not explain when, how, or why the lives of horses had become so entwined with their own, they were awestruck by horses' mysterious power and beauty and held them in high regard spiritually, as consorts of gods and goddesses, or as deities in their own right, all over the world.

Ceridwen is the Welsh mother deity of the moon and grain. She rides a white horse and sometimes takes on the form of a white mare herself. The tale of Lady Godiva is supposed to have derived from the Ceridwen goddess image, as did the Celtic horse goddess adopted by the Roman cavalry, Epona.

Odin, or Wodan, northern god of the wind, rode his magical eight-legged horse, Sleipnir, through the sky, especially during the Yule period. Farmers always left the last sheaf of wheat or corn in the field until after Yule so that when he passed, Sleipnir would have something to eat.

In the Quran, Muhammed rode a horse-like creature called Al-Buraq on his spiritual night journey from Mecca to Jerusalem and back. Al-Buraq was a white horse from the heavens with a beautiful face and wings on his thighs that made him able to travel as fast as lightning.

Pegasus is another well-known winged horse, from Greek mythology. Where he stamped his hoof, a spring was created that was the source of poetic inspiration.

The speedy Hippogriffe, a fantastical medieval creature, was half horse and half griffin, and the preferred mount of wizards.

Many people's favorite fabled horse creature is the unicorn. This remarkable single-horned horse, which symbolizes spiritual harmony, happiness, prosperity, and truth, is represented, in slightly different forms, in almost every culture around the world.

Cultural Impact Continues Today

Nowadays it seems impossible to see a real unicorn, and, for many people, it is rare to even see a horse. Even so, our historical relationship with horses still holds sway over us, so that when we do see one, we are filled with awe for his power, strength, swiftness, and beauty.

To this day, the horseshoe is considered a good-luck talisman, and toy horses are ever popular with children because of the deep subconscious magical worlds they can connect a child to.

Even if you are not easily able to come into regular contact with horses, there are many ways to connect with the magic of horses and the horse/human relationship and to use this magical power in spells, rituals, and visualization.

Lucky Horseshoe for Protection

The purpose of a horse's shoes are to protect his hooves from stony or hard road surfaces, thereby preventing the hooves from wearing down too fast if the horse is worked frequently on such

surfaces. This crescent moon-shaped metal plate can also protect you from harmful negative energies.

The horseshoe must be nailed up over a threshold with its "horns" pointing upwards where it invokes the moon's protection from evil intent, and collects and holds in good fortune. Hanging a horseshoe with its horns facing downward has the opposite effect.

Found horseshoes are the most powerful, but they are not so easy to come by unless you live someplace commonly frequented by shod horses. You can get a used one free from a riding stable, any horse owner, or blacksmith; however, the you must make sure that it had been worn by a horse. Brand-new ones will not work.

Paint it with acrylics any way that pleases you, using your lucky color or colors, and decorate it with tiny decoupage pictures and glitter glue, if desired. Finish with a coating of transparent acrylic paint, and, when completely dry, string a piece of wire or fishing line through the two holes closest to the tips of the "horns."

On the evening of the full moon (or else the last evening of the month, whichever comes first), drive a nail above your chosen threshold, making sure it is high enough so that the hung shoe will not obstruct the moving door, and perform a short ritual before hanging up the horseshoe.

Horse Dreaming for Improved Love/Sex/Body Image

Everybody dreams, even if you think you do not. Dreams are messages from our subconscious and can be used for positive transformation in your waking life. It is said that horses in dreams symbolize the animal life within the human body. Getting in touch with your own subconscious animal self will help you be more grounded and balanced—and will likely improve your body image, as well as your love and sex life.

If you do not usually remember your dreams, start keeping a notepad and pen next to your bed, and, upon waking, write down any tiny insignificant scrap of dream thought you remember. If you do this faithfully, within a week you will be able to remember entire dreams in detail.

On the night of the full moon, cut the corners off a sheet of plain white paper and burn them. Using a new pen with red ink, write down the following words:

Epona, reveal myself to me.

Fold the paper up, all the while visualizing a lovely white mare watching you from a few feet away. Tie a red ribbon or thread around the folded paper.

Put the tied paper under your pillow and leave it there for three nights until you dream of a horse.

Upon waking, write down your dream. Was the horse docile, hurt, wild, healthy, frightened, big, small, angry, etc.? Use your intuitive powers to analyze your horse dream, and use your analysis to help transform your life accordingly.

Toy Horse Spell for Money and Luck

Buy an inexpensive small toy horse at a dime store or supermarket, but choose it carefully—you should like it. By the light of the noontime sun on a Sunday, anoint the toy horse all over with a blend of basil and ginger essential oils. Name your horse according to some quality you see in him or something he brings to your mind. Repeat his name eight times while holding him in the palm of your hand, exposed to the sun. Tie a tiny golden thread or a gold or yellow ribbon around him to form a bow, like a gift.

Keep your toy horse with you, in your purse or pocket, for eight days, repeating his name eight times to him once each day.

On the ninth day, set him down discreetly in some public place—a fence rail, stairway, waiting room—where he is likely to be picked up by a stranger. As you walk away, repeat his name silently eight times, for the last time, and add, "Come back to me soon!"

As soon as someone else picks up and keeps your toy horse, money and/or luck will come to you.

Horse Power Vision for Healing, Well-Being, Bravery

Find a quiet place where you will not be disturbed. It can be outdoors or in, but you should be able to sit comfortably with your eyes closed.

Take some time to get comfortable and relaxed, and to banish all worrisome thoughts and irritations from your mind. Take several long, deep breaths. When you breathe in, see yourself inhaling sparkling golden light. You will exhale smoky gray smog. Continue these breaths until you feel yourself completely filled with the sparkling golden light and no more smog comes out when you exhale.

A white horse arrives, prancing softly, and stands near you. You feel her soft breath against the hairs of your arm. You feel her strong and quiet presence. Reach out to her and feel her velvety muzzle against the palm of your hand. She stretches her neck down, moving her face gently near yours and you see a white light emanating from her, a steady positive energy that soon wraps itself all around you, enclosing you in its strength and joyfulness of the moment. Continue breathing deeply, inhale the horse's light and see yourself becoming as strong, as swift, and as honest as the horse mother. If you have any particularly weak spots or parts that need healing, visualize the horse's magical white light entering that part of your self and cleaning it, filling it with healing energy.

Before she leaves you, thank the horse.

This visualization can be repeated every day for as long as necessary.

~

If you are lucky enough to be in contact with a real live horse, appreciate him for all he is worth. And if you should meet one by chance, do not hesitate to ask his rider if you may touch him.

Proactive Pagans

by Boudica

The Pagan community seems to be a culture that focuses on causes. Check out any Pagan's Facebook page and you will see memes ranging from animal protection to reproductive rights, gay rights, environmental issues and political causes. We sign petitions till we are blind, lobbying through internet-centric collection points. The web has made it easier for our voices to be heard on any topic we may want to discuss.

But being "for a cause" is not just about signing petitions—it's about face time. We seem to forget that while it is good to be out there to make sure that the proper parties are well informed as to what we think, it is not enough to sign petitions on the web. We need to put a face to the signature.

Informing such and such organizations that we do not want our local animal shelter closed down because of funding cuts is good, we also need to realize that it is necessary to find solutions to make sure this threat does not occur again. Offering our opinion and demanding resolution can get the cause the attention it needs. But follow-through is necessary to make sure the problem is resolved.

I recently moved to a new location. I hit the local library and started looking for volunteer opportunities. I don't mind volunteering my time. My passion is reading, and many libraries have adult reading tutoring. However, the face of that has changed. The library offers "online" reading courses for those who need tutorials. My chosen volunteer service has been replaced by online courses. While it is a good idea, it lacks the human element. So much for my thoughts on volunteering. I will examine other avenues of volunteer work. My husband is looking at the local animal shelter.

The local animal shelter needs volunteers. They require donations more than anything else right now. Along with animal foods (which they always need), dollars for medical supplies and spaying services are their primary needs. Hubby and I are talking about making monthly donations once we are able to work that into our budget. Their volunteer needs are for greeters, community outreach, animal care and foster parenting. Our house is at max capacity with animals, so we will be looking at community outreach or animal care once we have settled in.

Many Pagans do volunteer their time in their local communities or make donations to their chosen causes. Some are very proactive when it comes to walking the walk. And my hat goes off to them for their tireless efforts.

But what about those who want to do more than sign petitions on the web? As we have found out, many people cannot do everything they'd like. What else can we do to take our concerns to the action level? What can we do that will not break our budgets yet help further our causes?

Personal contact is important. Whether it is the sound of our voices on the phone to voice our opinion further with our local politicians or just a voice at the other end of an outreach service, human interaction has more impact than a petition with thousands of signatures. Mind you, politicians do take notice of reams of paper with signatures attached. However,

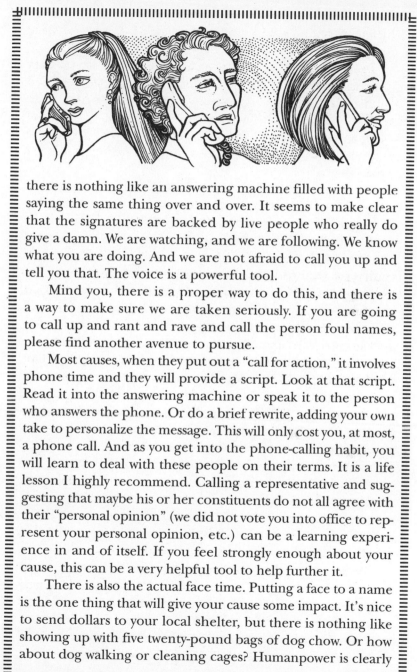

there is nothing like an answering machine filled with people saying the same thing over and over. It seems to make clear that the signatures are backed by live people who really do give a damn. We are watching, and we are following. We know what you are doing. And we are not afraid to call you up and tell you that. The voice is a powerful tool.

Mind you, there is a proper way to do this, and there is a way to make sure we are taken seriously. If you are going to call up and rant and rave and call the person foul names, please find another avenue to pursue.

Most causes, when they put out a "call for action," it involves phone time and they will provide a script. Look at that script. Read it into the answering machine or speak it to the person who answers the phone. Or do a brief rewrite, adding your own take to personalize the message. This will only cost you, at most, a phone call. And as you get into the phone-calling habit, you will learn to deal with these people on their terms. It is a life lesson I highly recommend. Calling a representative and suggesting that maybe his or her constituents do not all agree with their "personal opinion" (we did not vote you into office to represent your personal opinion, etc.) can be a learning experience in and of itself. If you feel strongly enough about your cause, this can be a very helpful tool to help further it.

There is also the actual face time. Putting a face to a name is the one thing that will give your cause some impact. It's nice to send dollars to your local shelter, but there is nothing like showing up with five twenty-pound bags of dog chow. Or how about dog walking or cleaning cages? Humanpower is clearly

in short supply, with local county governments shorting what they consider nonessential services in favor of funding for more human-centered services. You cannot argue there is a need in the human sector for more funding, so when they cut your local shelter budget in favor of children's services, volunteer rather than complain.

If you are allergic to animals, there are alternatives. What about showing up for cleanup day at your local park? I have noticed that some of our local parks are suffering from budget cuts, and cleanup days are becoming a monthly event. From roadside cleanup to playground sprucing up, people are needed to fill in the funding gaps. Funds for these types of services are drying up, no thanks to current political thinking, and while we are petitioning the governments to reinstate funding for these necessary services, we can also make our own personal impact by showing up to pick up the slack.

Face time can also be put into the private sector. From volunteering to help feed the elderly and the homeless to working craft projects for children in hospitals, we can provide necessary services that can make the human condition just a bit more comfortable for those in need.

There are many of you out there who will say, yeah, we are just as "in need" as the rest of the population. Well, yes, you may be. But are you going to be the victim that everyone is going to stare at or are you going to be an example of a survivor? How can you use your position to better the human condition?

Volunteers do not need to be well-to-do and comfortable in order to do their work. Rather, volunteers who are in the same or maybe just a bit better place as the people they help can serve as a mile marker for those being served. Take a look at the example of Alcoholics Anonymous—where those who were helped now turn around and become sponsors for those who come to be helped. They are examples of how you can survive such a devastating disease and move on with their lives.

Same is true for those who volunteer. You are saying, yes, I was where you are now. Your example says, I may be just a little bit better off than you are, but you are going to get where I am by taking the same baby steps I am taking. You offer hope for their future. As for your own situation, success is measured by each day you move forward and not backwards. How much better can you feel than by knowing you helped raise one more person out of a bad situation today?

We all have our causes. If you are not keen on the human condition because you can't deal with it, which is fine, there are so many other places to put your time into.

What about charity events? Some of these require minimal time once a year for some of their biggest events. What about being a water provider at a charity run? Or setting up for a gala event once a year? There are plenty of nondenominational events held that need volunteers. And remember, face time docs not require donations. So, yes, you can set up tables, assist at the food stalls, or do cleanup after a large event and all you are giving is your time.

Let's move on to what we get out of this. Yes, there is a return on being proactive in your community. One of the biggest returns is the improvement of your community. Every time another person is added to the list of people helping their personal cause or aiding their community, the community improves and the cause expands and becomes more successful. Every time we do something to further our cause, the cause has that much more of a chance to succeed. Imagine, if you will, an animal shelter that never has to refuse incoming animals because we succeed in finding homes for all the animals housed there. Imagine watching one more animal leave the shelter and going to their "furever" home. But think about it. How about not having to keep expanding shelters in order to house the ever-expanding amount of homeless animals? Or making the shelters self-sufficient, with outgoing fees paying for the needs of those animals coming in? Imagine free drop off—and never having to turn away another animal, or never having to kill another animal to make room for more.

We can step that up to the human level as well. Imagine saying goodbye to a homeless person because they have gotten a place to live or a job to support themselves, rather than saying goodbye as they are moved to a hospital or another homeless facility. Imagine children having enough food that you helped serve, or maybe a knit sweater you made to keep warm this winter. Even donations of your old clothes that go directly to shelters will help one more child be warmer this winter.

How about one less cleanup day a month because your local government has restored funding so they can hire sanitation one more day a month? Or maybe fences can be repaired, or picnic tables and facilities can be repaired because your voice added to the clamor for more funding for these needs. This then provides a better park experience for the families in your community, who hold family reunions, or birthday parties, or charity events at your local parks. Parks then collect more fees to further expand their funding base. This is a spiral up—not a spiral down—in bettering life in your community. You can say you are part of the cure. How do you think this will make you feel? And what better way to do honor to your gods or the universe than by bettering the human experience, starting with our environment and working our way up through all the small parts that comprise the world we live in.

~

Online petitions are good. They are but the first steps in being proactive. Use the web to find out where you can add your voice and your face to take your cause to the next level. Make what you do really count. Be a proactive Pagan, no matter what you can contribute to your cause.

Food and the Four Elements: Bread and Wine

by Emyme

The lightning cracks and the thunder rolls and they run from the open ground into the cave. A man, a woman, and two children. They gather around the large open pit, fire blazing, and dry off. This fire is never extinguished, tended by the old woman seated on a grass mat, a place of honor. Several families live in this cave. Their home, their community, carved from earth. Just outside the entrance to the cave sits a large log, hollowed out and coated with tree sap so as to be waterproof. This collects the rain that pours down, providing some of the water they use every day. Deep in the cave, a fresh cold spring bubbles up, another source of life-giving water. Surrounding them is air, the most basic of all needs—the air they breathe, the air that feeds the fire, the breeze

65

that cools them in summer and carries the heat from the fire pit, which warms them in winter. The wind that brings the good smell of food and the warnings of predators.

The children lay more sticks across the fire pit and the younger woman commences to prepare a meal. She scoops kernels of grain from a large stone jar into a smaller stone bowl and grinds it into a coarse powder with a rock. Adding water makes a paste, which she then pours onto the smooth, hot stones by the fire—soon several flat, chewy discs of bread are ready. The women of the other families have been busy preparing vegetables and meats—each family brings something to the communal evening meal. Meanwhile, the men tend the containers fashioned from animal skins hanging just inside the opening to the cave, where the sun shines in a few hours almost every day. That sun has warmed the mixture of grapes and berries and water within those skins. Every few weeks, the mixture is tested, tasted—today it is finally sweet enough. The heat and air working on the fruit of the earth and water have created a potable liquid as if by magic. The heat and the air working on the grain from the earth and water have created an edible food—as if by magic.

And that is what is talked of—magic—as the families sit and eat around the fire, drinking the liquid in their earthen shelter, comfortable in the temperate air. Magic—the old woman, the matriarch of this clan, weaves a tale of gods and goddesses. She tells a story of the magic of the air and the earth and the water and the fire. She points to the bread and the wine and explains and exclaims how these are truly gifts of the heavens. Many of the clan have heard these stories before, but there is always some new twist or some new child to take in this wonderment, and so these tales are told again and again. No written language is created yet, but somewhere off to the side one of the children records pictures from the old woman's stories, carving in a rock wall, or on a piece of wood, or painting with food dye on a leftover piece of hide. So we have come to know how early man created shelter and sustenance.

Air...Earth...Water...Fire.
Breath...Foundation...Hydration...Energy.

The elements are universally shared, and are integral to life—consider the Survival Rule of Three:

In any extreme, emergent situation, it is wise to recall one cannot survive more than three minutes without air, Three hours without shelter (earth/fire), three days without water, or three weeks without food (earth/fire).

The Four Elementals are fundamental to the earth-based belief system. We call upon them and bow to them in the casting of every spell. Great honor is awarded the elements, for they enable not just basic survival or getting by, but getting by with comfort.

References to and evidence of bread may be found in history going back more than ten thousand years. Grain was easily stored and transported, to be ground and prepared for baking wherever there was fire. At its most basic level, bread is made from numerous types of grain grown from earth, nourished by water (rain), air (breezes), and fire (the sun). This grain is gathered and separated, and the edible part is ground into a meal. The meal or flour is then again touched by earth through fermentation after adding water and then baked into a solid via air and fire. Bread is a whole food—with almost everything needed to live—that holds the four elements twice over.

As with bread, references to wine are found throughout recorded history. It has been and continues to be a potentially life-saving option in parts of the world with little or no potable water. Wine of the far past was most likely not quite as potent as the wine we now imbibe—even the young could and did drink it. Like grain, it too was easily stored and transported in a variety of containers. Grapes are grown from earth and nourished by water, air, and fire. Once harvested, the liquid is extracted and, similar to bread, fermentation is employed to complete the process of juice to wine. In this case however, fermentation involves earth and air and fire, all three at once. Again, it's nourishment that holds all of the four elements twice over.

Recipes

To anyone new to an earth-based belief system, a kind reminder—any creation in a kitchen, be it food, drink, or spellcasting should begin with blessings and intention. Prepare your workspace, much as you prepare your altar. Ground and center. Bow to the directions. Call to the elements. Ask blessings from the Lady and Lord and your personal deity. Do not forget the Kitchen Witch!

First the Grain

Keeping with the theme of fermentation as part of the earth influence in bread, sourdough is a great example. It requires natural fermentation from bacteria, which is always in the air. This recipe, considered medium-complicated and time-consuming, takes about a week. But the results are incredibly delicious. There is nothing quite like the taste of homemade sourdough bread. Enjoy.

Make the Sourdough Yeast (The "Starter")

The first step is mixing some flour and water. That is one-half cup of rye flour and one-half cup of wheat flour with one cup of warm water. Give it a stir and that is called the "starter." This recipe calls for homegrown yeast, not any commercial yeast. Wild yeast in the air and the flour will create the yeast for this starter.

Cover the mixture loosely and leave it out at room temperature. Every twenty-four hours, take out and discard half, and add one-half cup of wheat flour and one-half cup of warm water. Continue for three to seven days until the starter is fermented and bubbling with wild yeast.

After those three to seven days, depending on the weather and your locale, the mixture will be bubbly and smell "beer-y" with a nice sour smell.

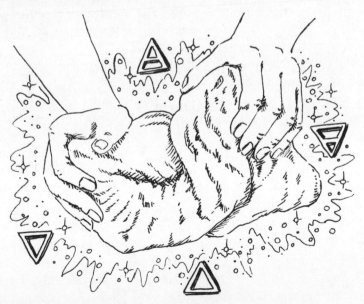

Make the Sourdough Sponge

Now to make the sponge. Pour the starter into a bowl and add one cup of bread flour and one cup of water. Cover that and leave it overnight. This is called a sponge, which is simply a fermented batter. This is used to make the dough.

Prepare the Sourdough Bread Dough

Give the sponge a stir and add two cups to a bowl. Then add:

1 teaspoon sugar	2 teaspoons salt
2 tablespoons oil	1 cup bread flour

Stir that up until it becomes wet, sticky dough. Add another cup of flour and that will make a dough firm enough to pour on to the cutting board. Then we're going to work in approximately a cup of flour. Go by feel. Add a little at a time and keep kneading until you have a smooth, elastic dough. This should take about ten to fifteen minutes.

You know you are done if you can stretch a piece of dough and see light through it. This is called the "window pane" test. Once the dough is ready put a teaspoon of oil in a bowl and oil the bowl and dough so it doesn't dry out.

The next step is allowing the dough to rise. Cover with a wet towel and let rise to double in size, about eighteen hours. Sourdough rises much slower than regular yeast dough. When it is ready, pat it down on the board, completely deflate it. Make it into a square shape and roll it into a loaf.

Put it onto a cornmeal coated pan (oiled, with two tablespoons of cornmeal shaken to cover surfaces), and place it seamside down. Place an oiled piece of plastic wrap loosely over the dough. Let that double in size, between eight and twelve hours.

When that is ready make some slices in the top of the bread, about one-half inch deep, for looks and to help the bread rise. Put a pan of water in the bottom of a cold oven, and place the bread pan in that. Turn on the oven to 425 degrees F., and bake for forty to forty-five minutes.

Should you want a beautiful, blistered, crispy crust, spray with plain water a few times during the baking. When it is done it will have a hollow sound when tapped.

Now the Grape

The essential steps in winemaking can be summarized as follows (this is an extreme simplification):

Extract the flavor and aroma from the base ingredients by chopping, crushing, pressing, boiling, or soaking them.

Add sugar, acid, nutrients, and yeast to the fermentation media or liquor to achieve the proper ratio and ferment, covered, for three to ten days in a primary fermentation vessel (crock, jar, or polyethylene pail) at 70 to 75 degrees Fahrenheit.

Strain off the liquid from the pulp, put the liquid into a secondary fermentation vessel (a carboy or jug), fit a fermentation trap (airlock) on the mouth of the bottle, and allow fermentation to proceed at 60 to 65 degrees Fahrenheit until all bubbling ceases (after several weeks).

Siphon the wine off the sediments (lees) into another clean secondary fermentation vessel. Reattach the fermentation trap. Repeat after another one or two months and again before bottling.

When wine is clear and all fermentation has stopped, siphon into wine bottles and cork the bottles securely. Leave corked bottles upright for three to five days and then store them on their side at 55 degrees Fahrenheit for six months (white wine) to a year (red wine) before sampling. If not up to expectations, allow to age another year or more.

~

Air, Earth, Water, Fire: bread and wine. The elemental world embodied in historical tradition and magical nutrition and imbued with romantic love.

Air: obviously the air we breathe, the breezes and wind; the all important conductor of the heat in baking, and bacteria necessary for fermentation.

Earth: the medium in which seeds grow and become the grain and the grapes; on a much smaller scale the bacteria which enable fermentation.

Water: first, rain to nourish crops; then, any water called for in recipes; also water added to wine for everyday consumption.

Fire: the sun, encouraging crop growth; the heat produced during fermentation; and literal fire to bake breads.

The vignette at the beginning of this essay illustrates how humankind had progressed to a certain level of comfort. While it may seem primitive to us in the twenty-first century, that community had obviously evolved from merely scrabbling for nourishment to preparing it. This underscores another way to look at the elements, and their necessity in creating a higher level of food/sustenance. On almost every continent, early humans lived this life. Wheat, barley, rye, oats, and maize are just some of the grains used to make primitive breads. Grapes of white and red, and every shade in between, provided a nourishing (sometimes intoxicating) liquid.

Thousands of years later children hurry into their home as the storm breaks. Inside, logs blaze in the fireplace. Wonderful smells emanate from the kitchen. Friends and family gather, each bringing something to the communal meal. Loaves of bread cool on the counter. Bottles of wine breathe in the pantry. Bread baked and wine bottled in factories of sparkling white and chrome can be purchased the world over. However, this family prefers a more personal option. During the meal everyone exclaims over the taste and texture of home-baked bread. Everyone partakes of the home-brewed wine, with water added for the children. After the meal, there are requests for recipes, and some pause to look over the brewing system. Wood is added to the fire. Lively conversation ensues. In one corner a grandmother reads to youngsters about ancient history and magic. Off to the side a teenager is engrossed in a sketchbook. Throughout the human experience, from the cave to the twenty-first century home, this scene has repeated too many times to count. No doubt this will continue into the future. People gather to prepare and share their own slice of bread and cup of wine: home-grown magic from air and earth, water, and fire.

The Perfect Magical Host

by James Kambos

Candles and herbs, a vase of flowers, or a strategically placed houseplant. These and many other everyday items, when used with magical intent prior to entertaining, can create a peaceful environment in any home. With some magical tricks and by planning ahead, you can become the perfect magical host/hostess. By using a few of the magical tips I'm going to share with you, your guests will be ensured of a pleasant visit. As an example, last year a severe storm knocked out electrical power to a wide area near where I live. As a result I had two houseguests stay three days until their power was restored. By using some magical tactics I turned what could have been a stressful situation into an enjoyable time. When my guests were ready to leave they remarked, "We feel like we've been on vacation." I guess my magic must have worked!

As magical folk, many of us may have spaces in our homes devoted to the tools of magic or the Craft—statues of deities, pentagrams, or a cauldron—are just a few. We must remember some of our guests aren't magically inclined and may misunderstand the symbols of our faith. Or perhaps you live in an area where Pagans aren't tolerated. Considering this to be a fact of life, I've found that when practicing magic while entertaining it's best to keep your magic subtle and low-key. With the magical advice I'm going to give you, nobody will realize your magical intentions. But everyone will benefit from it.

Cleansing Your Home

What I'm primarily talking about here is giving your home a psychic cleansing. This is especially important to perform before a party or before house guests arrive. If you do this on a regular basis, your home shouldn't need more than a light smudging with an herbal wand or incense of your choice. But if you haven't cleared the energy recently, or if you've had some discord in your home, I suggest a more thorough cleaning.

Here are two methods. Open all windows and doors, then, using a white sage smudge stick, walk through each room, and let the smoke penetrate all nooks and crannies. Or simmer some dried white sage leaves in a small pan, then carry it through each room. You may use a white feather to fan the steam into all corners. End by anointing each threshold and windowsill with a drop of lavender oil. Once the negative energy is removed, lavender will invite soothing energy into your home.

To assure your environment is cleared, take a broom and vigorously sweep your front steps/walk away from your home toward the street. If you have any throw rugs, roll them up tightly, then give them a good shaking outside. Visualize that you're shaking out any trapped negative energy. According to magical tradition, this sweeping or rug cleaning should be done before sunset to attract good luck.

Now that your space is cleansed, scenting the air with a suitable fragrance is a good way to maintain the positive energy you've created. Before company arrives, use an herbal fragrance mist. Warm scents such as vanilla or cinnamon are good because they impart a sense of well-being.

Candles

Almost everyone likes candles. Candles are a discreet way to practice your magic while entertaining. Here are a few ideas for you to consider.

First of all, when in doubt about which color to use, I suggest white. To charge your candles, magically "dress" your them with a drop of olive oil. To do this, as you think of your magical intent, rub each candle with the oil. If you wish to use other colored candles, here are some choices:

Cream: A cream candle will have a calming effect.

Light blue: Promotes peace.

Orange: Helps create a warm environment.

Violet: Excellent to use to balance emotions. Use violet if one or your guests is known to be a gossip.

Yellow: This color will help create lively conversation.

I try to avoid red candles because they may cause some heated conversations, which is something you don't want. If using pillar candles, try carving a peace sign in the bottom prior to use. Before your guests arrive light the candles. Around at least one candle, artfully arrange some fresh bay leaves—this will stop any negativity before it even starts. And you'll notice wherever you place the candles is probably where guests will sit first. And one last candle tip: to create a calm and welcoming atmosphere in the bathroom, you can't go wrong with a lavender-scented candle.

Using Plants and Flowers

To use plants for magical purposes while entertaining, use only living plants or fresh-cut flowers—no dried arrangements. This is especially true for centerpieces.

First let's take a look at houseplants. For magical entertaining a few of the best plants I've used are English ivy, ferns, and African violets. Peace lilies are also highly recommended, but I've never had one myself. English ivy is very protective, and its trailing habit makes it a good choice for mantels, or a dining room sideboard. Ferns are used to trap and hold negative energy, preventing it from entering the home. For

these reasons, place a fern near a door or window. To send out spiritual vibrations, place an African violet wherever you think guests will have conversations. On an end table or on a coffee table are good locations.

Fresh-cut flowers in a vase aren't only attractive, they're magical. To get your home ready magically for company, one of the best all-purpose healing flowers to use is the carnation. Place them in a vase with some fern foliage to create some powerful magic. To banish any evil influences in the home chrysanthemums are an excellent choice. And if you're entertaining for a romantic occasion, asters are a strong love-attracting flower.

Crystals and Stones

Like plants, crystals and stones can help create a soothing environment for your guests without anyone realizing their magical purpose. In fact, you can combine some of your crystals with your plants to increase their magical power. Simply arrange some of your crystals around a potted plant. The plant will grow even better and emit more magical energy.

Stones, beads, or crystals are a beautiful way to magically influence your entertaining. Here are some top choices to use to promote peace, stability, and friendship.

To keep your guests in a good mood, set out a wooden bowl filled with polished amber pieces. The amber will help improve anyone's disposition. If you're concerned about keeping things peaceful, place blue lace agate beads in a bowl and sprinkle with some dried lavender. To strengthen friendships it's not a bad idea to have a piece of tumbled garnet in the room where you'll be entertaining the most.

~

So, the next time your doorbell rings, you can relax, smile and greet your guests with confidence. Your home is now filled with positive energy, which will put you and your guests at ease.

Air Magic

Smudging Around the World: Cleansing Rituals Across Cultures

by Blake Octavian Blair

The practice of energetically and spiritually cleansing and purifying people, places, and objects prior to engaging in sacred practices is a fundamental magical practice. Religious, spiritual, and mystical traditions around the world and through time have practiced rituals of cleansing and purification. The details, tools, procedures, and the terms used to describe them may vary, however, the underlying intent and desired effect remains quite similar—energetic and spiritual purification.

Among present-day magickal and Pagan folk this practice of energetic cleansing is commonly called "smudging," a term stemming from the practices of the indigenous peoples of the Americas and involves the ritual burning of various herbs (commonly various sages) to bathe the subject (human or otherwise) needing cleansing in sacred smoke. Often a feather or one's hand is used to waft the smoke toward and around the subject. Despite the origins of the term we now commonly use in our magickal vernacular for the practice, smuding has existed in various forms for eons across cultures. Practitioners who have had exposure to Catholicism are well familiar with the Catholic Church's affection for censing with frankincense and myrrh. (Heck, even Pagans have an affection for frankincense and myrrh!) It cannot be denied that Catholicism knows how to run a ritual and its metaphysical symbolism runs deep. For example, in Roman Catholicism, the censer is generally swung in triplicate motions to represent the holy trinity from their cosmology.

Logically, various peoples around the world have traditionally tended to sway toward the use of plants available in their geographic area for their purification and smudging practices. Some classic mainstay plants among indigenous peoples in North America are white sage (also often referred to as California or desert sage), cedar, and sweetgrass. White sage is commonly used for its magical properties of purification, healing, and driving off malevolent forces. In contrast, sweetgrass is often burned after sage for the purpose of drawing in benevolent and helpful energies and spirits. Due to this attribute, many magical practitioners like to burn sweetgrass before their spells and rituals. Cedar, while offering healing and protection, also has a masculine energy. I find burning a small amount of cedar (in large quantities it can be irritating to the lungs) along with white sage, complements the feminine energy of sage very nicely.

While plants such as white sage are and were popular among those in North America due to being native to the southwestern region of what is now the United States, it doesn't grow wild in Europe or Asia. However, frankincense comes from the Oman area on the coast of the Arabian Sea. Its trade history through North Africa and the Arabian Peninsula spans at least 5,000 years. Myrrh resin is also harvested in abundance relatively nearby in places such as Yemen and Somalia. Thus, it is not surprising that the purificatory blend of choice among spiritual practitioners throughout the region is a blend of these two resins.

The purificatory rituals of the Aboriginals of Australia have even become a traditional way of culturally welcoming people to the country. These rituals are often referred to as "smoking ceremonies" and often are conducted by building a large central fire on which the herbs of various plants are burned to create the purifying smoke. Three of the most commonly used plants are wattle, cherry ballart, and river red gum (a type of eucalyptus)—all three plants are indigenous to Australia. The wattle is said to be symbolic of and an offering to the elders, the cherry ballart representative of youth, and the red river gum is used to represent the entire community of all Australians, aboriginal and non-aboriginal alike and equal and respective use to and of the land. Visiting groups and dignitaries are often treated to such a ceremony which is literally entitled "Welcome to Country."

The Q'ero shamans of the Andean region of Peru use the wood from the Bursera graveolens or palo santo tree, also known as "Holy Tree," which is indigenous to Central and South America. In addition to the general cleansing, blessing, and purifying properties associated with smudging, palo santo is said by the Q'ero to be especially effective at driving away evil spirits and misfortune. Many feel that palo santo has a light, pleasant, and sweet scent similar to a combination of sandalwood and frankincense, which is not surprising, as the tree is in the same family as frankincense and myrrh, Burseraceae. One interesting character-istic of palo santo is that a stick of it when burning tends produce smoke that is not as thick or seemingly heavy as other smudges. This makes it a good choice for those who are sensitive to smoke and/or have respiratory issues. It also thusly works well for small and enclosed spaces.

In Buddhist and Hindu shrines and temples, large and small, smoking incense is a staple feature. Its purpose is multifold. The incense is indeed used as an offering to the various deities, however, incense is also used in these traditions as a purificatory element. Visitors to Buddhist temples in the East will often place incense in a large bowl of sand used as an incense burner, light the incense, and then use their hands to waft the smoke over their bodies for healing and purification. Often these large vessels of smoking incense are placed outside or just inside a temple and people gather around in large numbers to cleanse themselves before even entering the temple proper. As we can see, this is already akin to many smudging rituals and customs familiar to Westerners. In fact, the temple incense of Tibetan Buddhists comes in a variety of blends, some specifically for healing others specifically for purification—both common reasons for smudging. The blends are intri-cate formulas typically consisting of over thirty different herbs and botanicals and are widely prized in Tibetan cul-ture. I find their energetic effects to be so effective that I carry purificatory Tibetan temple incense in my witch-on-the-go bag for house blessings and cleansings.

Similarly in Hinduism, incense is crafted from sacred woods, plants, and botanicals for their energetic and spiritual properties. Interestingly though, among many Hindus, the catalyst for purification from burning the incense, and thereby the plant matter, is not the smoke itself but rather the scent of the smoke. The divine scent of the burning materials is said not only to cleanse the entire environment it fills and those individuals within it, but also creates a sort of shared communion between the deity and the practitioner, as they both share in the consumption of the divine scent.

Be sure to properly research any smudging materials you plan to burn. The smoke and fumes of some substances when burned, like cedar, can be toxic—especially in large quantities. Be sure to take proper precautions when using these materials. Use proper ventilation and proper quantities and proportions. Some materials are okay only in small quantities. Additionally, many suggest that pregnant individuals not be exposed to the smoke of some materials, such as white sage. Some people feel that a light smudging outside with these substances is fine, however, others suggest avoiding them altogether. If you have any health concerns with the smoke of any smudging materials, please research the material, consult a medical professional and/or employ an alternative "smokeless smudging" method.

Smokeless Smudging Alternatives

There are many reasons and situations for which burning smudge and creating smoke is not possible, whether it be asthma or another medical concern, or an environmental or building code that prohibits burning anything. The good news is that there are many smokeless alternatives to smudging that are equally as effective, such as spirit or holy waters, gem elixirs, and flower waters or essences. Simply use your favorite method of asperging the water over the person, object, or area you wish to cleanse. While doing so, hold your intent in mind and/or accompany the ritual by reciting any mantras or prayers you'd like as you would when doing any other smudging ritual (do be mindful that whatever you are sprinkling will not be damaged by the bit of moisture). These "liquid smudges" can also be used to anoint a person or object in addition to asperging.

Sound is another excellent method of cleansing. I have been blessed with a few different opportunities to see Tibetan monks who were visiting the United States. You could almost tangibly feel the energy in the space shifting as they would chant their mantras and prayers. When they were finished, you could fully tell their intonations had transformed the energy of the space! You, too, can employ this technique by chanting your favorite mantra or blessing aloud in a space while visualizing a cleansing light filling the area. A nonvocal method of conducting a "sound smudge" is the playing of a singing bowl in an area you wish to cleanse. The vibrational frequency of the the bowl does an excellent job of clearing out unbeneficial energies. Rattling is another popular way to smudge a place or a person and is a common technique among shamanic practitioners for both cleansing and "sealing" healing work upon its completion. Simply rattle in the space or around a person in their auric field, it will break up and help dissolve detrimental energies and blockages.

Reiki and other energy and lightwork methods can also be used as a method of energetic cleansing. Smudging and purification rituals are all about shifting energy for various cleansing and healing effects, so it would only make sense that using an energy-based system, even without physical tools, can be just as effective. If you are trained in such a modality, experiment with it and see how you can apply it to this need. In this way, you have a method of cleansing anytime and anywhere in impromptu situations.

Tailor Your Practice

For many of us our spiritual practice is highly personal and individualized. Therefore, it is important to develop smudging rituals and practices that fit your needs and are relevant to you. Pick methods and materials that both resonate with you and are practical to your situation. Choose ritual incantations, prayers, or mantras to accompany according to your traditions. Depending on the choice of tools, a smudging ritual can invoke the four elements: earth (via plants), fire (via the action of burning), air (via smoke), and water (if a shell is used). In my opinion, regular smudging practices constitute good "spiritual hygiene." In addition to the typical situations that call for smudging (cleansing tools, before ritual, after traumatic events, house blessings, etc.). I also smudge myself on a daily basis and my entire home on a weekly basis. This is good maintenance and upkeep—as the old saying goes, "An ounce of prevention is worth a pound cure!" I think this is especially true for spiritual hygiene! So develop a routine that works for you, whether it be a smudging yourself daily, your home a certain day each week, or doing a cleansing ritual on the New and Full Moon.

The basic tools you will want for what we'd think of as more "traditional" smudging rituals, where plant matter is burned, are not hard to come by and you have several

options. You will need a fireproof bowl or clay pot of some type. I recommend a nonflammable substance such as sand or aquarium gravel to put in the bottom of the bowl. This safety measure helps absorb some of the heat as well as aid you in extinguishing the smudge. Many people like to use an abalone shell for this purpose, and while they can work just fine, they are not fireproof or heatproof and you can burn through the bottom. The shell can also become quite hot quite fast, so if you choose to use one purchase, definitely use sand or gravel. The bowl will serve as a vessel to catch ashes or burning embers and to rest the smudge in as you carry it about during your ceremony. Many people like to waft the smoke using a feather or their hand. At this point, all you are missing is your smudging material itself. If you choose to use a smudge stick or bundle, you are good to go, just be sure to fully tamp out and extinguish the bundle when you are finished by tapping and grinding it into the gravel or sand in the bowl. If you use loose resins and herbs, you will also need a small incense charcoal (and tongs to handle it) to place on top of the sand in the bowl to burn the smudge upon. But as always, never leave things burning unattended.

As I mentioned earlier, I like to smudge myself daily as a cleansing and an act of prayer. While you should work to create personalized rituals, I'll share here the basics of mine that you can use as an inspirational springboard. Remember, rituals need not be elaborate nor lengthy to be effective! For my daily smudging, I use a stick of palo santo wood and a medium-sized seashell I found at the beach. I stand before my altar and light the palo santo. I waft the smoke over my altar area as an offering and cleansing. I pass it down my body a couple times in the front and in the back (as best I can). I make sure to smudge under my feet and I then make prayers and requests to my spirits for protection and guidance throughout the day as I use my hand to waft the smoke again into my heart chakra, and then up over my brow and crown areas. I then hold the smoldering stick in front of me and focus on my intentions for the day and let the smoke carry them into the realm of spirit. (Smoke is a traditional method in many cultures to carry prayers into the spiritual realms.) I then declare to myself or aloud "Blessed be. So mote it be." I close the simple ritual by extinguishing the smudge by tamping it out in the shell I store it in on my altar.

～

Whether by smoke, sound, liquid, or other method, smudging can be a powerful practice to implement on a regular basis, not just prior to rituals. As you can see, smudging can be made into a powerful ritual in and of itself. Hopefully the information, techniques, and ideas shared in this article will provide the inspiration you need to implement and carry on the sacred tradition of smudging.

Thoughts Frozen in Time
by Charlie Rainbow Wolf

Think of energy, preserved throughout history. How marvelous would it be to be able to go back in time and space and touch that energy with our own? What if we could touch those who walked before, hear their thoughts, get a glimpse of who they were, or perhaps leave our own energies for those yet to come? Most of us do this every day without even thinking. We leave behind traces of ourselves, frozen in time, for many to see. We not only convey our thoughts, but also glimpses of our personality, and yet we do so almost automatically. The mystery is in our handwriting.

The study of handwriting—called graphology—has intrigued many people over the years. The brain guides the hand to make marks on the paper, and in the words formed by those marks, energy is captured. Now the message becomes twofold; the interpretation of the words being written, and the interpretation of the handwriting itself. On a mundane level, it is just handwriting; a quick note, a shopping list, a signature on a document. On a deeper level, though, this is a snapshot of the person behind the writing.

The Signature

The way that we write words on paper can reveal a lot about who we are. Much of what is written today is electronically produced. Even though important documents are usually computer-generated, in most cases they still require an actual signature. We sign checks, receipts, contracts, licenses, and other permanent records. Our signatures are as unique as we are.

Many people will sign their name with a slightly different handwriting than their normal penmanship. Perhaps there is a flourish underneath the name or some other embellishment around it. Subconsciously, our signature indicates how we want others to see us. This also makes sense because our signature is the piece of handwriting that we share the most often with others—it is our public expression of who we are. We might not consider putting flourishes in our normal handwriting, but with our signature it seems okay to do so because it is accepted that we can be artistic with our name. Large signatures tend to belong to bold people who want to be noticed while smaller signatures might belong to those of a more introverted nature. The exception to this is a signature that is unusually small when compared to the rest of the body of handwriting. This can indicate that someone is seeking attention, but perhaps in a less obvious way.

The Body of Work

The main piece of writing—a note or a letter, for example—will often display very different characteristics than the signature. First, let's look at the margins. They should be well balanced, so that the writing sits on the paper framed by empty space. If the margins are too wide, it can be a sign of insecurity or inhibitions on the part of the writer. If they are too narrow, this can indicate that the writer of the piece spreads himself too thinly in most areas of life. Wider left-hand margins can indicate that the writer is ready to leave the past behind; while if the right-hand margin is wider, it might reveal that this person was more comfortable in previous circumstances than the current situation—living in the past, perhaps. Sometimes the margins will start narrow and get progressively wider. A left-hand margin that steadily increases is often indicative of those who start out reserved but then find their confidence. The negative expression could be that this person is somewhat lacking in self-control; they mean well but then get carried away. The opposite tends to be true, too. A left-hand margin that starts wide but gradually narrows can indicate someone who may have big ideas but not the confidence or the diligence to see them manifested.

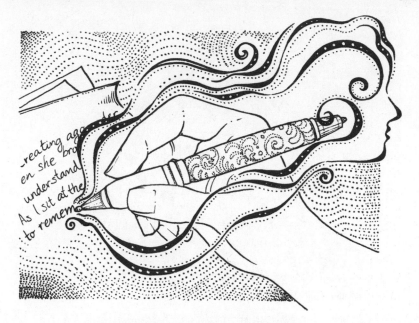

Encrypted in the Details

Another important factor in examining handwriting is the way that the lowercase *i* is dotted, or the *t* is crossed. Sometimes these will be precise and neat, showing self-discipline and control. Sometimes these marks will seem to be placed to the right of the letter, almost as an afterthought. This can be interpreted as a sign of eagerness or impatience. These writers are assertive and may also have a bit of a temper. It stands to reason then, that if the cross on the "t" or the dot of the "i" is too far to the left, it can indicate someone who lacks confidence, and may be indecisive. Markings that are too high above the letters can indicate imagination and a sense of adventure—or that the person may be setting unattainable goals. Some writers may curve these markings over the letters, indicating that they are trying to curb their own desires and goals. Sometimes the dot of the "i" or the cross of the "t" may look like a knot; this is usually a sign of persistence or stubbornness.

Loops—or lack of them—have a lot to say about a person, too. There are two kinds of loops in handwriting; those that reach up, such as on the lowercase letters *h*, *k*, or *l*; and those that reach down, as in the lowercase *g*, *p*, and *y*. Loops that reach up indicate how the writer feels about his goals and ambitions. We touched on that briefly when we looked at the crosses and dots on the *t* and the *i*. Loops that reach high, but are in proportion to the rest of the writing, often point to someone who is ambitious—individuals who have both goals and the ability to achieve them. The lower loops indicate the writer's relationship with more mundane things: their physical activity and possessions.

In both zones (upper and lower), loops that are wide and similar in size indicate that the individual is likely to be well-balanced and adaptable. Pointed loops can show that the writer has some discomfort with that area of life. Wide loops indicate an open-minded person, but loops that are unusually wide can show that the writer may be prone to daydreaming and fantasy. Narrow loops point to a narrow-minded outlook; thin and narrow loops often show an unwillingness to explore. Broken loops can point to areas that are missing, and that need specific attention.

The way that the words start and end is important too. They can tell us much about how the writer approaches their goals and aspirations. The lead-in strokes can reveal whether or not the writer is confident, easily led, or nursing a past hurt. When the lead-in stroke is long, it reveals someone who is sentimental, emotional, and who wants to be accepted; unless the stroke dips unnaturally lower than the rest of the word. A low lead-in points to low self-esteem and someone who may be quite gullible. If the lead-in stroke is angular, hurt may be being nursed.

If the ending strokes are truncated, rather than flowing to a close, it can indicate those people who are frugal, self-sufficient, and perhaps a bit closed to others. Ending strokes that point up relate to a person who is generous and optimistic; if they point up and out, this person may be prone to extravagance. If the word ending fills the gap between that word and the next, it can mean that the writer is responsive and giving, but perhaps trying to fill some gap in his or her life.

～

By now it should be apparent that, to the trained eye, our handwriting does more than just convey words. It shares who we are with others. Of course, there is much more to graphology than loops and hoops; handwriting analysis is a skill that takes much diligence and study to learn. Can changing our handwriting change who we are? Not really, but when we make changes in the way we approach life, it is often reflected in our penmanship. It's fun to look back over the years and see how our writing changes as we progress and grow. This is particularly true in signatures, reflecting the way we adapt as we progress through our lives. Remember, writing is the energy of our thoughts, frozen in time: what impression do we really want to leave?

For Further Study:

Amend, Karen. *Handwriting Analysis: The Complete Basic Book.* Newcastle Pub. Co. Inc., 1980.

Branston, Barry. *Graphology Explained: A Workbook.* Weiser Books, 1991.

McNichol, Andrea, and Jeffrey Nelson. *Handwriting Analysis: The Complete Basic Book.* McGraw Hill, 1994.

A Short History of Rosicrucians

by Magenta Griffith

Rosicrucian refers to both the groups and the members of any of several lodge organizations, some secret, which trace their lineage back to an order said to have been founded in fifteenth-century Germany. They hold a doctrine "built on esoteric truths of the ancient past," which, "concealed from the average man, provide insight into nature, the physical universe and the spiritual realm." Rosicrucianism is usually symbolized by the Rose Cross, a many-petaled rose superimposed on a cross, often equal-armed. The cross is supposed to symbolically represent the human body while the rose represents the individual's unfolding consciousness.

In 1614, an anonymous pamphlet entitled the *Fama Fraternitatis Rosae Crucis* (The Fame of the Brotherhood of the Rose Cross) was published in Cassel, Germany. This was followed in 1615 by the *Confessio Fraternitatis* (the Confessions of the Brotherhood), a publication in the same vein as the first but much more apocalyptic. It told of a society that had obtained the secrets of enlightenment and of a forthcoming reformation of the age, returning it to a state of grace. These pamphlets tell the story of one Christian Rosencreuz (the name *Rosenkreuz* can be translated as "Rosy Cross"), a young man who wandered through the Near East learning the esoteric wisdom of the Arabs and Egyptians. Upon returning to Germany in the early fifteenth century, he and a few like-minded people formed a society called the Fraternity of the Rose Cross and built a temple called the Spiritus Sanctus. There were only eight members at the beginning; all men, all bachelors, and all virgins. They had certain principles: they would be healers without asking for payment, they would have no uniform, they would adopt the customs of the country where they lived, they would meet once a year at the Spiritus Sanc-

tus, and each would find someone to be his successor. Also, the fraternity would remain secret for one hundred years.

Presumably, the *Fama* was published after the hundred years had elapsed since it describes the fraternity to the outside world. In that time, scientific, philosophical, and religious freedom had grown so that the public might benefit from the Rosicrucians' knowledge. The pamphlets don't explicitly ask people to join, but says the group's members will be watching for those in tune with their thinking.

A third document appeared in 1616 entitled *The Chemical Wedding of Christian Rosencreuz*. This is a highly symbolic treatise following Rosencreuz through a mystical "wedding" that is actually an alchemical allegory. Alchemy is presented not as the physical transformation of base metals into gold, but rather as a spiritual process in which the "base" person is enlightened, turning into spiritual "gold." The idea that Rosi-crusians were not just offering free healing but also spiritual enlightenment comes from this writing.

Major Rosicrucian Organizations

Many groups have used the word "Rosicrucian" in their name. The earliest ones are difficult to find information about; this is an overview of some of the nineteenth- and twentieth-century orders, especially the largest and most influential.

Fraternitas Rosae Crucis (the Rosicrucian Fraternity) claim they existed in America prior to the American Revolution, but the evidence is that this group was started in 1858, by Paschal Beverly Randolph after he was initiated by a German Rosicrucian fraternity. It is the oldest Rosicrucian Order in the United States and continues to provide mail-order instruction. They teach that there is one God and that within each of us is buried a particle of a Divine Spark, of and from God. To develop this celestial spark, we must transmute our lower nature. This state of spiritual development is termed Soul Consciousness or Soul Illumination, which is symbolized by the fully bloomed rose in the center of the Rosy Cross. Their mission is to guide individuals, one by one, on the path toward Soul Consciousness followed by God Consciousness.

The **Societas Rosicruciana in Anglia** (Society of Rosicrucians in England, or SRIA) was founded in 1867 by Robert Wentworth Little. This offshoot of **Societas Rosicruciana in Scotia** (Society of Rosicrucians in Scotland) requires its members to be both Masons and Christians. SRIA was popularized by William Wynn Wescott, who later helped to start the Hermetic Order of the Golden Dawn; the Golden Dawn had an inner order called the **Ordo Rosae Rubae et Aureae Crucis**, (Order of the Red Rose and Cross of Gold), whose rituals were based on Rosicrucian ideas. The American branch of this group, **Societas Rosicruciana in Civitatibus Foederatis, Society of Rosicrucians in the Civil Republic**, was founded in 1880. It still exists; membership is by invitation only.

The **Societas Rosicruciana in America, (Society of Rosicrucians)** SRIA is an American organization started in 1907 and incorporated on September 8, 1912, by Sylvester C. Gould and George Winslow Plummer, both prominent Freemasons. In 1916, the Society began to admit women into its ranks. This group doesn't require any prior membership in any other organization, Masonic or Rosicrucian, or restrict members from joining other groups, and is not affiliated with the Societas Rosicruciana anywhere else. They offer a number of correspondence courses and have an extensive website with links to many articles on a variety of occult subjects.

The **Rosicrucian Fellowship** was founded by Max Heindel in 1907. A largely Christian organization, it has closer ties with theosophy than with any other Rosicrucian group. It is composed of men and women who study the Rosicrucian Philosophy, and heal the sick—primarily spiritual healing. They offer correspondence courses on the Bible, Esoteric Christian Philosophy, and related topics. Because their founder felt strongly that no price should be put on spiritual teachings, only the Rosicrucian Fellowship books cost money—everything else they do is on a free-will "love-offering" basis, and there are no membership dues or fees. The Rosicrucian Fellowship has no connection with any other organization.

Lectorium Rosicrucianum (LRC) officially began in 1935, but had been developing years earlier. In 1924 the brothers Zwier Willem Leene and Jan Leene joined Het Genootschap Rozekruisers, the Dutch organization of the Rosicrucian Fellowship. Soon, the brothers took a prominent place, and were entrusted with its leadership in 1929. In 1935 they decided to proceed on the spiritual path with their own group, independent of the Rosicrucian Fellowship. In 1935, the Leene brothers went to London, visited the British Library and discovered the forgotten manifestos of the classical Rosicrucians of the seventeenth century. They carefully translated these manuscripts, republishing them in 1936 in Dutch under the title *The Book M*, and made these spiritual works available to a wider audience. New editions of the classical writings, including their

commentaries, were published several years later, and are now available in many languages. The Lectorium Rosicrucianum say they are a "Gnostic Spiritual School."

In 1912, Annie Besant, a prominent member and leader of the Theosophical Society, Marie Russak, and James Wedgwood founded the **Order of the Temple of the Rosy Cross** in England. However, during the First World War, the group's activities were suspended; Besant and Wedgwood returned to other work. Russak contacted Harvey Spencer Lewis in California and helped Spence compose the rituals of the AMORC, which is discussed below.

Rosicrucian Order Crotona Fellowship (ROCF) was started around 1924 by George Arthur Sullivan. It is important in occult history because they created the "**New Rosicrucian Theatre**" in Christenchurch, Hampshire. In this group, in the late 1930s, that Gerald Gardner, the founder of modern Witchcraft, first encountered witchcraft in some form. Also, Sullivan was the occult mentor of Peter Cady, one of the founders of the Findhorn Society. Not much is known about what happened to this unusual group, but it seems that it didn't last after the death of its founder and the chaos of World War II.

The Ancient Mystical Order Rosea Crucis (AMORC), was founded in 1915 in New York City by H. Spencer Lewis, an American occultist and mystic. Today, it is probably the largest and best-known Rosicrucian group in the world. From the beginning, men and women have had equal roles in this Rosicrucian Order. AMORC considers its traditions to go back to ancient Egypt; it is believed that these teachings were used by many people, including Francis Bacon, Benjamin Franklin, Thomas Jefferson, Leonardo da Vinci, Isaac Newton, Pascal, and Spinoza. While none of these historical figures can be confirmed, it is known that Walt Disney was once a member of AMORC, as was *Star Trek* creator Gene Roddenberry.

In 1909, Harvey Spencer Lewis visited France in search of Rosicrucians, was duly initiated in Toulouse, France, and given the mandate to establish an order in North America. After further qualification and preparation, the first official Manifesto was issued in the United States in 1915, announcing the establishment of Rosicrucian activity in America. Lewis also may have been given a charter from the magical order Ordo Templi Orientis (OTO) by Theodore Reuss, its head, perhaps as a way of getting support in his battle for leadership with Aleister Crowley.

In 1927 the Order moved its headquarters to San Jose, California. The AMORC headquarters now includes the Rosicrucian Park, the Rosicrusian Egyptian Museum, the fifth planetarium built in the USA, the Rosicrucian Peace Garden, Rosicrucian Research Library, Grand Temple, an administration Building, Fountain Plaza and gardens. AMORC is a worldwide organization, with the primary purpose of advancing of its principles and teachings for charitable, educational, and scientific purposes. It is financed mainly through fees paid by its members. Income is used by the organization to pay expenses, develop new programs, expand services, and carry out educational work. AMORC publishes several periodicals, including a public magazine called the *Rosicrucian Digest*. They have always used media technology of the day—in 1928, they erected a radio tower and began regular broadcasts, which continue on a regular radio station in San Jose. Their ads on the backs of magazines with the motto: "A split second in eternity—the ancients called it Cosmic Consciousness" are widely remembered. Now they have an extensive website, podcasts, and YouTube videos, and can be found on Facebook and Twitter.

AMORC is not a religion and does not require any specific beliefs; their students come from a variety of cultural and religious backgrounds. They claim that much of the material in their teachings cannot be found anywhere else, and goes back to the mystery schools of ancient Egypt and Europe. Their system of study is supposed to enable students to achieve their highest potential and bring about a transformation on all levels of being: physical, mental, emotional, psychic, and spiritual. Weekly lessons for study and practice that lead to three introductory degrees comprising an overview of the Rosicrucian course of study. This is followed by nine additional degrees, each having its own particular emphasis. The basic program of lessons, from the introductory courses up through the end of the ninth degree, takes approximately five years. There are teachings past the ninth degree for those who wish further development.

While they charge dues, there is no charge to members for their lessons, which are available online as well as by mail. They have local groups that offer classes and lectures as well. Initiations can be performed at home, or at an AMORC lodge. No Rosicrucian member is obligated to associate with a local Rosicrucian group, but it is highly recommended. They state on their website that students will discover how to achieve vibrant health and increased vitality, learn how to bring the life they want into physical manifestation, develop a greater sense of confidence and inner peace, waken their deeper psychic senses, and finally, achieve a gradual inner awakening, leading to a permanent awareness of the unity of all creation and a personal relationship with the "oneness" of the universe.

There are other Rosicrucian organizations in existence; new ones start and old ones fold over time. Some are small, or strictly invitational, and don't make themselves known to the general public. I found websites for several that seem to have been started since 2000, but have no recent activity, suggesting they were short-lived. These groups wax and wane, and there is no way to make a complete list of Rosicrucians orders. The larger, well-established groups serve an important purpose of providing training to seekers, especially those who need to use correspondence or online courses. All are part of a larger, ongoing Western tradition seeking spiritual enlightenment.

For Further Study:

Greer, John Michael. *Inside a Magical Lodge*. St. Paul, MN: Llewellyn, 1998.

———. *New Encyclopedia of the Occult*. St. Paul, MN: Llewellyn, 2003.

Conflict Resolution for a Magickal Community

by Emily Carlin

Conflict is a natural and inevitable part of life. We argue with a friend, disagree with a co-worker, or a fight with a parent. If you are a part of a school, coven, or any larger community, most likely you have seen your share of conflict. Whenever people with their own thoughts and feelings come together for a common purpose, they eventually come into conflict. How to best accomplish a common goal and how to behave during that process tends to reveal conflicts. As much as we'd like to think otherwise, the magickal community is not above this sort of behavior.

Whether you are directly involved or are only witness to a conflict, it can create stress. An unresolved conflict can ruin your day—and the day of others if you take that stress out on the people around you. It's rarely a good thing. When you're a magickal practitioner, the stress and tension of conflict can have a far deeper impact. Those who practice magick have been trained to make their thoughts and intentions go out into the world and manifest themselves. After all, that's what magick is. At the best of times, it takes practice, concentration, and a clear head to make sure what you get is what you intended and only what you intended. When a practitioner is in the midst of an ongoing conflict, it can throw off that delicate balance. At best, these challenges with friends, family, co-workers, or other practitioners are distracting and reduce the effectiveness of our magick.. At worst that imbalance can manifest itself as unintentional negative thoughtforms or hexes (but that's a problem for another day). Therefore, it is incredibly important that all people who practice magick take the time to learn how to deal with conflict thoroughly, efficiently, and productively so that we can maintain our equilibrium, our control, and our happiness.

The first step in dealing with conflict is to bring it out into the open. It is far too easy to slip into anger and resentment in a one-sided conflict. People rarely want their actions to breed conflict, but they can't do anything about it if they're never told it's happening. Letting something bother you and never saying anything does nothing but reinforce the actions that trouble you and make you miserable. Most people, particularly those working toward being a part of a happy and productive community, want to know when their actions have negative effects on those around them. Nobody wants to be the bad guy.

Acknowledging a conflict exists, the first step in resolving a conflict, can in itself create conflict. Bringing a problem out into the open might expose thoughts and feelings that you'd rather keep hidden, but in the end it is the only way to actually solve the problem. Be brave and face potential conflicts, rather than hiding from them. Respect the other members of your community

enough to call them on bad behavior and give them an opportunity to do something about it. Once a conflict is brought out into the open, there are a few simple things you can do to help resolve the situation fairly and effectively.

There are three basic techniques that will help you to help yourself and your community when conflict arises: recognizing a position from an underlying interest, taking the time to check your understanding and the understanding of others, and validating and respecting emotions without buying into them.

Positions vs. Underlying Interests

A position in a conflict is what a person is asking for: what they want to happen or what they want someone else to do. They are often statements like "I want you to buy the decorations for our next event" or "I think that we should all submit proposals for Pantheacon events this year." A position is the means by which someone hopes to accomplish his or her ends.

An underlying interest is the root motivation behind a person's positions—the reason those positions were proposed. These deeper interests are often very basic needs, such as the need for respect, safety, or to feel valued.

One of the difficulties in distinguishing between positions and underlying interests is that we often don't consciously understand what our underlying interests are. We can determine someone's underlying interest by starting with the position being proposed and asking why. If Rowan asks Pat to go to the store, ask why. Why does Rowan want something from the store, and why should it be Pat who goes? Is it that Rowan just wants something and doesn't feel like getting it, or is it something else? Or is Rowan asking because she feels like Pat hasn't been pulling his weight in the group? Why does Rowan think that Pat's going to the store will fix that? Ask why and dig deep to find the real underlying motivation for the position.

You'll know you've hit on an underlying interest when you ask why and there is no other answer but the interest itself. For example, if the underlying interest is respect, there isn't an answer to "Why do you want respect?" that goes beyond "Because respect is important to me." Underlying interests are basic universal values. You don't really need to ask someone why they want to feel loved or safe.

Let's look at these concepts in action. Pretend that we have a magickal group called Coven of the Sacred Star. This is a small group with only about eight people, two of which are Skye and Riley. For the last few months, Skye has bought nearly all of the supplies for the group's workings (candles, herbs, spell components, etc.) and Riley hasn't pitched in at all. The week before the group's next meeting, Skye calls Riley and tells him that he needs to buy the supplies for that meeting. Riley, feeling rather put out, says no. There is our conflict. Skye's position is: "Riley needs to buy next week's supplies"; and Riley's position is: "Skye should continue to buy the supplies." In this case, Skye's position initiated the conflict, so let's look at her underlying interests. Why does Skye want Riley to buy the supplies? Skye feels that it isn't fair for her to buy the supplies every week while Riley buys nothing. Why doesn't she think that's fair? She doesn't feel like her contribution to the group is being appreciated when people just assume that she'll keep paying for things without even asking her. Why is that a problem? Skye doesn't feel like she's being respected by the rest of the group, particularly Riley. There we have Skye's underlying interest: the need for respect.

Distinguishing between positions and underlying interests is critical in a conflict because, while positions can only be agreed to or refused, underlying interests can be satisfied in many different ways. In the scenario above, Riley will either buy the supplies or he won't, but perhaps there's another way to meet Skye's need for respect. What if instead of going up to Riley and making a demand of him, Skye had said, "Riley, I don't feel right about how everyone always assumes that I'm going to buy the supplies. It feels like my contribution to the group isn't being respected. We need to change things so I don't feel like I'm being taken for granted." That would have created a completely different conflict, one where Riley doesn't feel he's being attacked, guilt-tripped, or put upon—and one where there are many possible solutions. Arguing over a position versus arguing over an underlying interest is the difference between a fight—one winner and one loser—and an important discussion between reasonable people.

Recognizing people's underlying interests is critical to the healthy resolution of conflict. When everyone in a conflict feels respected and has their underlying interests addressed, then everyone wins and the community is better for it.

Check Your Understanding

The most common cause of conflict is miscommunication. In a conflict, emotions tend to run high and we don't always speak as clearly as we think we do. Those same emotions can color our understanding of what others say; our expectations and imaginings of what other mean becoming what we believe they actually said. Misunderstandings can reduce even the most reasonable and sophisticated people to squabbling children. While such miscommunications cannot be avoided altogether, they can be greatly reduced by simply taking a step back.

When emotions are heated, you have to take the occasional time-out to make sure what you're hearing is the message they meant to communicate—and that they actually understand what you were trying to communicate in response. To do this, simply paraphrase what you understand the other person's argument to be and let them correct you if you misunderstood. Then have the other person paraphrase what he or she thinks you meant to say and clarify as necessary. Do this until everyone agrees that people

have understood what they meant to communicate. It takes some time to do it right, but uncovering a misunderstanding early in the conflict-resolution process is well worth the effort.

When you reflect back someone else's argument, it is crucial that you do so honestly and respectfully. You have to genuinely want to understand what they're trying to say or your effort will come off as mockery. For example, here is a good way check your understanding: "What I'm hearing is that you don't want us to do a public Samhain ritual because you don't think we have enough practice to do a good job. Is that what you meant?" A bad way to do so would be: "Look, you're saying that you just don't want to a public ritual because you think we're not good enough. Is that it?" The first statement is respectful and tries not to make assumptions. It leaves room for the person on the receiving end to correct misunderstanding. The second statement is combative and disrespectful and will likely make the person on the receiving end defensive and unreasonable.

Checking your understanding is critical for both correcting our own misunderstandings and correcting what you may have misspoken. People often don't say what they intend to under the best of circumstances, and the emotional tension and speed of an evolving conflict is hardly an ideal circumstance for clearheadedness. You will say the wrong thing at some point. So will everyone else involved in the conflict. When you check your understanding, you give the other person in the conflict a safe space to correct what he or she may have misspoken while saving face.

Respecting Emotions without Buying into Them

In almost any conflict worthy of the name, you will run into emotions. Strong feelings like anger, sorrow, betrayal, and grief are unfortunately common. Such strong emotions often muddle our thinking and can make resolving a conflict extremely difficult. The best way to deal with such feelings is to validate and respect them without actually taking them on ourselves. Just because someone else is feeling a strong emotion doesn't mean that we have to.

Emotions are deeply personal experiences that an individual has in a given moment and they are always valid. Emotions aren't right or wrong; they are what someone is feeling, regardless of whether we think that's reasonable or appropriate. Emotions are always real to the person experiencing them. Never, ever invalidate or belittle someone else's emotions. It is a surefire way to assure that you will be reduced in that person's eyes from a member of their community to "the enemy." Making the effort to recognize someone's emotional experience in a conflict shows that you care and respect that experience. It's not only kind, it's essential to making the other person feel heard and respected.

That's as far you need to take your recognition of someone else's emotions. As said above, emotions are merely an individual experience in a given moment. You can respect someone's experience without agreeing with it or going so far as to take that emotion on to yourself and feel it with them. If you feel yourself becoming too involved in someone else's emotions take a step back and remain objective. Getting outraged on a friend's behalf might look supportive of them, but in reality it doesn't help solve the problem at all and can, in fact, make it worse. It's up to you to decide what's more important in a given situation: showing empathy for a friend or remaining objective enough to think clearly.

For Further Study:

Brinkman, Rick, and Rick Kirschner. *Dealing with People You Can't Stand.* New York: McGraw-Hill, 2002.

Cloke, Kenneth. *Mediating Dangerously: The Frontiers of Conflict Resolution.* San Francisco: Jossey-Bass, 2001.

Fisher, Roger, and William Ury. *Getting to Yes: Negotiating Agreement Without Giving In.* New York: Penguin Books, 1991.

McLeod, Saul. "Maslow's Hierarchy of Needs." http://www.simplypsychology.org/maslow.html.

Stone, Douglas, Bruce Patton, and Sheila Heen. *Difficult Conversations: How to Discuss What Matters Most.* New York: Penguin Books, 1999.

Going Postal:
Magickal Uses for Mail

by Raven Digitalis

Swiftness of communication is at an all-time high in human civilization. No more than a minute before typing this, I sent an email to a friend in the Caribbean and another to a friend in the UK, both of whom received the message and responded immediately. Yesterday I spoke on the phone to my buddy in New Delhi. Earlier today I was watching the CCTV News (China Central Television). Last week, I listened to an EDM podcast from Egypt and briefly webcammed on a friend's computer with a guy from Kashmir. Amazing!

While occurrences like these can easily be taken for granted, particularly by members of younger generations (like me!), it's honestly miraculous that global communication can be transmitted instantaneously. Humanity has never seen this before—and there's no telling what the future holds. Our level of immediate communication has reached such a fever pitch that it's almost *unique* for you to be reading these words in a book made of real paper. Younger generations in the Western world tend to be incredibly proficient at screen-based communication, yet often encounter obstacles when faced with person-to-person dialogue.

Mail of one kind or another has been in existence for as long as we've had written communication. Our modern electronic mediums allow for instant gratification. Like all things, this can be for better or worse. I would consider electronic communication a big "pro" if compassion and global progression were the motivators. While I genuinely believe we are meant to be entering an age of global empathy and awareness, I find that many uses of electronic communication are instead "cons," motivated by these malicious forces such as greed and exploitation. But, just like magick, emotions, mental prowess, or any other force in reality, electronic advancements are *neutral* rather than inherently good or bad.

That said, physical mail, or snail-mail, has its own properties and advantages. Utilizing the physical plane for our magick, we can help create potentially reverberating positive change simply by writing a letter. According to the Crowleyan or Thelemic definition of magick, simply writing a letter or postcard to a company would be a great way to harness change by physical means. Whereas emails are empty in many ways, when we get postal mail we can feel the energy or personality of the person sending the letter or item—unless it's mass-manufactured junk mail! Postal mail is a magickal thing and has the potential to carry great amounts of energy and power from point A to point B. It's also the only form of long-distance communication that is *confidential*, as phones and emails can be tapped. For less than 50 cents (at the time of this writing, in America), we can write a letter, stick it in a blue box, and kick back while it zips across the country in a few days. That truly is amazing.

Snail-mail Sorcery

So, how can someone work their magick through snail-mail? Let's start by looking at something that most people don't think of as necessarily "magickal."

Corporations and political institutions often regard *one* consumer's opinion as the voice of *many* more—hundreds or thousands of additional consumers, depending on the market. Most people never take the time to make corporate contact. By taking a few minutes to express sentiments, a company or institution may be more inclined to change in progressive ways. It literally only takes a few minutes and a bit of couch-change to pay for a stamp. In my opinion, this is an incredibly small sacrifice for a piece of activism that could potentially have rippling effects that could help people, animals, or the earth. Is this not our duty as magicians and seekers of consciousness? Indeed I've seen these sorts of positive changes happen due to my own brief letter-writing.

I should also add that *postcards* are also more likely to get read by ultra-large corporations or institutions. Postcards can be quickly written and are very inexpensive to send. If someone is receiving mounds upon mounds of mail, they are more likely to read the postcards before opening letters. However, both have their times and places and both can be effective.

Revitalize Long-Distance Relationships

My coven and I enjoy sending "care packages" to friends and relatives around the world, whether at Yuletide, harvest time, when someone falls ill, or whenever the mood strikes us. Sharing is caring. Care packages can be a fun and creative act of personal magick. Simply piece together a number of fun items from around the house or from local shops, write a note, channel energies of your choice into the package, seal it up, and send off the love. Opening a random package of random stuff is a fun experience, especially if it's imbued with intentions of bonding or healing.

Creating a spiritual piece of art in collaboration with a long-distance friend can also be fun. Begin the piece—regardless of the medium—and mail it to your friend to add to, alter, and imbue. They can mail it back to you to do the same. This can continue for as long as you wish, until you both feel the piece is a completed work of magickal art that carries the intentions you set forth to create.

Enhance Your Practice Postally

Postal magick is something I've utilized in some of my Men's Rituals for the Dark Sun. In the Order and Coven I cofounded, called Opus Aima Obscuræ (OAO), we utilize the Dark Sun or New Sun as the masculine equivalent to the women's Dark Moon or New Moon. This occurs when the sun enters a new zodiac sign in tropical astrology.

During a ritual marking the sun's entrance into Virgo (a sign ruled by Mercury, a planet/god of communication), we once performed postcard magick for the Men's Ritual. Each of us took a small stack of postcards and visualized a place we wished to travel. Upon creating this traveling to-do list, we performed a series of magickal exercises to enchant and empower the postcards, which were to be mailed to those destinations. Magick included the creation of sigils to represent these traveling goals. (Note: there are multiple ways to create a sigil or magickal seal aligned to a specific purpose. Please consult a book or internet source for more about sigilry, particularly the methods given by Austin Osman Spare.) Our sigils represented these personal goals, acting a visual anchors for our intentions, which were worded in the form of "I will effortlessly and joyously travel to _____ in this lifetime," or similar affirmations.

Once the sigils were created, drawn, and enchanted on the left sides of the postcards, the symbols were layered overtop in a series of fun stickers like smiley faces and hearts. Many of these stickers entirely covered up any given sigil. On the right side of each postcard, the address was written. We researched addresses of hotels in any given national or global location we picked, and addressed them as such. For example, if I wanted to travel to Ireland, I would research a functioning hotel in Ireland and address it to the hotel—this would ensure the postcard's delivery to the city or country of manifestation. Additionally, we wrote a bit of text on the left sides of each postcard so they wouldn't look *too* suspicious or strange—the goal is not to scare the randomized recipient! Because these were being sent to hotels, each postcard got a silly little message, like, "Thanks for the great stay! Love your hotel! Cheers!" or we simply made it look as if a child had written the postcard and an adult addressed it.

To conclude, each participant pricked the pointer finger of his left hand (to represent the future and the fiery command of one's own energy) and put a small "blood stamp" in the right-hand uppermost part of the postcard. Once dried, proper national or international postage was secured atop the blood prints, leaving the blood hidden beneath the stamps.

To summarize, each of these were magically charged, odd-but-happy-looking postcards addressed to hotels across the globe. The postcards we had chosen had pleasant nature scenes on the front sides of each. The postcards were properly stamped depending on the area they were being mailed to (postage rates can be looked up online), and no postcards had a return address (this *anonymity* is important with this sort of magick). Postcards should be put in a public mailbox, not mailed from your place of residence, as to send off these energies without an obvious link to your person.

When each hotel receives any given postcard, it's likely that the recipient would briefly read the postcard, look at it strangely, perhaps give a little chuckle, and then toss it in the trash. Once tossed in the trash, it ensures that the magician's energy, through the sigil and bloodprint, is connected to the location being manifested for travel. If the address of the hotel is expired, the post office in that area will simply "dead letter" the postcard, which will also make its way into the trash. The magician, then, can choose when to astrally connect to the city or country of choice, helping pull the area closer energetically, thus making traveling to that location easier with time.

Anonymous Activism
Another type of magickal postal activism can be utilized, but it requires a different kind of creativity.

I'm not a liar. I don't lie. I greatly dislike lying. But sometimes (and I mean very seldomly) untruths can be used for reverse effects *without* causing harm—and ideally perpetuating the contrary. Allow me to give an example. A church in my area was using severe, hellfire-and-brimstone messaging in their roadside letterboard, saying things like, "Don't believe in Christ? You might believe once He sends you into a sea of eternal flame!" Of course, this sort of extreme religious musing is meant to shock people into conforming to their line of thinking (which, incidentally, is *far* from Christlike). In response, I wrote a postcard saying something along the lines of, "As a Christian woman, I encourage you to direct people to the Light of Christ. I feel this is most effective by professing the Love and Goodness that our Lord and Savior expressed through His teachings. I believe that more and more individuals can be saved by encouraging brotherly and sisterly love rather than perpetuating messages of hatred. What would Jesus do? Thanks for doing the good work of the Good Book." Upon signing the letter with a fake name ("Yours in Christ, Amanda") and *not using a return address*, I witnessed the local church entirely and immediately change their roadside letterboard to weekly messages of God's love and compassion. Score! This was ten years ago, and they haven't changed to this day. I can only hope their sermons also reflect this more progressive and unifying line of thinking.

~

However you choose to utilize the postal system to carry your magick, give thanks to Mercury, Hermes, or Thoth: three of the classical gods of communication. I often draw the alchemical symbol for Mercury on pieces of mail I send. This not only ensures safe delivery, but aligns the essence of the god to the postal system itself, giving thanks for the miracles of modern communication.

Will the Real Santa Claus Please Stand Up?

by Sybil Fogg

In my home, we celebrate Yule, the Winter Solstice, but we also celebrate Christmas. When I first began to delve seriously into Paganism, I dropped many of the holidays I had been raised celebrating and replaced them with their Pagan brothers and sisters. Easter became Ostara, Halloween became Samhain, and Christmas became Yule. Over time, I realized that aspects of the holidays of my childhood began to creep back in, particularly surrounding the celebrations on the dark half of the year. My fourth child was born on the Winter Solstice and, in an attempt to give him this sacred day as his own, we began pushing back Yule until Christmas pretty much reappeared as if it had never left. My older children taught my younger ones about Santa Claus as they knew him from literature and before I realized it, he had taken up residence in my home. I also discovered I knew very little about the old gent. My youngest child was born on December 6, which I knew to be Odin's day and hence, that is his middle name. I learned quickly that it is also Saint Nicholas's Day and Krampusnacht (Krampus Night). More research dug up where the popular red and white Santa Claus originated, as well as Kriss Kringle and the Christkind. I began to wonder if the real Santa Claus would ever stand up.

Today, there is much information on the internet connecting the Norse God, Odin to the origins of Santa Claus. It is true that Odin was often depicted as an old man with a bearded face moving through the sky on his eight-legged horse, Sleipnir, who could leap great distances. On December 25, he leads the Wild Hunt, a ghostly procession through the sky. He often leaves small gifts and trinkets for children in their shoes as they slept. He is honored by his followers on December 6.

The story of Santa Claus begins with Saint Nicholas, who lived during the third century. History states that St. Nicholas was wealthy but gave up his material possessions to the poor and focused his energies on helping those in need. He became known throughout the land as a patron of children, sailors, and ships. The name Santa Claus very likely stems from the German name for Saint Nicholas, *Sinterklass*. We celebrate the anniversary of his death on December 6.

There are many legends surrounding Saint Nicholas telling of his life and deeds. He was loved and renowned for his kind character and protective nature, always seeking to assist those most needy.

One of the most popular tales of Saint Nicholas's kind deeds tells of how he granted dowries to three sisters whose father was preparing to sell them into slavery or prostitution because he could not pay for their weddings. Saint Nicholas tossed bags of gold, one for each daughter, through their window and the money landed in stockings or shoes that had been laid out to dry by the fire. It is believed that this led to the custom of hanging a stocking or putting out shoes to be filled with gifts from Saint Nicholas.

Popular in Europe, Saint Nicholas's Day was celebrated in a variety of ways. In Germany and Poland, boys would dress as bishops begging alms for the poor. In the Netherlands, candy was tossed through doorways. In Holland and Germany, children left out shoes to be filled with treats and small gifts. Bad children received coal.

In Germany, Austria, and many other parts of Europe, Saint Nicholas comes to bring treats for the well behaved and mannered children, while his counterpart, The Krampus appears to punish those who have misbehaved. The visual appearance of Krampus (also known as Knecht Ruprecht, Certa, Perchten, Black Peter, Schmutzli, Pelznickel, Klaubauf[1]) is close to the depiction of the Christian devil—cloven foot, horned, tailed, and covered in fur. He would appear

---

1 http://www.krampus.com/who-is-krampus.php

with whip in hand to discipline bad children before whisking them away in a basket to whence he came. Today, Krampusnacht is enjoying a comeback, mostly amongst adults who hold Krampus parties and parades, where Krampuses will dance down the street carrying switches accompanied by Saint Nicholas, white winged angels and children in cages.

Another well-known Santa Claus reference is Kriss Kringle, who derives his name from the German, Christkindchen, meaning ChristKind, a figure introduced by Martin Luther to deter people from honoring Saint Nicholas. The Christkind is a sprite-like, winged child with golden hair and clothed in white, bringing presents to children on Christmas Eve, effectively moving the date away from December 6 and all reference to Saint Nicholas. The Christkind was meant to be a version of Jesus as an infant, but over time, the figure of Saint Nicholas replaced the Christkind and the name became Americanized.

Sometime in the sixteen century, England was introduced to the concept of Father Christmas, likely by King Henry VIII. Father Christmas embodied the spirit of the holiday and he was honored and celebrated with great feasting and merrymaking on Christmas Day, moving the holiday further from the sixth and cementing its connection to the birth of Jesus. His celebrations and visage became quite popular during the Victorian era and immortalized in Charles Dickens's work, *A Christmas Carol.*

The poet, Clement Moore penned the famous work, "A Visit from St. Nicholas" in 1822, drawing on solstice traditions, German and Scandinavian lore, and what he had learned of the church teachings of Saint Nicholas. He gave Saint Nicholas a fey touch and added the flying reindeer.[2]

And as time went on, more people added flourishing touches to Saint Nicholas, adding a backstory that includes the North Pole outpost complete with a toy shop and Christmas

---

2 http://www.unmuseum.org/santa.htm

elves. These days, many people are familiar with the fact that the Coca Cola Company outfitted our hero in the white and red fur that we know and love. In our household, we honor Santa Claus on Saint Nicholas's Day by hanging stockings. We each choose a family member randomly from a hat and then leave treats in their stocking each day, culminating on Christmas Eve. Then we announce our identity and feast and celebrate together. Santa Claus represents charity and kindness towards our fellow beings. The winter holidays are an excellent time to remember and practice this. So mote it be.

Weather Witching

by Charlynn Walls

Weather is a driving force that surrounds and affects us on a daily basis. However, in this day and age, we rarely give it a second thought. As stewards of the earth, we are vested not only in the conservatorship of the earth itself, but also to the preservation and protection of its inhabitants. As the world continues to become more polluted and desecrated, its natural rhythms and responses become unbalanced. Now Pagans and Witches are being looked to again to be the force of positive change in the world. With increasingly violent storms, periods of drought, or severe flooding, we are the ones that can work to keep the balance and bring the equilibrium back.

Weather is a part of our everyday lives. It determines how we go about our business, but it is not usually an aspect we feel we have any control over. That is, unless you consider yourself to be a Weather Witch. Weather Witches have long been tasked as the stewards of the earth and its elements. We are the facilitators of balance and restoration. We work with Mother Nature and Gaia to bring about stability to each of our parts of the world.

In the past during times of drought, we were sought out to restore the natural patterns of weather by conjuring the rain to save the crops. We also work to harness the energies that come from the weather and apply those in our magick. However, this article will focus solely on how one goes about altering the weather responsibly. Sadly, it is an aspect of our heritage that has gone by the wayside as an agrarian lifestyle has morphed into a more industrial and technological one.

Ethics

Whenever weather and magick are uttered in the same conversation, there is an ensuing discussion of ethics. People are either for weather witching—or they're against it. Some do not think we should ever interfere with the process in any way. Then there are those who think if we can do it responsibly, then it is our duty to do so.

As with everything we do, we must take into account what would be for the highest good of all—of the flora and fauna in our care. Ethical considerations should be at the forefront of our minds before we cast any type of magick or spell. Your intent will be paramount to the outcome of any magickal working. If we can assess the situation and be assured that the impact is not detrimental to the environment or its inhabitants, then it would be reasonable to proceed.

So, how do you know if the spell would be detrimental? You need to ask yourself if it would have a positive or negative influence on your immediate area. Then ask yourself the same question regarding the larger zone in which you reside. Then you must consider and weigh its long-reaching effects on other regions. What may be good for one area may not be good for another area.

Another consideration is that of imminent danger. If you are protecting yourself and others from a hazardous situation, then you should consider all options at your disposal. After all, Witches protect. They protect life in all of its forms.

Weather Witching Checklist:
Are you in imminent danger?
Does the region benefit from the spell?
Is the impact on other regions negligible?

If the answer to at least two of the above questions is yes, then you will probably be fine to work your ritual or spell.

Practical Applications

There are often practical ways that Witches will be called upon to intervene with the elemental conditions that control the weather. Our connection to nature and the ability to direct the energy around us allows us to effectively become a conduit for those energies. We can then harness them and alter them if necessary.

One way that Weather Witches work with the natural forces surrounding them is in an emergency situation. If there is drought, flooding, hurricane, tornado, or other natural event befalling an area, the Witch will seek to protect not only the land, but those that dwell there. We may not always be able to stop the event, but we can work toward balancing energies to prevent or minimize a devastating loss of life. The floodwaters can be encouraged to recede more quickly. Hurricanes and tornadoes can be lessened in intensity. It is also possible to increase the chances of survival by slowing them down before they strike.

Also, as practitioners of a spirituality based on nature, we often hold our rites and events outdoors. In order to ensure the safety of those in attendance, a common practice (at least where I live) is to enlist the help of a Weather Witch to do work for fair weather. This does not typically preclude the typical rain shower. Rather, it helps keep any storms that develop from becoming severe. Should a storm become severe, it skirts the space that has been shielded. The area of the event is protected and the impact on the surrounding area is minimal.

Ritual to Diminish a Storm

The following is a full ritual if you know that a large storm is bearing down on your area and you have ample time to prepare. This ritual can be performed by an individual or adapted to accommodate a coven or working group.

Items Needed: Protection powder, liquid lightning elixir, tealight candle, and yourself.

The protection powder and liquid lightning are two items that you can create and store before they are needed. These are a great addition to your magickal toolbox and can keep for up to a year before their potency begins to diminish.

Protection Powder: Take equal parts of the following herbs and grind them together with a mortar and pestle.

Sea salt	Dragon's blood	Willow
Alder	Laurel	

Liquid Lightning Elixir

Set out and collect water during a lightning storm. The water will be charged with the lightning's energy. Once you've collected the water, filter out any impurities. If you can find a piece of fulgurite, add it to the collected water. Check for sales online or at any local rock shop. I like to shop locally and if they do not have it in stock they can usually acquire it for you. Fulgurite is a tube created from lightning striking sand. The structures of fulgurite range from the size of a finger to pieces that are many meters long. A small part of it is sufficient for use in this elixir. Store the water in a light, tight container for future use.

Before you cast the circle, you'll want to prepare the ritual area. I like to take the protection powder and walk the perimeter of the circle or the property that is to be protected. Walk the space thrice about while sprinkling the powder as you walk. Please note, that dragon's blood can stain skin and clothing, so take care what it is sprinkled on.

Cast the Circle

You can be as formal or informal as you like when casting the circle. The following technique has always worked well for me. Envision a ball of bluish white light forming between your hands. Center them in front of your solar plexus. See the light pulse and become more defined. Slowly, move your hands apart, allowing the energy between them to grow. Continue to do this until your arms are fully extended out at your sides. The sphere of energy now encircles you. If you need the space to be larger, just push it out with your mind until it is the appropriate size for your needs.

To complete the casting of the circle say:

I now stand between the worlds, an instrument of the elements for the purpose of this work. The circle is cast.

Call to the Quarters

My group begins in quarter calls in the North, but you may choose to alter this to what feels most comfortable for you.

North: *Boreas, Guardian of the North Wind, lend to us the strength of your mountain home to provide the support we need for our work. Hail and welcome!*

East: *Euros, Guardian of the East Wind, bring to us clarity of thought in order to provide prospective on the situation. Hail and welcome!*

South: *Zephyrus, Guardian of the South Wind, allow the passion of our convictions to be felt through our rite. Hail and welcome!*

West: *Notos, Guardian of the West Wind, temper our emotions that we may see clearly our task at hand. Hail and welcome!*

Call to the God/Goddess

You may invoke deity from any pantheon you choose. I find that those associated with aspects of the weather such as wind, thunder, and rain seem to work better than others for this purpose, since it is their domain. For this ritual I am choosing to work with the Greek deities, but you can substitute for what works best for you.

Iris, goddess of sea and sky, you are a bridge between the worlds. Bring forth our message to the gods so that they may hear our plea. Hail and welcome!

Great god Zeus, who commands the energies of the skies, hear our petition lay before you this day. Hail and welcome!

Magickal Working/Petition

You will need to be able to visualize the approaching storm and be aware of its size and intensity. Radar images might help to see the

storm's path and speed as it moves toward your location. When you can clearly see the storm in your mind's eye, you can begin.

Sit comfortably within the sacred space of the circle. Picture the storm, feeling its intensity as it draws near. Take the tealight and anoint it with the liquid lightning elixir. Light the candle and visualize the components that make up the storm, the wind, the lightning, the pouring rain. You will want to picture each aspect decreasing in intensity as the candle burns down. For instance, strong cloud-to-ground lightning will reduce down to cloud-to-cloud lightning with each instance taking longer to occur.

Envision the storm as a whole made up of wedges, and as it approaches breaking off into smaller wedges that will reduce the intensity of the main storm. Each sliver provides a disruption to the continuation of the storm. The more shards you can see the storm breaking into, the better the chances of the storm lessening.

If you have difficulty visualizing this and have time to print out the radar image, you can cut it into pieces. While you are focusing your intent on breaking the storm, recite this chant:

This storm's intensity I seek to shake;
Calling for the storm to break.

Repeat the chant over and over as you envision the storm breaking apart within your mind until you see the last part splinter off and weaken.

Release the God/Goddess

Lord Zeus, we thank you for being receptive to our plea and hope to have your blessing over the sky. Hail and farewell!

Lady Iris, we thank you for bearing our message to the gods. We hope that your symbol of the rainbow brings us blessings to our endeavor. Hail and farewell!

Release the Quarters

West: *Notos, we thank you for allowing us clear sight in the midst of turbulent emotions. Hail and farewell!*

South: *Zephyrus, we thank you for sharing with us our passions. Hail and farewell!*

East: *Euros, we thank you for providing us prospective in this time of need. Hail and farewell!*

North: *Boreas, we thank you for aiding us with your strength. Hail and farewell!*

Release the Circle

Now that the quarters have been released you can begin to release the circle. See in your mind's eye the sphere of energy you created. Extend out your arms from your body and feel the energy contract till you feel the warmth of it on the palms of your hands. Draw your hands inward slowly, until your palms are facing one another in front of your solar plexus. See the energy begin to dissipate. Once it is completely gone the circle is open.

Quick Version for Imminent Danger

There may not always be time to conduct a full ritual when a storm is bearing down on your location. When you need to batten down the hatches quickly, here is a quick spell to help you protect yourself and your family. If you practice the circle-casting technique in the previous ritual, it will become second nature. It will make the following spell much quicker and easier to do on the spur of the moment.

Visualize the sphere of bluish white energy spread out and envelope you and your family. See and hold that light in your mind. Now, call upon the god or goddess of your choice and state your intention for protection against the pending storm and your desire to make the storm diminish in its size and intensity.

The following is an example of what you could say as a petition.

Lord and Lady, hear my plea for the storm to quickly pass us by and weaken in strength. Protect what we hold most dear in our time of need, harming none along the way. Blessed be!

See yourself riding out the storm by seeing it split around you. Picture a canoe or wedge shape that allows the storm to flow around you, but does not inhibit its path.

When the danger has passed give thanks to deity for their protection against the storm. See the protective light from the sphere contract and then dissipate.

～

As curators of the earth, we have a responsibility to help provide stability. When the forces of nature are out of sync, it is difficult to sustain such a balance. The more we strain the earth's resources, the more it seems that she pushes back. As we struggle to cut back on our consumption of natural resources, we must also work to bring harmony back to its natural functions.

The weather is one of those functions that can easily be thrown out of balance by our actions. While impossible to control, we can promote restoration of the equilibrium that is necessary to the system. Weather witching is still a controversial topic to some there are no clear-cut black and white areas.

When the forces of nature bring too much rain, snow, or heat, those who work with the earth's energies are tasked with the important role of reining in the excess and redistributing it to correct the imbalance. This is all in an effort to protect not only ourselves, but those who are entrusted to our care. Anything else is far too self-serving of a concept.

Zodiac Spells

by Ellen Dugan

I have a confession to make. I am terrible at astrology. It makes me crazy. My theory has always been that this is because serious astrological charts are too much like math. I see the words *degrees* and *trine,* and I get twitchy. However, maybe even perversely, I made up my mind a few years ago to try and learn something—anything—about astrology.

I approached this topic not unlike someone else would move toward a bomb—very, very carefully. I stood back, considered the options, and asked myself what would be the simplest thing I could take apart to see how it magickally ticked.

Maybe if I just sort of eased in? Being a perfectionist, I worried that it would blow up in my face, and I'd end up only confusing myself more. Then I had to snicker and think how my astrologically talented Witch friends would roll their eyes and accuse me of being such a worrywort Virgo.

I finally decided to focus on the Sun signs. To my surprise, I really enjoyed learning more about the magickal possibilities of the twelve signs of the zodiac. Also, I think I gravitated to this topic because sun signs correspond with some of the Major Arcana cards in the tarot, *and* the twelve sun signs all break down into four elemental categories. The fire signs are Aries, Leo, and Sagittarius. The earth signs consist of Taurus, Virgo, and Capricorn. The air signs encompass Gemini, Libra, and Aquarius. Finally, the water signs cover Cancer, Scorpio, and Pisces. I had explored the elemental sign angle before, but now it was time to really see what I could learn. I have to admit it was a lot of fun. (Somewhere, some hardcore astrologer just slumped over in a dead faint because I dared to use the word "fun" while describing the zodiac and magick. We can give them a few moments to recover.) In the meantime, I urge you to remember my motto: *magick is a joyous thing.* So let's have some fun, shall we?

In my opinion, the best part about working magick with the different zodiac signs is that this allows you to work seasonal witchery as the year progresses. You can tap in to the magickal energy that is present during each sun sign and ride the wheel of the cosmos—no matter what your personal sun sign happens to be. Yes, that's right. A serious Capricorn can sit and work the "Happy Home" zodiac spell during the sensitive time of Cancer the Crab. A dreamy, mystical Pisces can work the "Organization and Completion" spell during the time of the sun sign of Virgo to finish projects and to get (dare we say) organized. The possibilities are endless.

Zodiac Correspondence Charts and Spells

In the information below, you will see a correspondence chart with the date of the zodiac sign and its symbol, element, and planetary information. There are also coordinating candle colors, complementary herbs and crystals, and the associated tarot cards from my Witches Tarot for you to consider. Finally, you will see the magickal energy of the zodiac sign that is present while the sun is in this time, and, lastly, the spell verse.

Having the correspondences for each zodiac sign at your fingertips will allow you to choose your complementary spell accoutrements with a minimum of fuss, thereby helping the spell link together and the magickal energy to flow more smoothly. Choose your spell accessories from the correspondences and personalize these twelve zodiac spells as you like. Happy casting and blessed be.

Aries Spell Correspondences

The Ram's zodiac energy consists of courage, victory, motivation, confidence, passion, and personal energy. Aries is also connected to the element of fire, the planet Mars, and the candle color red. Its Witches Tarot card is IV, The Emperor.

Crystal & Stones: Ruby, bloodstone
Herbs & Flowers: Coriander, thistle

Confidence and Victory Spell

In this time of the sun sign of Aries,
I call for courage and confidence please.
Now let this fiery springtime energy swirl around,
So victory and good energy will always be found!

Taurus Spell Correspondences

The Bull's zodiac energy consists of sovereignty, commitment, finances, gardening, enjoyment, and pleasure. Taurus is also connected to the element earth, the planet Venus, and the candle color green. Its Witches Tarot card is V, The High Priest.

Crystal & Stones: Emerald, lapis lazuli
Herbs & Flowers: Thyme, violet

Connecting to the Earth Spell

In the time of the sun sign of Taurus,
May the earth's power sustain and bless us.
The witchery of the garden true pleasure brings,
Ground and center me now while this spell I do sing.

Gemini Spell Correspondences

The Twins's zodiac energy consists of change, variety, communication, study, and duality. Gemini is also connected to the element air, the planet Mercury, and the candle color yellow. Its Witches Tarot card is VI, The Lovers.

Crystal & Stones: Agate, aventurine

Herbs & Flowers: Parsley, iris

Communication Spell

In the Gemini cycle of the zodiac signs,
Clear communication will surely be yours and mine.
Magickal change spins out swiftly on a breeze,
While the Twins aid my spell that is sure to please.

Cancer Spell Correspondences

The Crab's zodiac energies include Home and family, self-control, comfort, and protection. Cancer is also connected to the element water, the Moon, and the candle colors white and silver. Its Witches Tarot card is VII, The Chariot.

Crystal & Stones: Moonstone, sapphire

Herbs & Flowers: Mallow, lotus

Happy Family Spell

The zodiac sign of Cancer the Crab has now begun,
Combining the summer's magick of the moon and the sun.
May my family know comfort, in all possible ways,
While affection and love illuminate all our days.

Leo Spell Correspondences

The Lion's zodiac energies include charisma, pride, standing out, believing in yourself, and creativity. Leo is also connected to the element fire, the Sun, and the candle color gold. Its Witches Tarot card is VIII, Strength.

Crystal & Stones: Carnelian, topaz

Herbs & Flowers: St. John's wort, rosemary

Creativity and Charisma Spell

The sun cycle of Leo the Lion has arrived,
I conjure creativity, charisma, and pride.

My work now stands out, and my confidence will soar,
This spell radiates out on Leo's mighty roar.

Virgo Spell Correspondences

The Earth Goddess's zodiac energies include healing, mental clarity, pride in doing a job well, and concentration. Virgo is also connected to the element earth, the planet Mercury, and the candle colors light green and brown. Its Witches Tarot card is IX, The Hermit.

Crystal & Stones: Tourmaline, jasper
Herbs & Flowers: Valerian, lily

Organization and Completion Spell

While the down-to-earth sun sign of Virgo is in play,
Organization will be the order of the day.
With a call now for clarity, and a job well done,
I'll complete projects easily as this spell is spun.

Libra Spell Correspondences

The Scales's zodiac energies include harmony, love, justice, and walking in balance. Libra is also connected to the element air, the planet Venus, and the candle colors pale blue and pink. Its Witches Tarot card is XI, Justice.

Crystal & Stones: Opal, turquoise
Herbs & Flowers: Primrose, goldenrod

Justice and Balance Spell

The harmonious time of Libra has now blown in,
Bringing balance as the season of autumn begins.
May justice be served in the best possible way,
Granting peace and stability to all my days.

Scorpio Spell Correspondences

The Scorpion's energies are transformation, passion, endurance, concealment, intuition, and willpower. Scorpio is connected to the element water, the planet Pluto, and the candle colors burgundy and black. Its Witches Tarot card is XIII, Death.

Crystal & Stones: Garnet, jet
Herbs & Flowers: Chrysanthemum, basil

Protection Spell

When Scorpio is the current zodiac sign,
Protection is conjured with the sound of a rhyme.
With resolve, all baneful energy is now washed away,
Bringing light and transformation to the darkest of days.

Sagittarius Spell Correspondences

The Archer's zodiac energies are wisdom, inspiration, long journeys, prophecy, and clarity. Sagitarrius is also connected to the element fire, the planet Jupiter, and the candle colors purple and magenta. Its Witches Tarot card is XIV, Temperance.

Crystal & Stones: Amethyst, topaz
Herbs & Flowers: Sage, carnation

Spell to Increase Psychic Talents

During this zodiac sign, prophecy abounds.
In the time of the archer, insight will be found,
Sagittarius brings fiery energy,
With this divine wisdom may I gain clarity.

Capricorn Spell Correspondences

The Goat's zodiac energies are binding, conquering fear, determination, persistence, practicality, and a drive to succeed. Capricorn is also connected to the element earth, the planet Saturn, and the candle colors black and deep blue. Its Witches Tarot card is XV, The Shadow Side.

Crystal & Stones: Onyx, obsidian
Herbs & Flowers: Comfrey, snowdrop

Spell for Conquering Fear

When the zodiac time is earthy Capricorn,
Many practical aspirations may be born.
Any fear can be conquered if you but stand your ground,
With persistence and common sense, success will be found.

Aquarius Spell Correspondences

The Water Bearer's element is water, and its zodiac energies are bringing change, optimism, peace, inspiration, and a love of personal freedom. Aquarius is also connected to the planet

Uranus, and the candle color ultramarine blue. Its Witches Tarot card is XVII, The Star.

Crystal & Stones: Aquamarine, jet
Herbs & Flowers: Solomon's seal, pansy

Spell for Peace and Positive Change

Now arrives the water-bearer Aquarius's time
Even though it is an "airy" zodiac sign.
This spell for peace gently flows out on the winter wind,
Granting me positive change, hope and inspiration.

Pisces Spell Correspondences

The Fishes' zodiac energies are intuition, imagination, empathy, dreams, mystical, and emotional. Pisces is also connected to the element water, the planet Neptune, and candle colors turquoise and green. Its Witches Tarot card is XVIII, The Moon.

Crystal & Stones: Quartz crystal, coral
Herbs & Flowers: Honeysuckle

Spell for Empathy and Dreams

Now the zodiac sign of Pisces the fishes is here,
Bringing dreams and sharing emotions, often crystal clear.
This mystical time encourages visions and insight true,
Using this knowledge wisely, I'll be blessed in all that I do.

The To-Go Tarot Kit

by Deanna Anderson

When I first started studying tarot, I took my deck with me wherever I went. I never knew when I would get a chance to read the cards for someone, and I had a goal to read for at least fifty people as part of my studies. As instructed, I recorded with the customer's initials and had customers complete surveys. In addition to seeing what worked and what did not, this was done to help students develop a routine and a sense of professionalism. At first, I did not have a formal tarot kit, but further into my studies, I read about the use of tarot cloths, gemstones, incense, or candles to enhance a reading or add ambience. As I started collecting these items, and a few extra decks, I knew I needed a better option than throwing items in my purse—and thus my first tarot kit was made!

Tarot kits, which you may create for yourself or as a gift, can be as unique as the person who makes it. No matter how the kits end up, they are convenient and easy to just grab and go, whether you're heading to a friend's house, a party, a festivals, or out of town. However, before we get into making a tarot kit, there is an issue worth mentioning since this kit is meant for travel.

When doing readings for "fun" (that is, for no monetary exchanges), legal issues are not a concern, as tarot can be deemed a party trick. However, when money is exchanged, you should know the business and legal side of things. In some regions, a person has to be licensed to charge money for a reading (like any other business), in other areas, readings may not be allowed at all as "divination" or "fortune-telling" may be considered an illegal act (along the lines of fraud or deception). Laws vary, so make it a point to know what they are wherever you are going. It is also poor etiquette to perform a reading in another's business or at festivals without a vendor's agreement, randomly hitting up people for readings, or to do readings in someone's house without permission. Whether money is exchanged or not, it is always advisable to state that tarot is "for entertainment purposes only."

Legal issues aside, having a tarot kit ensures that you always have what you need when you need it. Always having what you want or need on hand gives you the confidence to perform readings. The first thing you need to do is to decide what purpose you want your kit to serve: Is it an at-home kit or a travel kit? Do you want a simple kit for just general outings (consisting of perhaps just a deck) and a kit to take when traveling out of town? Your answers will determine the size of your kit and its contents.

The Tarot Kit

My tarot kit is in a handbag that was probably once used for toiletries, which I purchased from a thrift store for under $3.00. So far, it has worked well. It is big enough for one deck, a few accessories, and two of my favorite books. However, as I acquire more tarot decks, I am contemplating getting a larger case. I also recently created a "mini-kit" that has one deck and a simple reference sheet

with keywords, phrases, and elemental and numerological corre-spondences. The cards and reference sheet all fit in a camera case that stays in my purse. My larger kit at home has a candle, pendu-lum, a couple decks, my tarot journal, gemstones, pen and paper, and a tarot cloth.

Obviously, the size of your tarot kit and its contents can vary based on its purpose—and, like me, you can have more than one kit. Take some time to think about what you prefer and how large of a casing you need. If your tarot journal is in a three-ring binder, then a small handbag will not work, but a backpack or tote bag will. If all you want is a tarot deck and small tablet, then a cam-era case, small handbag, or makeup bag works great. Some peo-ple may choose something sturdier, such as a box or plastic tote. Wooden and cardboard boxes can be bought in department stores or craft stores. Decorate your kit with paint or decoupage pictures on it (for wooden or cardboard totes), use fabric paints or iron-on appliqués for fabric totes, or use colored permanent markers for plastic totes. Wood and fabrics anointed with a drop or two of essential oil, or a sachet bag of herbs placed in a plastic totes, will bless and consecrate the kit.

Accessories

If you haven't yet performed a reading for others (or yourself), you need to think about the items you want to use. Creating a routine or performance is always beneficial. Not only does it set the ambience to put the reader and the customer in the right frame of mind, it can also aid in opening the psyche and tap-ping into our subconscious and intuitive reasoning. While there is nothing wrong with a quick-read (I often will just grab a deck, shuffle, and pull one card to see what the day will bring), setting the mood is imporatant for a full reading. This is the same for all tasks we perform. When we clean the house, we dress in comfort-able clothes that we don't mind getting dirty. When we go to bed, we dress in pajamas, adjust the lighting, or turn off television sets. We "set the mood" for other areas in life—tarot is no different. And while these tools will not help you understand tarot cards (only studying and practicing with them can do that) a routine can be beneficial.

Pendulums

Pendulums are great to keep in a tarot kit because they are small and portable. A pendulum can be made with any weight on the end of a string, but those generally available at metaphysical stores are made of wood or gemstone, both of which have their own energy and properties. They can aid in understanding a reading by asking "yes or no" questions or choose the cards to read. They can also choose a significator card (represents the one receiving the reading). To select cards for a reading or a significator card (sometimes referred to as a power of querant card), hover the pendulum over each card, face down, and ask it to select by rotating clockwise. If it does not rotate, go on to the next card, stopping only when it has chosen a card or you have enough for a reading.

Pendulums can also be used to cleanse a deck by holding it over the stacked deck (or spread the cards out on a flat surface) and ask the pendulum to rotate counterclockwise (also known as widdershins, a direction believed to cast away or get rid of things) over the cards. When the pendulum slows or stops, the deck has been cleansed. This same method can also be used to cleanse a space, often the table or surface on which you spread the cards.

Crystals

Crystals or gemstones can enhance a reading because of their natural properties. Keeping stones in your tarot kit helps cleanse the cards, protects them from unwanted energies, and facilitates psychic intuition. Malachite is a good stone for divination and amethyst is great for psychic powers and opening the Third Eye. Sodalite is also good for physic powers and grounding. Hematite is good for grounding and if magnetic it can "absorb" unwanted energies. Clear quartz is a good stone in general as it can aid in energy work, cleansing, and divination. Check out some websites or books devoted to stones and choose a few that will work for you. They can be bought online or in metaphysical shops and don't cost very much, but make sure you look for raw or polished stones. Stones can also be used for a protective circle around the cards. Lay a stone at each corner of the surface area (north, east, south, and west). The stones can be any kind but I prefer to us the elemental correspondences for stones and their directions.

Candles

Candles and incense can be used for ambience or to open the psyche, particularly if the scent or color corresponds to psychic powers. When using candles or incense, always ask permission in case your client has allergies or might be irritated by the smoke. In public venues, candles and incense might not be allowed. If this is the case, add a drop of essential oil to a cup of water in a spray bottle and spray around the area in between readings. Reed diffusers and sachet bags can also be used, but again, allergies are always an issue and a reed diffuser may leak in a tarot kit. If you do place candles and incense in your kit, don't forget matches or a lighter—and never leave that tarot kit in the hot sun!

Runes

Runes are another wonderful divination method and can enhance a reading. If you already know how to read runes, they can lend a lot of insight into a reading. (Likewise, tarot cards can aid in rune readings, too.) However, don't feel that they are mandatory. Runes and tarot are their own divination methods, and while they can go hand in hand, they are just as powerful alone. If you think you would like to read with either method, you can also make a rune kit that is separate from a tarot kit.

Tarot Cloth and Bags

A cloth or bag to wrap the tarot cards in is another key item to have. The very act of wrapping cards in a cloth or placing them in a bag can cleanse them and keep them safe from unwanted residual energies. The cloth can be anointed with a drop or two of essential oil, but let it dry well before wrapping around the cards so the oil doesn't damage the deck. Some people prefer to keep their cards in the original box and others do not. Either way, the cards can still be wrapped in cloth or placed in a bag. In addition to protecting the cards physically and metaphysically, a tarot cloth may also be used as a barrier from residual energy when laid between the surface area and the cards.

Bags can be purchased just about anywhere and can be zipper, Velcro, button, or drawstring closures. A personal favorite of mine is an idea I heard of when I worked at a fabric store years ago. A customer purchased fabric to sew squares from. Then she would sew a pocket in the center of the square. The tarot cards would be

placed in the square and the remaining fabric wrapped around the cards. When unfolded it could be used as a tarot cloth.

For my tarot cloth, I purchased a bandanna for 99 cents at a department store and wrapped my deck of cards in that. Bandannas are great to use for tarot cloths because they are cheap and come in a variety of designs. Plus, for the sewing-challenged, it is a square piece of fabric already hemmed on four sides. However, the crafty folks can find directions online for sewing or crocheting tarot cloths or bags and the non-crafty can purchase bags or cloth in stores or online.

Tarot Journals, Reference Books, Recording Devices

If you are the kind of person who keeps a tarot journal or likes to have a reference book on hand, you will want to consider adding these to your kit as well. I have a tarot journal in which I record personal reflections, readings, and just random thoughts concerning tarot. I do not record readings for others in this journal aside from a small notation such as date, time, name, and maybe if I think the reading went well or not.

As stated before, I also have two of my favorite books in my kit but there is a third book that I created for myself, which I use in a reading if needed. It is a quick-flip reference book that I printed up and had bound. I then purchased tab dividers so I could flip to a section quickly. The book includes all of the cards with key words, phrases, and brief descriptions. I also have a checklist on preparing for a reading, numerological and elemental correspondences, and spaces to record the date of each reading I do.

Pen and paper are always beneficial: a small tablet, journal, or day planner can be added to a kit to keep up with events you are attending, a scheduled reading, or to take notes on readings you perform or little tidbits of tarot wisdom you may glean here and there. A person never knows when they may need to write something down.

Recording your tarot sessions (or not) is another important consideration, for personal and professional reasons. When in the tarot business, people often will record a session so that they can give the customer a copy of their reading as well as retaining a copy for themselves (in case legal issues come up). Digital recorders have multiple files and hold more information so several readings can be recorded without changing tapes or uploading immediately to a computer. Make sure to let the customer know you are recording and state the date, time, their name, and within the reading state each card's name. It does no good to refer back to a tape and hear "this card" and not know which card it is. Finally, except in extreme cases, keep tapes confidential—clients have a right to privacy.

~

Having a tarot kit is the perfect way for a person to further connect with tarot and to feel confident that wherever they go they will have the means to perform a reading either for themselves or for others. Think of it as a tarot emergency kit, carrying all the essentials you need for performing a reading anytime, anywhere.

Cauldrons, Black Cats, Brooms, and Pointy Hats

by Autumn Damiana

One of the most vivid and enduring symbols of Halloween and one that everyone is acquainted with is the stereotypical Halloween witch. Dressed head to toe in black, gleefully stirring up trouble in her bubbling cauldron, her trusty broom and black cat familiar at her side, she is by far the most popular and iconic embodiment of the Halloween celebration. But who is she, and where did she originate? What do her attributes represent? And what significance does this witch have in an era of modern witchcraft? (Please note that in this article I only capitalize the word "witch" when talking about Neopagan Witches, or when the word requires capitalization, such as in a title.)

Witch History

To understand the Halloween witch today, we have to look at the beliefs people had about witches in the past. The idea of the witch is about as old as time, and witches have been in the collective unconscious since the beginning. Descriptions of witches in classical Greek and Roman literature reveal that witches were not always maligned and reviled figures, but were once highly respected, revered, and sometimes even considered holy. This may be because these witches emerged from the priesthood and were wise women (and sometimes men) of power, skilled in the arts of divination, prophecy, and healing, and entrusted with the most sacred religious rites. In addition, many of these women came from Goddess cults and were seen as embodying the divine feminine, making their seemingly magical works proof of their connection to the Goddess.

Although the Bible mentions witches and is pointedly clear about avoiding and condemning them, the real problems for witches don't come about until the 1300s. Up until this time, those who lived in rural areas and away from the political institutions concentrated in major cities were free to practice religion as they saw fit, and this often included rituals dedicated to the old, pre-Christian gods and the observance of folkloric customs. Then, two things happened: one was the Bubonic Plague, also known as the "Black Death," which killed almost one-third of the European population, and the other was that witchcraft was declared heresy by the Pope, who authorized the persecution of witches through the Inquisition. Intense fear generated by the Black Death caused many to blame supernatural powers, which is when the witch-hunts officially began. Much of what the general population today believes about witches dates back to this period lasting from the fifteenth to the eighteenth century, which was an unstable time full of witch hysteria. Witch stereotypes arose from a complex collection of sources, including:

Religion: Medieval Christian Churches spread the belief that all power came from God and that to work outside the Church (i.e., as a healer, midwife, herbalist, diviner, spiritual consultant, etc.) was heresy. Because women were not allowed to be part of the clergy, all women that previously employed these practices were seen as being in league with Satan.

Politics: Because the Patriarchy of the Church was the dominant power of the times, women were targeted—particularly those who were thought to be wise, talented, and powerful—in order to promote the Church's belief that "the One True God" was male and that power belonged to men alone. However, anyone who fell out of favor in society could be denounced as a witch, and this included men and even children, often because of a personal grudge or long-standing suspicion of "malicious" behavior.

Sexuality: Unfortunately, during the witch-hunt craze, women were often accused of witchcraft simply because they had captured a man's sexual imagination and he believed himself to be "enchanted," or under her spell. Based on the Biblical story of the Fall of Man through Eve, the Church's official stance on women was that they were especially prone to the lure of sin and would induce carnal desires in men to lead them into evil. Thus many women, pretty and homely alike, were executed as witches based on nothing more than one man's testament of "unclean thoughts," temptations, and desires.

∼

So what does all of this have to do with the Halloween witch? To understand why she exists in her present form, it is necessary to examine these historical ideas and how they have impacted popular opinion on what a witch supposedly is and is not. Much of what the Halloween witch symbolizes is based on Medieval ideas, including classic European myths and fairy tales about witches, peppered with biases left over from the Inquisition. Much of what a witch is thought to be can be traced back to a few common, influential, and often repeated myths surrounding witches.

Misconceptions About Witches

Myth #1: A witch is always female.

In mythology, folktales, and popular culture today, a witch is always portrayed as a woman. Typically, magical males are called "wizards" (like in J. K. Rowling's Harry Potter series), or sometimes "warlocks." Yet historically, men were also decried as witches, usually because of past grievances with the accuser and other politics or because the man was ill-tempered, odd, suspected of homosexuality, or generally served as the village scapegoat.

Myth #2: A witch is an ugly, old, or deformed crone.

This idea comes from a couple of sources. One is the belief from Medieval times that only old and/or ugly women were skilled in sorcery because oftentimes it was older, unmarried, or widowed women who served the community as herbalists, midwives, soothsayers, etc. Some of these women were also disabled or had some sort of physical deformity and could not engage in a more traditional livelihood, such as farming or weaving. Medieval sentiments also stated that if you were ugly, hunchbacked, warty, had excessive moles, were born with a birth defect, etc., you might be targeted as a witch by the Church because you were "marked" as evil by your afflictions.

Myth #3: All witches are evil.

You would think that this myth comes entirely from the Inquisition and the demonization of witches by the Church, but there's actually more to this idea. It's simple psychology: people who appear to have supernatural powers are often misunderstood, and therefore feared. While the image of the Halloween witch is rooted in European traditions, the idea of the witch has existed in every culture around the globe and often serves as a figure to blame when misfortune strikes. Most of the people accused of witchcraft during the Inquisition were entirely innocent and had nothing to do with the magical arts, but anyone will admit to consorting with Satan under extreme torture. And while the modern stereotype of the witch is typically depicted as more naughty and mischievous than flat-out evil, she is still more often associated with negativity than not.

The Facts about Witches

Here are the most common symbols of the Halloween witch and what they represent:

Black cats: Cats have been associated with Goddess worship for centuries—Freyja's chariot was drawn by cats, Artemis/Diana could transform into a cat, and cats were thought to be living manifestations of the Goddess Bast. Many households kept cats to control the rodent population, but like several other nocturnal animals (frogs, bats, owls, etc.) cats were often thought to be witches' familiars. A black cat, like the color black itself, was thought to be particularly evil.

Brooms: A familiar tool of housekeeping, a broom is also a potent symbol of fertility, as its appearance brings to mind the union of the male and female sex organs. "Jumping the broom" is an old custom thought to bestow fertility on a newlywed couple and was used as a way to cement a common-law marriage. Many are also familiar with stories of earlier Pagans jumping and running around astride brooms, shovels, pitchforks, etc., in rituals meant to bless their crops and fields. The witch "riding" her broom, along with the broom's fertility aspect, were crude sexually suggestive ideas that became associated with witches, who were thought to be wicked and immoral.

Cauldrons: The cauldron represents the life-giving womb of the Goddess and is an ancient symbol of transformation, birth and rebirth, abundance, and plenty. It was also an extremely practical tool the witch used to cook food, brew potions, and mix medicines. During the Inquisition, it was suspected that witches used the cauldron to concoct poisons and drugs, cast storm spells, cook babies, etc. Because women had such low status, the cauldron, just like the broom, became connected to witchcraft because it was a symbol of domesticity.

Witch hat: The conical shape of a witch's hat is meant to signify what is now commonly referred to as the "cone of power." It was believed that by wearing a hat of this shape, cosmic energy would be drawn down into the head of the person and flow into the rest of the body to be used for magic. This is, incidentally, why dunce caps are the same shape—in order to funnel knowledge into the head of the wearer.

The Ever-Evolving Witch

No other image quite captures the spirit of the Halloween witch like Margaret Hamilton's portrayal of the Wicked Witch of the West in the 1939 classic *The Wizard of Oz*. Her

cackling, green-faced, black-clad character—complete with witch hat and broom—is undoubtedly what many people think witches really are and is still one of the top Halloween costumes of all time. Other well-known and similar witches come from literature, legend, and even pop culture, like the witch in "Hansel and Gretel," the Three Witches in Shakespeare's *Macbeth* (who were loosely based on the Fates from Greek mythology), the Crone aspect of Triple Goddesses such as Hecate, the "Mistress of Magic," Baba Yaga from Slavic myth, and some Disney witches like Ursula the Sea Witch in *The Little Mermaid* and the witch at the end of *Snow White* (both of which originated from classic fairy tales).

Thanks to the modern Neopagan movement, Witches are coming "out of the broom closet" and helping to tear down these and other stereotypes of the witch, but not everyone wants to see the Halloween witch fade into obscurity. While it's true that some Witches see the witch stereotypes as harmful distortions, it seems that many more

Witches embrace them and are helping to transform these stereotypes into something positive. You can see this attitude in Witches who sport pointy hats and put bumper stickers on their cars that poke fun at witch clichés, like "Life's a Witch and then you fly!" "My other car is a broom!" and "Something Wiccan this way comes." Possibly in part because of this lighthearted approach, there are also some newer witch counterparts that seem to hint at the idea that the witch as a symbol is evolving into a more benign figure. Take the popularity of TV shows like *Charmed* and *Sabrina the Teenage Witch* as well as contemporary children's books like the Little Witch series and the aforementioned Harry Potter. Movies like *Practical Magic, The Craft,* and *The Skeleton Key,* while chock-full of Hollywood exaggeration and special effects, do actually contain elements of real Witchcraft beliefs and practices today. Newer Disney witches, like Madame Odie in *The Princess and the Frog,* are downright cheery. And witch costumes and images now range from cute or goofy to even beautiful or sexy.

Although the stereotype of the witch is linked with Halloween, as it is one of the most (if not THE most) important Pagan holidays, the Halloween witch herself is an archetype and a symbol born out of history, myth, and culture. Whether or not you see her as positive or negative, good or evil, dismissed as a silly superstition or worth some serious scrutiny is up to you. However, I think that whatever your feelings on the Halloween witch, you will agree that upon closer inspection, she is a much more complex and misunderstood figure than people, even modern Witches, give her credit for.

Almanac Section

Calendar

Time Changes

Lunar Phases

Moon Signs

Full Moons

Sabbats

World Holidays

Incense of the Day

Color of the Day

Almanac Listings

In these listings you will find the date, day, lunar phase, Moon sign, color, and incense for the day, as well as festivals from around the world.

The Date

The date is used in numerological calculations that govern magical rites.

The Day

Each day is ruled by a planet that possesses specific magical influences:

MONDAY (MOON): Peace, sleep, healing, compassion, friends, psychic awareness, purification, and fertility.

TUESDAY (MARS): Passion, sex, courage, aggression, and protection.

WEDNESDAY (MERCURY): The conscious mind, study, travel, divination, and wisdom.

THURSDAY (JUPITER): Expansion, money, prosperity, and generosity.

FRIDAY (VENUS): Love, friendship, reconciliation, and beauty.

SATURDAY (SATURN): Longevity, exorcism, endings, homes, and houses.

SUNDAY (SUN): Healing, spirituality, success, strength, and protection.

The Lunar Phase

The lunar phase is important in determining the best times for magic.

THE WAXING MOON (from the New Moon to the Full) is the ideal time for magic to draw things toward you.

THE FULL MOON is the time of greatest power.

THE WANING MOON (from the Full Moon to the New) is a time for study, meditation, and little magical work (except magic designed to banish harmful energies).

The Moon's Sign

The Moon continuously "moves" through the zodiac, from Aries to Pisces. Each sign possesses its own significance.

ARIES: Good for starting things, but lacks staying power. Things occur rapidly, but quickly pass. People tend to be argumentative and assertive.

TAURUS: Things begun now last the longest, tend to increase in value, and become hard to alter. Brings out appreciation for beauty and sensory experience.

GEMINI: Things begun now are easily changed by outside influence. Time for shortcuts, communication, games, and fun.

CANCER: Stimulates emotional rapport between people. Pinpoints need, supports growth and nurturance. Tends to domestic concerns.

LEO: Draws emphasis to the self, central ideas, or institutions, away from connections with others and other emotional needs. People tend to be melodramatic.

VIRGO: Favors accomplishment of details and commands from higher up. Focuses on health, hygiene, and daily schedules.

LIBRA: Favors cooperation, social activities, beautification of surroundings, balance, and partnership.

SCORPIO: Increases awareness of psychic power. Precipitates psychic crises and ends connections thoroughly. People tend to brood and become secretive.

Sagittarius: Encourages flights of imagination and confidence. This is an adventurous, philosophical, and athletic Moon sign. Favors expansion and growth.

Capricorn: Develops strong structure. Focus on traditions, responsibilities, and obligations. A good time to set boundaries and rules.

Aquarius: Rebellious energy. Time to break habits and make abrupt changes. Personal freedom and individuality is the focus.

Pisces: The focus is on dreaming, nostalgia, intuition, and psychic impressions. A good time for spiritual or philanthropic activities.

Color and Incense

The color and incense for the day are based on information from *Personal Alchemy* by Amber Wolfe, and relate to the planet that rules each day. This information can be taken into consideration along with other factors when planning works of magic or when blending magic into mundane life. Please note that the incense selections listed are not hard and fast. If you cannot find or do not like the incense listed for the day, choose a similar scent that appeals to you.

Festivals and Holidays

Festivals are listed throughout the year. The exact dates of many of these ancient festivals are difficult to determine; prevailing data has been used.

Time Changes

The times and dates of all astrological phenomena in this almanac are based on **Eastern Standard Time (EST)**. If you live outside of the Eastern time zone, you will need to make the following changes:

PACIFIC STANDARD TIME: Subtract three hours.

MOUNTAIN STANDARD TIME: Subtract two hours.

CENTRAL STANDARD TIME: Subtract one hour.

ALASKA: Subtract four hours.

HAWAII: Subtract five hours.

DAYLIGHT SAVING TIME (ALL ZONES): Add one hour.

Daylight Saving Time begins at 2 am on March 8, 2015, and ends at 2 am on November 1, 2015.

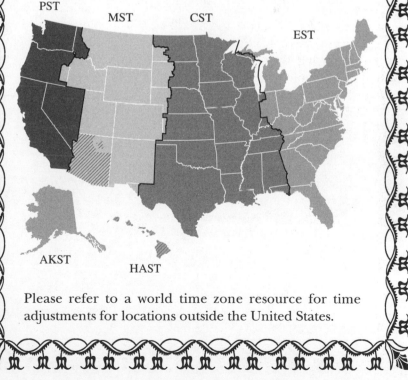

Please refer to a world time zone resource for time adjustments for locations outside the United States.

2015 Sabbats
and Full Moons

January 4	Cancer Full Moon 11:53 pm
February 2	Imbolc
February 3	Leo Full Moon 6:09 pm
March 5	Virgo Full Moon 1:05 pm
March 20	Ostara (Spring Equinox)
April 4	Libra Full Moon 8:06 am
May 1	Beltane
May 3	Scorpio Full Moon 11:42 pm
June 2	Sagittarius Full Moon 12:19 pm
June 21	Midsummer (Summer Solstice)
July 1	Capricorn Full Moon 10:20 pm
July 31	Aquarius Full Moon 6:43 am
August 1	Lammas
August 29	Pisces Full Moon 2:35 pm
September 23	Mabon (Fall Equinox)
September 27	Aries Full Moon 10:51 pm
October 27	Taurus Full Moon 8:05 am
October 31	Samhain
November 25	Gemini Full Moon 5:44 pm
December 21	Yule (Winter Solstice)
December 25	Cancer Full Moon 6:12 am

*All times are Eastern Standard Time (EST)
or Eastern Daylight Time (EDT)*

2015 Sabbats in
the Southern Hemisphere

Because Earth's Northern and Southern Hemispheres experience opposite seasons at any given time, the season-based Sabbats listed on the previous page and in this almanac section are not correct for those residing south of the equator. Listed here are the Southern Hemisphere sabbat dates for 2015:

February 2	Lammas
March 20	Mabon (Fall Equinox)
May 1	Samhain
June 21	Yule (Winter Solstice)
August 2	Imbolc
September 23	Ostara (Spring Equinox)
November 1	Beltane
December 21	Midsummer (Summer Solstice)

January

1 **Thursday**
New Year's Day • Kwanzaa ends
Waxing Moon
Moon phase: Second Quarter
Color: Green

Moon Sign: Taurus
Moon enters Gemini 12:09 pm
Incense: Nutmeg

2 **Friday**
First Writing Day (Japanese)
Waxing Moon
Moon phase: Second Quarter
Color: Rose

Moon Sign: Gemini
Incense: Yarrow

3 **Saturday**
St. Genevieve's Day
Waxing Moon
Moon phase: Second Quarter
Color: Black

Moon Sign: Gemini
Moon enters Cancer 8:08 pm
Incense: Rue

☺ **Sunday**
Frost Fairs on the Thames
Waxing Moon
Full Moon 11:53 pm
Color: Gold

Moon Sign: Cancer
Incense: Juniper

5 **Monday**
Epiphany Eve
Waning Moon
Moon phase: Third Quarter
Color: Ivory

Moon Sign: Cancer
Incense: Clary sage

6 **Tuesday**
Epiphany
Waning Moon
Moon phase: Third Quarter
Color: Scarlet

Moon Sign: Cancer
Moon enters Leo 6:03 am
Incense: Basil

7 **Wednesday**
Rizdvo (Ukrainian)
Waning Moon
Moon phase: Third Quarter
Color: Yellow

Moon Sign: Leo
Incense: Bay laurel

8   Thursday
Midwives' Day   Moon Sign: Leo
Waning Moon   Moon enters Virgo 5:58 pm
Moon phase: Third Quarter   Incense: Mulberry
Color: Crimson

9   Friday
Feast of the Black Nazarene (Filipino)   Moon Sign: Virgo
Waning Moon   Incense: Orchid
Moon phase: Third Quarter
Color: White

10   Saturday
Business God's Day (Japanese)   Moon Sign: Virgo
Waning Moon   Incense: Ivy
Moon phase: Third Quarter
Color: Blue

11   Sunday
Carmentalia (Roman)   Moon Sign: Virgo
Waning Moon   Moon enters Libra 6:57 am
Moon phase: Third Quarter   Incense: Almond
Color: Yellow

12   Monday
Revolution Day (Tanzanian)   Moon Sign: Libra
Waning Moon   Incense: Lily
Moon phase: Third Quarter
Color: Gray

○   Tuesday
Twentieth Day (Norwegian)   Moon Sign: Libra
Waning Moon   Moon enters Scorpio 6:44 pm
Fourth Quarter 4:46 am   Incense: Cinnamon
Color: White

14   Wednesday
Feast of the Ass (French)   Moon Sign: Scorpio
Waning Moon   Incense: Lilac
Moon phase: Fourth Quarter
Color: Brown

15 Thursday

Birthday of Martin Luther King, Jr. (actual)
Waning Moon
Moon phase: Fourth Quarter
Color: Purple

Moon Sign: Scorpio
Incense: Balsam

16 Friday

Apprentices's Day
Waning Moon
Moon phase: Fourth Quarter
Color: Coral

Moon Sign: Scorpio
Moon enters Sagittarius 3:01 am
Incense: Alder

17 Saturday

St. Anthony's Day (Mexican)
Waning Moon
Moon phase: Fourth Quarter
Color: Indigo

Moon Sign: Sagittarius
Incense: Magnolia

18 Sunday

Assumption Day
Waning Moon
Moon phase: Fourth Quarter
Color: Orange

Moon Sign: Sagittarius
Moon enters Capricorn 7:04 am
Incense: Marigold

19 Monday

Birthday of Martin Luther King, Jr. (observed)
Waning Moon
Moon phase: Fourth Quarter
Color: Silver

Moon Sign: Capricorn
Incense: Neroli

Tuesday

Breadbasket Day (Portuguese)
Waning Moon
New Moon 8:14 am
Color: Red

Moon Sign: Capricorn
Sun enters Aquarius 4:43 am
Moon enters Aquarius 7:59 am
Incense: Cedar

21 Wednesday

St. Agnes's Day
Waxing Moon
Moon phase: First Quarter
Color: White

Moon Sign: Aquarius
Incense: Lavender

January

22 Thursday
St. Vincent's Day (French)
Waxing Moon
Moon phase: First Quarter
Color: Turquoise

Moon Sign: Aquarius
Moon enters Pisces 7:48 am
Incense: Apricot

23 Friday
St. Ildefonso's Day (French)
Waxing Moon
Moon phase: First Quarter
Color: Pink

Moon Sign: Pisces
Incense: Cypress

24 Saturday
Alasitas Fair (Bolivian)
Waxing Moon
Moon phase: First Quarter
Color: Gray

Moon Sign: Pisces
Moon enters Aries 8:31 am
Incense: Patchouli

25 Sunday
Burns' Night (Scottish)
Waxing Moon
Moon phase: First Quarter
Color: Amber

Moon Sign: Aries
Incense: Eucalyptus

☽ Monday
Republic Day (Indian)
Waxing Moon
Second Quarter 11:48 pm
Color: Lavender

Moon Sign: Aries
Moon enters Taurus 11:37 am
Incense: Hyssop

27 Tuesday
Vogelgruff (Swiss)
Waxing Moon
Moon phase: Second Quarter
Color: Black

Moon Sign: Taurus
Incense: Ginger

28 Wednesday
St. Charlemagne's Day
Waxing Moon
Moon phase: Second Quarter
Color: Topaz

Moon Sign: Taurus
Moon enters Gemini 5:36 pm
Incense: Honeysuckle

January

29 Thursday
Marty's Day (Nepalese)
Waxing Moon
Moon phase: Second Quarter
Color: White

Moon Sign: Gemini
Incense: Carnation

30 Friday
Three Hierarchs Day (Eastern Orthodox)
Waxing Moon
Moon phase: Second Quarter
Color: Purple

Moon Sign: Gemini
Incense: Vanilla

31 Saturday
Independence Day (Nauru)
Waxing Moon
Moon phase: Second Quarter
Color: Brown

Moon Sign: Gemini
Moon enters Cancer 2:09 am
Incense: Sandalwood

Grounding (Connecting with Earth)

Many of us no longer live on the land, so we have to make more of an effort to connect with the element of earth outside of ritual. Still, it is as easy to do as walking outside and sitting down under a tree or on a patch of grass. If you don't have a yard or garden, take a few minutes from time to time to seek out a local park or public gardens. If you don't have a green space near you, you can use this easy substitute: take a medium-sized pot and fill it with soil (store-bought is okay, although it is nice if you can dig some up somewhere). Take five minutes to put your hands into the dirt and feel that connection.

– Deborah Blake

February

1 Sunday
St. Brigid's Day (Irish)
Waxing Moon
Moon phase: Second Quarter
Color: Orange

Moon Sign: Cancer
Incense: Frankincense

---

2 Monday
Imbolc • Groundhog Day
Waxing Moon
Moon phase: Second Quarter
Color: Lavender

Moon Sign: Cancer
Moon enters Leo 12:41 pm
Incense: Rosemary

Tuesday
St. Blaise's Day
Waxing Moon
Full Moon 6:09 pm
Color: Gray

Moon Sign: Leo
Incense: Geranium

---

4 Wednesday
Independence Day (Sri Lankan)
Waning Moon
Moon phase: Third Quarter
Color: White

Moon Sign: Leo
Incense: Marjoram

---

5 Thursday
Festival de la Alcaldesa (Italian)
Waning Moon
Moon phase: Third Quarter
Color: Purple

Moon Sign: Leo
Moon enters Virgo 12:46 am
Incense: Clove

---

6 Friday
Bob Marley's Birthday (Jamaican)
Waning Moon
Moon phase: Third Quarter
Color: Coral

Moon Sign: Virgo
Incense: Violet

---

7 Saturday
Full Moon Poya (Sri Lankan)
Waning Moon
Moon phase: Third Quarter
Color: Blue

Moon Sign: Virgo
Moon enters Libra 1:44 pm
Incense: Sage

February

8 Sunday
Mass for Broken Needles (Japanese)
Waning Moon
Moon phase: Third Quarter
Color: Amber

Moon Sign: Libra
Incense: Heliotrope

9 Monday
St. Marion's Day (Lebanese)
Waning Moon
Moon phase: Third Quarter
Color: Silver

Moon Sign: Libra
Incense: Narcissus

10 Tuesday
Gasparilla Day (Floridian)
Waning Moon
Moon phase: Third Quarter
Color: Maroon

Moon Sign: Libra
Moon enters Scorpio 2:05 am
Incense: Ylang-ylang

◑ Wednesday
Foundation Day (Japanese)
Waning Moon
Fourth Quarter 10:50 pm
Color: Yellow

Moon Sign: Scorpio
Incense: Bay laurel

12 Thursday
Lincoln's Birthday (actual)
Waning Moon
Moon phase: Fourth Quarter
Color: White

Moon Sign: Scorpio
Moon enters Sagittarius 11:46 am
Incense: Myrrh

13 Friday
Parentalia (Roman)
Waning Moon
Moon phase: Fourth Quarter
Color: Rose

Moon Sign: Sagittarius
Incense: Thyme

14 Saturday
Valentine's Day
Waning Moon
Moon phase: Fourth Quarter
Color: Brown

Moon Sign: Sagittarius
Moon enters Capricorn 5:24 pm
Incense: Pine

15   Sunday
      Lupercalia (Roman)   Moon Sign: Capricorn
      Waning Moon   Incense: Hyacinth
      Moon phase: Fourth Quarter
      Color: Gold

16   Monday
      Presidents' Day (observed)   Moon Sign: Capricorn
      Waning Moon   Moon enters Aquarius 7:13 pm
      Moon phase: Fourth Quarter   Incense: Clary sage
      Color: White

17   Tuesday
      Mardi Gras (Fat Tuesday)   Moon Sign: Aquarius
      Waning Moon   Incense: Bayberry
      Moon phase: Fourth Quarter
      Color: Black

☽   Wednesday
      Ash Wednesday   Moon Sign: Aquarius
      Waning Moon   Moon enters Pisces 6:47 pm
      New Moon 6:47 pm   Sun enters Pisces 6:50 pm
      Color: Topaz   Incense: Lavender

19   Thursday
      Chinese New Year (sheep)   Moon Sign: Pisces
      Waxing Moon   Incense: Jasmine
      Moon phase: First Quarter
      Color: Green

20   Friday
      Installation of the New Lama (Tibetan)   Moon Sign: Pisces
      Waxing Moon   Moon enters Aries 6:13 pm
      Moon phase: First Quarter   Incense: Rose
      Color: Pink

21   Saturday
      Feast of Lanterns (Chinese)   Moon Sign: Aries
      Waxing Moon   Incense: Rue
      Moon phase: First Quarter
      Color: Gray

February

22 Sunday
Caristia (Roman)
Waxing Moon
Moon phase: First Quarter
Color: Yellow

Moon Sign: Aries
Moon enters Taurus 7:28 pm
Incense: Eucalyptus

23 Monday
Terminalia (Roman)
Waxing Moon
Moon phase: First Quarter
Color: Ivory

Moon Sign: Taurus
Incense: Hyssop

24 Tuesday
Regifugium (Roman)
Waxing Moon
Moon phase: First Quarter
Color: Scarlet

Moon Sign: Taurus
Moon enters Gemini 11:54 pm
Incense: Basil

Wednesday
Saint Walburga's Day (German)
Waxing Moon
Second Quarter 12:14 pm
Color: Brown

Moon Sign: Gemini
Incense: Marjoram

26 Thursday
Zamboanga Festival (Filipino)
Waxing Moon
Moon phase: Second Quarter
Color: Crimson

Moon Sign: Gemini
Incense: Mulberry

27 Friday
Threepenny Day
Waxing Moon
Moon phase: Second Quarter
Color: Purple

Moon Sign: Gemini
Moon enters Cancer 7:50 am
Incense: Mint

28 Saturday
Kalevala Day (Finnish)
Waxing Moon
Moon phase: Second Quarter
Color: Black

Moon Sign: Cancer
Incense: Magnolia

March

1 Sunday
Matronalia (Roman)
Waxing Moon
Moon phase: Second Quarter
Color: Amber

Moon Sign: Cancer
Moon enters Leo 6:34 pm
Incense: Juniper

2 Monday
St. Chad's Day (English)
Waxing Moon
Moon phase: Second Quarter
Color: White

Moon Sign: Leo
Incense: Lily

3 Tuesday
Doll Festival (Japanese)
Waxing Moon
Moon phase: Second Quarter
Color: Gray

Moon Sign: Leo
Incense: Cedar

4 Wednesday
St. Casimir's Day (Polish)
Waxing Moon
Moon phase: Second Quarter
Color: Topaz

Moon Sign: Leo
Moon enters Virgo 6:58 am
Incense: Lilac

5 Thursday
Purim
Waxing Moon
Full Moon 1:05 pm
Color: Crimson

Moon Sign: Virgo
Incense: Apricot

6 Friday
Alamo Day
Waning Moon
Moon phase: Third Quarter
Color: Pink

Moon Sign: Virgo
Moon enters Libra 7:52 pm
Incense: Yarrow

7 Saturday
Bird and Arbor Day
Waning Moon
Moon phase: Third Quarter
Color: Blue

Moon Sign: Libra
Incense: Sandalwood

March

8 Sunday
International Women's Day
Waning Moon
Moon phase: Third Quarter
Color: Gold

Moon Sign: Libra
Incense: Almond

Daylight Saving Time begins

9 Monday
Forty Saints' Day
Waning Moon
Moon phase: Third Quarter
Color: Lavender

Moon Sign: Libra
Moon enters Scorpio 9:10 am
Incense: Rosemary

10 Tuesday
Tibet Day
Waning Moon
Moon phase: Third Quarter
Color: White

Moon Sign: Scorpio
Incense: Geranium

11 Wednesday
Feast of the Gauri (Hindu)
Waning Moon
Moon phase: Third Quarter
Color: Brown

Moon Sign: Scorpio
Moon enters Sagittarius 7:30 pm
Incense: Honeysuckle

12 Thursday
Receiving the Water (Buddhist)
Waning Moon
Moon phase: Third Quarter
Color: Purple

Moon Sign: Sagittarius
Incense: Nutmeg

☽ Friday
Purification Feast (Balinese)
Waning Moon
Fourth Quarter 1:48 pm
Color: Coral

Moon Sign: Sagittarius
Incense: Alder

14 Saturday
Mamuralia (Roman)
Waning Moon
Moon phase: Fourth Quarter
Color: Black

Moon Sign: Sagittarius
Moon enters Capricorn 2:40 am
Incense: Pine

March
♈

15 Sunday
Phallus Festival (Japanese)
Waning Moon
Moon phase: Fourth Quarter
Color: Orange

Moon Sign: Capricorn
Incense: Marigold

16 Monday
St. Urho's Day (Finnish)
Waning Moon
Moon phase: Fourth Quarter
Color: Gray

Moon Sign: Capricorn
Moon enters Aquarius 6:14 am
Incense: Neroli

17 Tuesday
St. Patrick's Day
Waning Moon
Moon phase: Fourth Quarter
Color: Maroon

Moon Sign: Aquarius
Incense: Bayberry

18 Wednesday
Sheelah's Day (Irish)
Waning Moon
Moon phase: Fourth Quarter
Color: Yellow

Moon Sign: Aquarius
Moon enters Pisces 6:58 am
Incense: Bay laurel

19 Thursday
St. Joseph's Day (Sicilian)
Waning Moon
Moon phase: Fourth Quarter
Color: Turquoise

Moon Sign: Pisces
Incense: Myrrh

☽ Friday
Ostara • Spring Equinox
Waning Moon
New Moon 5:36 am
Color: White

Moon Sign: Pisces
Moon enters Aries 6:28 am
Sun enters Aries 6:45 pm
Incense: Vanilla

21 Saturday
Juarez Day (Mexican)
Waxing Moon
Moon phase: First Quarter
Color: Indigo

Moon Sign: Aries
Incense: Ivy

March ♈

22 Sunday
Hilaria (Roman)
Waxing Moon
Moon phase: First Quarter
Color: Yellow

Moon Sign: Aries
Moon enters Taurus 6:40 am
Incense: Hyacinth

23 Monday
Pakistan Day
Waxing Moon
Moon phase: First Quarter
Color: Silver

Moon Sign: Taurus
Incense: Narcissus

24 Tuesday
Day of Blood (Roman)
Waxing Moon
Moon phase: First Quarter
Color: Black

Moon Sign: Taurus
Moon enters Gemini 9:23 am
Incense: Cinnamon

25 Wednesday
Tichborne Dole (English)
Waxing Moon
Moon phase: First Quarter
Color: White

Moon Sign: Gemini
Incense: Marjoram

26 Thursday
Prince Kuhio Day (Hawaiian)
Waxing Moon
Moon phase: First Quarter
Color: Green

Moon Sign: Gemini
Moon enters Cancer 3:45 pm
Incense: Balsam

◐ Friday
Smell the Breezes Day (Egyptian)
Waxing Moon
Second Quarter 3:43 am
Color: Rose

Moon Sign: Cancer
Incense: Thyme

28 Saturday
Oranges and Lemons Service (English)
Waxing Moon
Moon phase: Second Quarter
Color: Brown

Moon Sign: Cancer
Incense: Patchouli

29 Sunday

Palm Sunday
Waxing Moon
Moon phase: Second Quarter
Color: Gold

Moon Sign: Cancer
Moon enters Leo 1:48 am
Incense: Frankincense

30 Monday

Seward's Day (Alaskan)
Waxing Moon
Moon phase: Second Quarter
Color: White

Moon Sign: Leo
Incense: Hyssop

31 Tuesday

The Borrowed Days (Ethiopian)
Waxing Moon
Moon phase: Second Quarter
Color: Red

Moon Sign: Leo
Moon enters Virgo 2:12 pm
Incense: Ginger

❦

Thanks and Good Night!

Few people have perfect lives, but an attitude of appreciation can remind us of the good things we do have. And it is never a bad idea to say "Thank you." When times are tough, you may have to look for the smallest things, but there is always something to be grateful for. At the end of the day, take five minutes to say something like this:

"Great goddess, Great god (or your own deity), I greet you at the end of the day and thank you for the many blessings in my life. Thank you for _____ (people, pets, unexpected positive moments, food, home, etc.). And thank you for your presence in my life."

– Deborah Blake

April

♈

1 Wednesday
April Fools' Day
Waxing Moon
Moon phase: Second Quarter
Color: Yellow

Moon Sign: Virgo
Incense: Honeysuckle

2 Thursday
The Battle of Flowers (French)
Waxing Moon
Moon phase: Second Quarter
Color: White

Moon Sign: Virgo
Incense: Carnation

3 Friday
Good Friday
Waxing Moon
Moon phase: Second Quarter
Color: Rose

Moon Sign: Virgo
Moon enters Libra 3:07 am
Incense: Mint

☺ Saturday
Passover begins
Waxing Moon
Full Moon 8:06 am
Color: Brown

Moon Sign: Libra
Incense: Pine

5 Sunday
Easter
Waning Moon
Moon phase: Third Quarter
Color: Yellow

Moon Sign: Libra
Moon enters Scorpio 3:04 pm
Incense: Heliotrope

6 Monday
Chakri Day (Thai)
Waning Moon
Moon phase: Third Quarter
Color: Gray

Moon Sign: Scorpio
Incense: Clary sage

7 Tuesday
Festival of Pure Brightness (Chinese)
Waning Moon
Moon phase: Third Quarter
Color: White

Moon Sign: Scorpio
Incense: Ylang-ylang

April

8 Wednesday
Buddha's Birthday
Waning Moon
Moon phase: Third Quarter
Color: Brown

Moon Sign: Scorpio
Moon enters Sagittarius 1:08 am
Incense: Lavender

9 Thursday
Valour Day (Filipino)
Waning Moon
Moon phase: Third Quarter
Color: Purple

Moon Sign: Sagittarius
Incense: Clove

10 Friday
Orthodox Good Friday
Waning Moon
Moon phase: Third Quarter
Color: Pink

Moon Sign: Sagittarius
Moon enters Capricorn 8:47 am
Incense: Orchid

◗ Saturday
Passover ends
Waning Moon
Fourth Quarter 11:44 pm
Color: Black

Moon Sign: Capricorn
Incense: Sage

12 Sunday
Orthodox Easter
Waning Moon
Moon phase: Fourth Quarter
Color: Amber

Moon Sign: Capricorn
Moon enters Aquarius 1:44 pm
Incense: Eucalyptus

13 Monday
Thai New Year
Waning Moon
Moon phase: Fourth Quarter
Color: Silver

Moon Sign: Aquarius
Incense: Lily

14 Tuesday
Sanno Festival (Japanese)
Waning Moon
Moon phase: Fourth Quarter
Color: Maroon

Moon Sign: Aquarius
Moon enters Pisces 4:12 pm
Incense: Basil

15 **Wednesday**
Plowing Festival (Chinese)
Waning Moon
Moon phase: Fourth Quarter
Color: Topaz

Moon Sign: Pisces
Incense: Lilac

16 **Thursday**
Zurich Spring Festival (Swiss)
Waning Moon
Moon phase: Fourth Quarter
Color: White

Moon Sign: Pisces
Moon enters Aries 5:00 pm
Incense: Jasmine

17 **Friday**
Yayoi Matsuri (Japanese)
Waning Moon
Moon phase: Fourth Quarter
Color: Coral

Moon Sign: Aries
Incense: Cypress

Saturday
Flower Festival (Japanese)
Waning Moon
New Moon 2:57 pm
Color: Blue

Moon Sign: Aries
Moon enters Taurus 5:31 pm
Incense: Sandalwood

19 **Sunday**
Cerealia last day (Roman)
Waxing Moon
Moon phase: First Quarter
Color: Orange

Moon Sign: Taurus
Incense: Frankincense

20 **Monday**
Drum Festival (Japanese)
Waxing Moon
Moon phase: First Quarter
Color: Ivory

Moon Sign: Taurus
Sun enters Taurus 5:42 am
Moon enters Gemini 7:28 pm
Incense: Neroli

21 **Tuesday**
Tiradentes Day (Brazilian)
Waxing Moon
Moon phase: First Quarter
Color: Gray

Moon Sign: Gemini
Incense: Ginger

22 Wednesday

Earth Day
Waxing Moon
Moon phase: First Quarter
Color: Yellow

Moon Sign: Gemini
Incense: Bay laurel

23 Thursday

St. George's Day (English)
Waxing Moon
Moon phase: First Quarter
Color: Crimson

Moon Sign: Gemini
Moon enters Cancer 12:25 am
Incense: Apricot

24 Friday

St. Mark's Eve
Waxing Moon
Moon phase: First Quarter
Color: White

Moon Sign: Cancer
Incense: Violet

☽ Saturday

Robigalia (Roman)
Waxing Moon
Second Quarter 7:55 pm
Color: Indigo

Moon Sign: Cancer
Moon enters Leo 9:13 am
Incense: Ivy

26 Sunday

Arbor Day
Waxing Moon
Moon phase: Second Quarter
Color: Amber

Moon Sign: Leo
Incense: Marigold

27 Monday

Humabon's Conversion (Filipino)
Waxing Moon
Moon phase: Second Quarter
Color: Lavender

Moon Sign: Leo
Moon enters Virgo 9:07 am
Incense: Hyssop

28 Tuesday

Floralia (Roman)
Waxing Moon
Moon phase: Second Quarter
Color: Red

Moon Sign: Virgo
Incense: Bayberry

April

29 Wednesday
Green Day (Japanese)
Waxing Moon
Moon phase: Second Quarter
Color: White

Moon Sign: Virgo
Incense: Honeysuckle

30 Thursday
Walpurgis Night • May Eve
Waxing Moon
Moon phase: Second Quarter
Color: Turquoise

Moon Sign: Virgo
Moon enters Libra 10:03 am
Incense: Nutmeg

※

Just Breathe (Connecting with Air)

The element of air is all around us, but we rarely think to connect with it outside of ritual. Yet nothing could be simpler than to breathe—the thing that makes it magick is doing so with focus and purpose. Once a day, try to take five minutes to breathe with the intention of connecting with the element of air. Find a quiet space (even an elevator or a bathroom will do) and breathe in—pulling in energy and power from the universe. Breathe out—letting go of tension and negativity. Do this simple activity for five minutes, and you will be amazed how good it feels.

– Deborah Blake

May

1 Friday
Beltane • May Day
Waxing Moon
Moon phase: Second Quarter
Color: Coral

Moon Sign: Libra
Incense: Rose

2 Saturday
Big Kite Flying (Japanese)
Waxing Moon
Moon phase: Second Quarter
Color: Indigo

Moon Sign: Libra
Moon enters Scorpio 9:47 pm
Incense: Rue

3 Sunday
Holy Cross Day
Waxing Moon
Full Moon 11:42 pm
Color: Gold

Moon Sign: Scorpio
Incense: Juniper

4 Monday
Bona Dea (Roman)
Waning Moon
Moon phase: Third Quarter
Color: Ivory

Moon Sign: Scorpio
Incense: Rosemary

5 Tuesday
Cinco de Mayo (Mexican)
Waning Moon
Moon phase: Third Quarter
Color: Black

Moon Sign: Scorpio
Moon enters Sagittarius 7:13 am
Incense: Cedar

6 Wednesday
Martyrs' Day (Lebanese)
Waning Moon
Moon phase: Third Quarter
Color: Brown

Moon Sign: Sagittarius
Incense: Lilac

7 Thursday
Pilgrimage of St. Nicholas (Italian)
Waning Moon
Moon phase: Third Quarter
Color: Crimson

Moon Sign: Sagittarius
Moon enters Capricorn 2:16 pm
Incense: Myrrh

8 Friday
Liberation Day (French)
Waning Moon
Moon phase: Third Quarter
Color: White

Moon Sign: Capricorn
Incense: Alder

9 Saturday
Lemuria (Roman)
Waning Moon
Moon phase: Third Quarter
Color: Gray

Moon Sign: Capricorn
Moon enters Aquarius 7:22 pm
Incense: Patchouli

10 Sunday
Mother's Day
Waning Moon
Moon phase: Third Quarter
Color: Yellow

Moon Sign: Aquarius
Incense: Hyacinth

◐ Monday
Ukai Season Opens (Japanese)
Waning Moon
Fourth Quarter 6:36 am
Color: Silver

Moon Sign: Aquarius
Moon enters Pisces 10:53 pm
Incense: Narcissus

12 Tuesday
Florence Nightingale's Birthday
Waning Moon
Moon phase: Fourth Quarter
Color: White

Moon Sign: Pisces
Incense: Ylang-ylang

13 Wednesday
Pilgrimage to Fatima (Portuguese)
Waning Moon
Moon phase: Fourth Quarter
Color: Topaz

Moon Sign: Pisces
Incense: Lavender

14 Thursday
Carabao Festival (Spanish)
Waning Moon
Moon phase: Fourth Quarter
Color: Turquoise

Moon Sign: Pisces
Moon enters Aries 1:13 am
Incense: Mulberry

May

♊

15 Friday
Festival of St. Dympna (Belgian)
Waning Moon
Moon phase: Fourth Quarter
Color: Purple

Moon Sign: Aries
Incense: Orchid

---

16 Saturday
St. Honoratus' Day
Waning Moon
Moon phase: Fourth Quarter
Color: Black

Moon Sign: Aries
Moon enters Taurus 3:02 am
Incense: Sage

---

17 Sunday
Norwegian Independence Day
Waning Moon
Moon phase: Fourth Quarter
Color: Orange

Moon Sign: Taurus
Incense: Almond

☽ Monday
Las Piedras Day (Uruguayan)
Waning Moon
New Moon 12:13 am
Color: Lavender

Moon Sign: Taurus
Moon enters Gemini 5:27 am
Incense: Clary sage

---

19 Tuesday
Pilgrimage to Treguier (French)
Waxing Moon
Moon phase: First Quarter
Color: Maroon

Moon Sign: Gemini
Incense: Cinnamon

---

20 Wednesday
Pardon of the Singers (British)
Waxing Moon
Moon phase: First Quarter
Color: White

Moon Sign: Gemini
Moon enters Cancer 9:56 am
Incense: Bay laurel

---

21 Thursday
Victoria Day (Canadian)
Waxing Moon
Moon phase: First Quarter
Color: Purple

Moon Sign: Cancer
Sun enters Gemini 4:45 am
Incense: Balsam

May ♊

22 Friday
Heroes' Day (Sri Lankan)
Waxing Moon
Moon phase: First Quarter
Color: Coral

Moon Sign: Cancer
Moon enters Leo 5:42 pm
Incense: Mint

23 Saturday
Tubilustrium (Roman)
Waxing Moon
Moon phase: First Quarter
Color: Blue

Moon Sign: Leo
Incense: Ivy

24 Sunday
Shavuot
Waxing Moon
Moon phase: First Quarter
Color: Amber

Moon Sign: Leo
Incense: Eucalyptus

☽ Monday
Memorial Day (observed)
Waxing Moon
Second Quarter 1:19 pm
Color: White

Moon Sign: Leo
Moon enters Virgo 4:52 am
Incense: Rosemary

26 Tuesday
Pepys' Commemoration (English)
Waxing Moon
Moon phase: Second Quarter
Color: Gray

Moon Sign: Virgo
Incense: Basil

27 Wednesday
St. Augustine of Canterbury's Day
Waxing Moon
Moon phase: Second Quarter
Color: Yellow

Moon Sign: Virgo
Moon enters Libra 5:42 pm
Incense: Marjoram

28 Thursday
St. Germain's Day
Waxing Moon
Moon phase: Second Quarter
Color: Green

Moon Sign: Libra
Incense: Carnation

May

29 Friday
Royal Oak Day (English)
Waxing Moon
Moon phase: Second Quarter
Color: Pink

Moon Sign: Libra
Incense: Thyme

30 Saturday
Memorial Day (actual)
Waxing Moon
Moon phase: Second Quarter
Color: Brown

Moon Sign: Libra
Moon enters Scorpio 5:34 am
Incense: Sandalwood

31 Sunday
Flowers of May
Waxing Moon
Moon phase: Second Quarter
Color: Yellow

Moon Sign: Scorpio
Incense: Frankincense

❖

Healing Hoodoo

Many people think of "Voodoo dolls" as a part of Hoodoo practice, but Witches have been using poppets and other representations of the human body since ancient times. These aren't necessarily used to "curse" or harm another, but can in fact be a healing tool. If you have basic sewing skills, it is easy enough to make a rough dolly with a head, arms, and legs. Otherwise, you can cut one out of paper instead. Mark the places that need healing on the doll with thread or pen and sprinkle them with salt and/or waft with a sage stick. Visualize those places being healed and say:

"Healthy healing, cure all harm. Healthy healing with this charm."

Place it on your altar or someplace safe, and repeat as needed.

– Deborah Blake

June

♊

1 Monday
National Day (Tunisian)
Waxing Moon
Moon phase: Second Quarter
Color: Silver

Moon Sign: Scorpio
Moon enters Sagittarius 2:39 pm
Incense: Lily

☺ **Tuesday**
Rice Harvest Festival (Malaysian)
Waxing Moon
Full Moon 12:19 pm
Color: Scarlet

Moon Sign: Sagittarius
Incense: Bayberry

3 Wednesday
Memorial to Broken Dolls (Japanese)
Waning Moon
Moon phase: Third Quarter
Color: White

Moon Sign: Sagittarius
Moon enters Capricorn 8:50 pm
Incense: Lavender

4 Thursday
Full Moon Day (Burmese)
Waning Moon
Moon phase: Third Quarter
Color: Purple

Moon Sign: Capricorn
Incense: Jasmine

5 Friday
Constitution Day (Danish)
Waning Moon
Moon phase: Third Quarter
Color: Rose

Moon Sign: Capricorn
Incense: Yarrow

6 Saturday
Swedish Flag Day
Waning Moon
Moon phase: Third Quarter
Color: Gray

Moon Sign: Capricorn
Moon enters Aquarius 1:02 am
Incense: Rue

7 Sunday
St. Robert of Newminster's Day
Waning Moon
Moon phase: Third Quarter
Color: Amber

Moon Sign: Aquarius
Incense: Frankincense

June ♊

8 Monday
St. Medard's Day (Belgian)
Waning Moon
Moon phase: Third Quarter
Color: Lavender

Moon Sign: Aquarius
Moon enters Pisces 4:16 am
Incense: Hyssop

◖ Tuesday
Vestalia (Roman)
Waning Moon
Fourth Quarter 11:42 am
Color: White

Moon Sign: Pisces
Incense: Ylang-ylang

10 Wednesday
Time-Observance Day (Chinese)
Waning Moon
Moon phase: Fourth Quarter
Color: Brown

Moon Sign: Pisces
Moon enters Aries 7:14 am
Incense: Bay laurel

11 Thursday
Kamehameha Day (Hawaiian)
Waning Moon
Moon phase: Fourth Quarter
Color: White

Moon Sign: Aries
Incense: Myrrh

12 Friday
Independence Day (Filipino)
Waning Moon
Moon phase: Fourth Quarter
Color: Pink

Moon Sign: Aries
Moon enters Taurus 10:16 am
Incense: Rose

13 Saturday
St. Anthony of Padua's Day
Waning Moon
Moon phase: Fourth Quarter
Color: Black

Moon Sign: Taurus
Incense: Ivy

14 Sunday
Flag Day
Waning Moon
Moon phase: Fourth Quarter
Color: Gold

Moon Sign: Taurus
Moon enters Gemini 1:51 pm
Incense: Hyacinth

15 **Monday**
Father's Day
Waning Moon
Moon phase: Fourth Quarter
Color: Gray

Moon Sign: Gemini
Incense: Neroli

☽ **Tuesday**
Bloomsday (Irish)
Waning Moon
New Moon 10:05 am
Color: Red

Moon Sign: Gemini
Moon enters Cancer 6:51 pm
Incense: Geranium

17 **Wednesday**
Bunker Hill Day
Waxing Moon
Moon phase: First Quarter
Color: Topaz

Moon Sign: Cancer
Incense: Honeysuckle

18 **Thursday**
Ramadan begins
Waxing Moon
Moon phase: First Quarter
Color: Crimson

Moon Sign: Cancer
Incense: Clove

19 **Friday**
Juneteenth
Waxing Moon
Moon phase: First Quarter
Color: White

Moon Sign: Cancer
Moon enters Leo 2:23 am
Incense: Violet

20 **Saturday**
Flag Day (Argentinian)
Waxing Moon
Moon phase: First Quarter
Color: Blue

Moon Sign: Leo
Incense: Patchouli

21 **Sunday**
Midsummer • Summer Solstice • Father's Day
Waxing Moon
Moon phase: First Quarter
Color: Yellow

Moon Sign: Leo
Sun enters Cancer 12:38 pm
Moon enters Virgo 12:59 pm
Incense: Heliotrope

22 Monday
Rose Festival (English)
Waxing Moon
Moon phase: First Quarter
Color: White

Moon Sign: Virgo
Incense: Lily

---

23 Tuesday
St. John's Eve
Waxing Moon
Moon phase: First Quarter
Color: Black

Moon Sign: Virgo
Incense: Ginger

○ Wednesday
St. John's Day
Waxing Moon
Second Quarter 7:03 am
Color: Yellow

Moon Sign: Virgo
Moon enters Libra 1:41 am
Incense: Lilac

---

25 Thursday
Fiesta of Santa Orosia (Spanish)
Waxing Moon
Moon phase: Second Quarter
Color: Green

Moon Sign: Libra
Incense: Nutmeg

---

26 Friday
Pied Piper Day (German)
Waxing Moon
Moon phase: Second Quarter
Color: Purple

Moon Sign: Libra
Moon enters Scorpio 1:57 pm
Incense: Vanilla

---

27 Saturday
Day of the Seven Sleepers (Islamic)
Waxing Moon
Moon phase: Second Quarter
Color: Brown

Moon Sign: Scorpio
Incense: Magnolia

---

28 Sunday
Paul Bunyan Day
Waxing Moon
Moon phase: Second Quarter
Color: Orange

Moon Sign: Scorpio
Moon enters Sagittarius 11:21 pm
Incense: Juniper

June

29 Monday
Feast of Saints Peter and Paul
Waxing Moon
Moon phase: Second Quarter
Color: Lavender

Moon Sign: Sagittarius
Incense: Narcissus

30 Tuesday
The Burning of the Three Firs (French)
Waxing Moon
Moon phase: Second Quarter
Color: Gray

Moon Sign: Sagittarius
Incense: Cedar

Energy Anywhere

We could all use more energy from time to time. It is easy to drink coffee or cola, but don't forget that you can call on the energy of the universe around you as well. No matter where you are, the earth is always somewhere below you and the sky somewhere above (although this works best if you can actually stand outside). Take five minutes to close your eyes and connect with the energy of the planet. Feel it humming, pulsing, and shimmering all around you. Pull energy from below and above. If you want, you can say these words silently or aloud:

"I am part of earth and sky, as above and as below. On this connection I rely, as energy it does bestow."

– Deborah Blake

July

⊙ **Wednesday**
Climbing Mount Fuji (Japanese)
Waxing Moon
Full Moon 10:20 pm
Color: Topaz

Moon Sign: Sagittarius
Moon enters Capricorn 5:11 am
Incense: Lavender

---

2 **Thursday**
Heroes' Day (Zambian)
Waning Moon
Moon phase: Third Quarter
Color: White

Moon Sign: Capricorn
Incense: Carnation

---

3 **Friday**
Indian Sun Dance (Native American)
Waning Moon
Moon phase: Third Quarter
Color: Pink

Moon Sign: Capricorn
Moon enters Aquarius 8:21 am
Incense: Cypress

---

4 **Saturday**
Independence Day
Waning Moon
Moon phase: Third Quarter
Color: Black

Moon Sign: Aquarius
Incense: Sage

---

5 **Sunday**
Tynwald (Nordic)
Waning Moon
Moon phase: Third Quarter
Color: Yellow

Moon Sign: Aquarius
Moon enters Pisces 10:23 am
Incense: Marigold

---

6 **Monday**
Khao Phansa Day (Thai)
Waning Moon
Moon phase: Third Quarter
Color: Lavender

Moon Sign: Pisces
Incense: Clary sage

---

7 **Tuesday**
Weaver's Festival (Japanese)
Waning Moon
Moon phase: Third Quarter
Color: Red

Moon Sign: Pisces
Moon enters Aries 12:38 pm
Incense: Cinnamon

July

○ **Wednesday**
St. Elizabeth's Day (Portuguese)
Waning Moon
Fourth Quarter 4:24 pm
Color: Brown

Moon Sign: Aries
Incense: Bay laurel

---

9 Thursday
Battle of Sempach Day (Swiss)
Waning Moon
Moon phase: Fourth Quarter
Color: Green

Moon Sign: Aries
Moon enters Taurus 3:49 pm
Incense: Apricot

---

10 Friday
Lady Godiva Day (English)
Waning Moon
Moon phase: Fourth Quarter
Color: Purple

Moon Sign: Taurus
Incense: Alder

---

11 Saturday
Revolution Day (Mongolian)
Waning Moon
Moon phase: Fourth Quarter
Color: Indigo

Moon Sign: Taurus
Moon enters Gemini 8:16 pm
Incense: Sandalwood

---

12 Sunday
Lobster Carnival (Nova Scotian)
Waning Moon
Moon phase: Fourth Quarter
Color: Amber

Moon Sign: Gemini
Incense: Hyacinth

---

13 Monday
Festival of the Three Cows (Spanish)
Waning Moon
Moon phase: Fourth Quarter
Color: Gray

Moon Sign: Gemini
Incense: Rosemary

---

14 Tuesday
Bastille Day (French)
Waning Moon
Moon phase: Fourth Quarter
Color: White

Moon Sign: Gemini
Moon enters Cancer 2:14 am
Incense: Basil

☽ **Wednesday**
St. Swithin's Day
Waning Moon
New Moon 9:24 pm
Color: Yellow

Moon Sign: Cancer
Incense: Honeysuckle

16 **Thursday**
Our Lady of Carmel
Waxing Moon
Moon phase: First Quarter
Color: Purple

Moon Sign: Cancer
Moon enters Leo 10:15 am
Incense: Balsam

17 **Friday**
Ramadan ends
Waxing Moon
Moon phase: First Quarter
Color: Rose

Moon Sign: Leo
Incense: Orchid

18 **Saturday**
Gion Matsuri Festival (Japanese)
Waxing Moon
Moon phase: First Quarter
Color: Blue

Moon Sign: Leo
Moon enters Virgo 8:47 pm
Incense: Rue

19 **Sunday**
Flitch Day (English)
Waxing Moon
Moon phase: First Quarter
Color: Orange

Moon Sign: Virgo
Incense: Frankincense

20 **Monday**
Binding of Wreaths (Lithuanian)
Waxing Moon
Moon phase: First Quarter
Color: White

Moon Sign: Virgo
Incense: Hyssop

21 **Tuesday**
National Day (Belgian)
Waxing Moon
Moon phase: First Quarter
Color: Maroon

Moon Sign: Virgo
Moon enters Libra 9:23 am
Incense: Ylang-ylang

July

22 Wednesday
St. Mary Magdalene's Day
Waxing Moon
Moon phase: First Quarter
Color: White

Moon Sign: Libra
Sun enters Leo 11:30 pm
Incense: Lilac

23 Thursday
Mysteries of Santa Cristina (Italian)
Waxing Moon
Moon phase: First Quarter
Color: Crimson

Moon Sign: Libra
Moon enters Scorpio 10:07 pm
Incense: Mulberry

☾ Friday
Pioneer Day (Mormon)
Waxing Moon
Second Quarter 12:04 am
Color: Coral

Moon Sign: Scorpio
Incense: Yarrow

25 Saturday
St. James' Day
Waxing Moon
Moon phase: Second Quarter
Color: Black

Moon Sign: Scorpio
Incense: Pine

26 Sunday
St. Anne's Day
Waxing Moon
Moon phase: Second Quarter
Color: Gold

Moon Sign: Scorpio
Moon enters Sagittarius 8:24 am
Incense: Heliotrope

27 Monday
Sleepyhead Day (Finnish)
Waxing Moon
Moon phase: Second Quarter
Color: Silver

Moon Sign: Sagittarius
Incense: Narcissus

28 Tuesday
Independence Day (Peruvian)
Waxing Moon
Moon phase: Second Quarter
Color: Black

Moon Sign: Sagittarius
Moon enters Capricorn 2:47 pm
Incense: Ginger

July

29 Wednesday
Pardon of the Birds (French)
Waxing Moon
Moon phase: Second Quarter
Color: Brown

Moon Sign: Capricorn
Incense: Marjoram

30 Thursday
Micman Festival of St. Ann
Waxing Moon
Moon phase: Second Quarter
Color: Turquoise

Moon Sign: Capricorn
Moon enters Aquarius 5:40 pm
Incense: Jasmine

Friday
Weighing of the Aga Kahn
Waxing Moon
Full Moon 6:43 am
Color: White

Moon Sign: Aquarius
Incense: Mint

❖

Fast Candle Calm Down
(Connecting with Fire)

Life can be fast-paced and stressful, and sometimes it is hard to keep our minds from spinning around and around. Try this simple practice to connect with the element of fire while also giving yourself five minutes of peace and the space to catch your breath. Light a candle and sit or stand in front of it. Take slow deep breaths as you concentrate on the flame; its shape, its motion, its warmth, and its beauty. As you gaze at the candle, feel yourself becoming calm and centered. After five minutes, snuff out the candle and get on with your day.

– Deborah Blake

August

1 Saturday
Lammas
Waning Moon
Moon phase: Third Quarter
Color: Brown

Moon Sign: Aquarius
Moon enters Pisces 6:36 pm
Incense: Ivy

2 Sunday
Porcingula (Native American)
Waning Moon
Moon phase: Third Quarter
Color: Orange

Moon Sign: Pisces
Incense: Eucalyptus

3 Monday
Drimes (Greek)
Waning Moon
Moon phase: Third Quarter
Color: Silver

Moon Sign: Pisces
Moon enters Aries 7:24 pm
Incense: Rosemary

4 Tuesday
Cook Islands Constitution Celebration
Waning Moon
Moon phase: Third Quarter
Color: White

Moon Sign: Aries
Incense: Cinnamon

5 Wednesday
Benediction of the Sea (French)
Waning Moon
Moon phase: Third Quarter
Color: Yellow

Moon Sign: Aries
Moon enters Taurus 9:29 pm
Incense: Honeysuckle

○ Thursday
Hiroshima Peace Ceremony
Waning Moon
Fourth Quarter 10:03 pm
Color: Crimson

Moon Sign: Taurus
Incense: Clove

7 Friday
Republic Day (Ivory Coast)
Waning Moon
Moon phase: Fourth Quarter
Color: Purple

Moon Sign: Taurus
Incense: Rose

8 **Saturday**
Dog Days (Japanese)
Waning Moon
Moon phase: Fourth Quarter
Color: Black

Moon Sign: Taurus
Moon enters Gemini 1:40 am
Incense: Patchouli

9 **Sunday**
Nagasaki Peace Ceremony
Waning Moon
Moon phase: Fourth Quarter
Color: Yellow

Moon Sign: Gemini
Incense: Juniper

10 **Monday**
St. Lawrence's Day
Waning Moon
Moon phase: Fourth Quarter
Color: Lavender

Moon Sign: Gemini
Moon enters Cancer 8:08 am
Incense: Lily

11 **Tuesday**
Puck Fair (Irish)
Waning Moon
Moon phase: Fourth Quarter
Color: Black

Moon Sign: Cancer
Incense: Bayberry

12 **Wednesday**
Fiesta of Santa Clara
Waning Moon
Moon phase: Fourth Quarter
Color: White

Moon Sign: Cancer
Moon enters Leo 4:52 pm
Incense: Lavender

13 **Thursday**
Women's Day (Tunisian)
Waning Moon
Moon phase: Fourth Quarter
Color: Green

Moon Sign: Leo
Incense: Carnation

☽ **Friday**
Festival at Sassari
Waning Moon
New Moon 10:53 am
Color: Pink

Moon Sign: Leo
Incense: Violet

August

15 Saturday
Assumption Day
Waxing Moon
Moon phase: First Quarter
Color: Blue

Moon Sign: Leo
Moon enters Virgo 3:46 am
Incense: Sage

16 Sunday
Festival of Minstrels (European)
Waxing Moon
Moon phase: First Quarter
Color: Gold

Moon Sign: Virgo
Incense: Almond

17 Monday
Feast of the Hungry Ghosts (Chinese)
Waxing Moon
Moon phase: First Quarter
Color: Ivory

Moon Sign: Virgo
Moon enters Libra 4:23 pm
Incense: Hyssop

18 Tuesday
St. Helen's Day
Waxing Moon
Moon phase: First Quarter
Color: Scarlet

Moon Sign: Libra
Incense: Geranium

19 Wednesday
Rustic Vinalia (Roman)
Waxing Moon
Moon phase: First Quarter
Color: Brown

Moon Sign: Libra
Incense: Bay laurel

20 Thursday
Constitution Day (Hungarian)
Waxing Moon
Moon phase: First Quarter
Color: Turquoise

Moon Sign: Libra
Moon enters Scorpio 5:24 am
Incense: Balsam

21 Friday
Consualia (Roman)
Waxing Moon
Moon phase: First Quarter
Color: White

Moon Sign: Scorpio
Incense: Alder

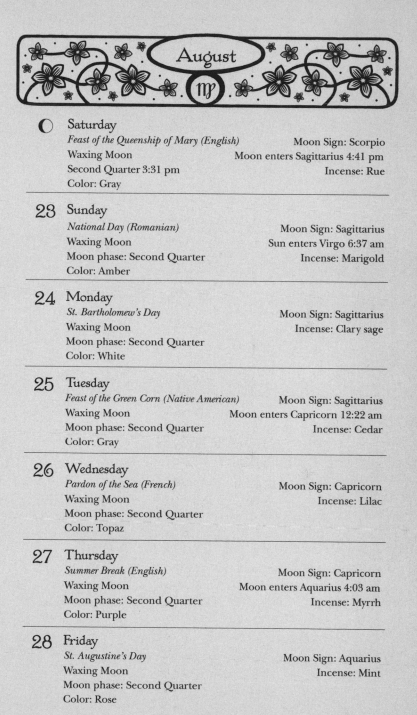

August ♍

○ **Saturday**
Feast of the Queenship of Mary (English)
Waxing Moon
Second Quarter 3:31 pm
Color: Gray

Moon Sign: Scorpio
Moon enters Sagittarius 4:41 pm
Incense: Rue

---

23 Sunday
National Day (Romanian)
Waxing Moon
Moon phase: Second Quarter
Color: Amber

Moon Sign: Sagittarius
Sun enters Virgo 6:37 am
Incense: Marigold

---

24 Monday
St. Bartholomew's Day
Waxing Moon
Moon phase: Second Quarter
Color: White

Moon Sign: Sagittarius
Incense: Clary sage

---

25 Tuesday
Feast of the Green Corn (Native American)
Waxing Moon
Moon phase: Second Quarter
Color: Gray

Moon Sign: Sagittarius
Moon enters Capricorn 12:22 am
Incense: Cedar

---

26 Wednesday
Pardon of the Sea (French)
Waxing Moon
Moon phase: Second Quarter
Color: Topaz

Moon Sign: Capricorn
Incense: Lilac

---

27 Thursday
Summer Break (English)
Waxing Moon
Moon phase: Second Quarter
Color: Purple

Moon Sign: Capricorn
Moon enters Aquarius 4:03 am
Incense: Myrrh

---

28 Friday
St. Augustine's Day
Waxing Moon
Moon phase: Second Quarter
Color: Rose

Moon Sign: Aquarius
Incense: Mint

August ♍

☺ **Saturday**
St. John's Beheading
Waxing Moon
Full Moon 2:35 pm
Color: Black

Moon Sign: Aquarius
Moon enters Pisces 4:51 am
Incense: Ivy

---

30 Sunday
St. Rose of Lima Day (Peruvian)
Waning Moon
Moon phase: Third Quarter
Color: Yellow

Moon Sign: Pisces
Incense: Frankincense

---

31 Monday
Unto These Hills Pageant (Cherokee)
Waning Moon
Moon phase: Third Quarter
Color: White

Moon Sign: Pisces
Moon enters Aries 4:33 am
Incense: Narcissus

Bless This Food

Many cultures say a blessing over a meal before it is eaten, often as a way of saying thank you to the god or gods who provided the food. I like to thank the people who labored to get the food to my table as well, in addition to expressing gratitude for the sacrifice if I am eating meat. Taking a moment to appreciate your food and where it came from is another easy way to integrate spirit into your everyday life. You can simply close your eyes and send out gratitude, or you can say something like this:

"I thank the gods for this food, and send appreciation to all those who got it to my table. May it nourish and support my body. So mote it be."

– Deborah Blake

September ♍

1 Tuesday
Greek New Year
Waning Moon
Moon phase: Third Quarter
Color: Red

Moon Sign: Aries
Incense: Bayberry

2 Wednesday
St. Mama's Day
Waning Moon
Moon phase: Third Quarter
Color: White

Moon Sign: Aries
Moon enters Taurus 5:02 am
Incense: Honeysuckle

3 Thursday
Founder's Day (San Marino)
Waning Moon
Moon phase: Third Quarter
Color: Turquoise

Moon Sign: Taurus
Incense: Nutmeg

4 Friday
Los Angeles' Birthday
Waning Moon
Moon phase: Third Quarter
Color: Pink

Moon Sign: Taurus
Moon enters Gemini 7:48 am
Incense: Vanilla

5 ☽ Saturday
Roman Circus • First Labor Day (1882)
Waning Moon
Fourth Quarter 5:54 am
Color: Gray

Moon Sign: Gemini
Incense: Magnolia

6 Sunday
The Virgin of Remedies (Spanish)
Waning Moon
Moon phase: Fourth Quarter
Color: Gold

Moon Sign: Gemini
Moon enters Cancer 1:40 pm
Incense: Hyacinth

7 Monday
Labor Day
Waning Moon
Moon phase: Fourth Quarter
Color: White

Moon Sign: Cancer
Incense: Neroli

8 Tuesday
Birthday of the Virgin Mary   Moon Sign: Cancer
Waning Moon   Moon enters Leo 10:36 pm
Moon phase: Fourth Quarter   Incense: Basil
Color: Gray

9 Wednesday
Chrysanthemum Festival (Japanese)   Moon Sign: Cancer
Waning Moon   Incense: Marjoram
Moon phase: Fourth Quarter
Color: Yellow

10 Thursday
Festival of the Poets (Japanese)   Moon Sign: Leo
Waning Moon   Incense: Apricot
Moon phase: Fourth Quarter
Color: Crimson

11 Friday
Coptic New Year   Moon Sign: Leo
Waning Moon   Moon enters Virgo 9:56 am
Moon phase: Fourth Quarter   Incense: Yarrow
Color: Rose

12 Saturday
National Day (Ethiopian)   Moon Sign: Virgo
Waning Moon   Incense: Pine
Moon phase: Fourth Quarter
Color: Blue

☽ Sunday
The Gods' Banquet (Roman)   Moon Sign: Virgo
Waning Moon   Moon enters Libra 10:41 pm
New Moon 2:41 am   Incense: Frankincense
Color: Orange

14 Monday
Rosh Hashanah   Moon Sign: Libra
Waxing Moon   Incense: Lily
Moon phase: First Quarter
Color: Gray

15 Tuesday
Birthday of the Moon (Chinese)
Waxing Moon
Moon phase: First Quarter
Color: White

Moon Sign: Libra
Incense: Ginger

---

16 Wednesday
Mexican Independence Day
Waxing Moon
Moon phase: First Quarter
Color: Topaz

Moon Sign: Libra
Moon enters Scorpio 11:43 am
Incense: Lilac

---

17 Thursday
Von Steuben's Day
Waxing Moon
Moon phase: First Quarter
Color: Purple

Moon Sign: Scorpio
Incense: Mulberry

---

18 Friday
Dr. Johnson's Birthday
Waxing Moon
Moon phase: First Quarter
Color: Coral

Moon Sign: Scorpio
Moon enters Sagittarius 11:32 pm
Incense: Orchid

---

19 Saturday
St. Januarius' Day (Italian)
Waxing Moon
Moon phase: First Quarter
Color: Black

Moon Sign: Sagittarius
Incense: Sage

---

20 Sunday
St. Eustace's Day
Waxing Moon
Moon phase: First Quarter
Color: Yellow

Moon Sign: Sagittarius
Incense: Heliotrope

◖ Monday
UN International Day of Peace
Waxing Moon
Second Quarter 4:59 am
Color: Silver

Moon Sign: Sagittarius
Moon enters Capricorn 8:33 am
Incense: Narcissus

22 Tuesday

Mabon • Fall Equinox
Waxing Moon
Moon phase: Second Quarter
Color: Maroon

Moon Sign: Capricorn
Incense: Cedar

23 Wednesday

Mabon • Fall Equinox • Yom Kippur
Waxing Moon
Moon phase: Second Quarter
Color: Brown

Moon Sign: Capricorn
Sun enters Libra 4:21 am
Moon enters Aquarius 1:51 pm
Incense: Lavender

24 Thursday

Schwenkenfelder Thanksgiving (German-American)
Waxing Moon
Moon phase: Second Quarter
Color: White

Moon Sign: Aquarius
Incense: Jasmine

25 Friday

Dolls' Memorial Service (Japanese)
Waxing Moon
Moon phase: Second Quarter
Color: Purple

Moon Sign: Aquarius
Moon enters Pisces 3:43 pm
Incense: Rose

26 Saturday

Feast of Santa Justina (Mexican)
Waxing Moon
Moon phase: Second Quarter
Color: Indigo

Moon Sign: Pisces
Incense: Patchouli

☺ Sunday

Saints Cosmas and Damian's Day
Waxing Moon
Full Moon 10:51 pm
Color: Amber

Moon Sign: Pisces
Moon enters Aries 3:29 pm
Incense: Eucalyptus

28 Monday

Sukkot begins
Waning Moon
Moon phase: Third Quarter
Color: Ivory

Moon Sign: Aries
Incense: Rosemary

29 Tuesday

Michaelmas
Waning Moon
Moon phase: Third Quarter
Color: Black

Moon Sign: Aries
Moon enters Taurus 2:57 pm
Incense: Cinnamon

30 Wednesday

St. Jerome's Day
Waning Moon
Moon phase: Third Quarter
Color: White

Moon Sign: Taurus
Incense: Bay laurel

Greet the Day

We all have good intentions about maintaining a vibrant, active spiritual practice, but our hectic and busy lives often get in the way. One simple addition to your daily routine can help. When you wake up in the morning, before you jump into life's whirlwind, take five minutes to greet the gods and tune in to spirit:

"Great goddess, Great god (or the names of your personal deities), I greet you at the start of another day and ask for the best day possible. Help me to feel my best so I might do my best for myself and for others. Guide me as I walk your path and send me _____ (whatever you need for the day). Watch over me and those that I love. So mote it be."

– Deborah Blake

October

1 Thursday
Armed Forces Day (South Korean)
Waning Moon
Moon phase: Third Quarter
Color: Green

Moon Sign: Taurus
Moon enters Gemini 4:03 pm
Incense: Carnation

2 Friday
Old Man's Day (Virgin Islands)
Waning Moon
Moon phase: Third Quarter
Color: Rose

Moon Sign: Gemini
Incense: Mint

3 Saturday
Moroccan New Year's Day
Waning Moon
Moon phase: Third Quarter
Color: Indigo

Moon Sign: Gemini
Moon enters Cancer 8:22 pm
Incense: Sandalwood

☾ Sunday
Sukkot ends
Waning Moon
Fourth Quarter 5:06 pm
Color: Amber

Moon Sign: Cancer
Incense: Almond

5 Monday
Republic Day (Portuguese)
Waning Moon
Moon phase: Fourth Quarter
Color: White

Moon Sign: Cancer
Incense: Hyssop

6 Tuesday
Dedication of the Virgin's Crowns (English)
Waning Moon
Moon phase: Fourth Quarter
Color: Gray

Moon Sign: Cancer
Moon enters Leo 4:31 am
Incense: Bayberry

7 Wednesday
Kermesse (German)
Waning Moon
Moon phase: Fourth Quarter
Color: Yellow

Moon Sign: Leo
Incense: Honeysuckle

October
♎

8 Thursday
Okunchi (Japanese)
Waning Moon
Moon phase: Fourth Quarter
Color: Purple

Moon Sign: Leo
Moon enters Virgo 3:50 pm
Incense: Myrrh

9 Friday
Alphabet Day (South Korean)
Waning Moon
Moon phase: Fourth Quarter
Color: Coral

Moon Sign: Virgo
Incense: Alder

10 Saturday
Health Day (Japanese)
Waning Moon
Moon phase: Fourth Quarter
Color: Black

Moon Sign: Virgo
Incense: Ivy

11 Sunday
Medetrinalia (Roman)
Waning Moon
Moon phase: Fourth Quarter
Color: Yellow

Moon Sign: Virgo
Moon enters Libra 4:45 am
Incense: Marigold

☽ Monday
Columbus Day (observed)
Waning Moon
New Moon 8:06 pm
Color: Silver

Moon Sign: Libra
Incense: Clary sage

13 Tuesday
Fontinalia (Roman)
Waxing Moon
Moon phase: First Quarter
Color: Scarlet

Moon Sign: Libra
Moon enters Scorpio 5:38 pm
Incense: Ylang-ylang

14 Wednesday
Islamic New Year
Waxing Moon
Moon phase: First Quarter
Color: Brown

Moon Sign: Scorpio
Incense: Marjoram

15 Thursday
The October Horse (Roman)
Waxing Moon
Moon phase: First Quarter
Color: Green

Moon Sign: Scorpio
Incense: Apricot

16 Friday
The Lion Sermon (British)
Waxing Moon
Moon phase: First Quarter
Color: White

Moon Sign: Scorpio
Moon enters Sagittarius 5:18 am
Incense: Vanilla

17 Saturday
Pilgrimage to Paray-le-Monial
Waxing Moon
Moon phase: First Quarter
Color: Blue

Moon Sign: Sagittarius
Incense: Rue

18 Sunday
Brooklyn Barbecue
Waxing Moon
Moon phase: First Quarter
Color: Orange

Moon Sign: Sagittarius
Moon enters Capricorn 2:52 pm
Incense: Frankincense

19 Monday
Our Lord of Miracles Procession (Peruvian)
Waxing Moon
Moon phase: First Quarter
Color: Lavender

Moon Sign: Capricorn
Incense: Rosemary

◐ Tuesday
Colchester Oyster Feast
Waxing Moon
Second Quarter 4:31 pm
Color: White

Moon Sign: Capricorn
Moon enters Aquarius 9:38 pm
Incense: Geranium

21 Wednesday
Feast of the Black Christ
Waxing Moon
Moon phase: Second Quarter
Color: White

Moon Sign: Aquarius
Incense: Lilac

October ♏

22 Thursday
Goddess of Mercy Day (Chinese)
Waxing Moon
Moon phase: Second Quarter
Color: Turquoise

Moon Sign: Aquarius
Incense: Lavender

23 Friday
Revolution Day (Hungarian)
Waxing Moon
Moon phase: Second Quarter
Color: Pink

Moon Sign: Aquarius
Moon enters Pisces 1:18 am
Sun enters Scorpio 1:47 pm
Incense: Mulberry

24 Saturday
United Nations Day
Waxing Moon
Moon phase: Second Quarter
Color: Gray

Moon Sign: Pisces
Incense: Rose

25 Sunday
St. Crispin's Day
Waxing Moon
Moon phase: Second Quarter
Color: Gold

Moon Sign: Pisces
Moon enters Aries 2:22 am
Incense: Marjoram

26 Monday
Quit Rent Ceremony (English)
Waxing Moon
Moon phase: Second Quarter
Color: Gray

Moon Sign: Aries
Incense: Marigold

☺ Tuesday
Feast of the Holy Souls
Waxing Moon
Full Moon 8:05 am
Color: Red

Moon Sign: Aries
Moon enters Taurus 2:07 am
Incense: Marjoram

28 Wednesday
Ochi Day (Greek)
Waning Moon
Moon phase: Third Quarter
Color: Topaz

Moon Sign: Taurus
Incense: Cinnamon

October

29 Thursday
Iroquois Feast of the Dead
Waning Moon
Moon phase: Third Quarter
Color: Crimson

Moon Sign: Taurus
Moon enters Gemini 2:24 am
Incense: Balsam

30 Friday
Meiji Festival (Japanese)
Waning Moon
Moon phase: Third Quarter
Color: White

Moon Sign: Gemini
Incense: Yarrow

31 Saturday
Halloween • Samhain
Waning Moon
Moon phase: Third Quarter
Color: Brown

Moon Sign: Geminni
Moon enters Cancer 5:09 am
Incense: Pine

A Walk in the Rain
(Connecting with Water)

Our connection with the elements (earth, air, fire, and water) is one of the things that comes with a witchcraft practice. But you don't have to be standing in a ritual circle in order to do it. Why not take five minutes to renew that connection in between magickal workings? Water is probably the easiest element to connect to. Here are some simple ways to do it:

Take a walk in the rain. Concentrate on how the rain sounds and feels. If you are comfortable doing so, leave the hat or the umbrella at home, and let the rain fall on your face. Or sit by running water—a stream, or river, or the ocean. Put your hands or feet in the water. Drink some water mindfully.

– Deborah Blake

November ♏

1 Sunday
All Saints' Day
Waning Moon
Moon phase: Third Quarter
Color: Orange

Moon Sign: Cancer
Incense: Heliotrope

---

2 Monday
All Souls' Day • Daylight Saving Time ends
Waning Moon
Moon phase: Third Quarter
Color: White

Moon Sign: Cancer
Moon enters Leo 10:48 am
Incense: Narcissus

◯ Tuesday
Election Day (general)
Waning Moon
Fourth Quarter 7:24 am
Color: Black

Moon Sign: Leo
Incense: Ginger

---

4 Wednesday
Mischief Night (British)
Waning Moon
Moon phase: Fourth Quarter
Color: Brown

Moon Sign: Leo
Moon enters Virgo 9:22 pm
Incense: Lavender

---

5 Thursday
Guy Fawkes Night (British)
Waning Moon
Moon phase: Fourth Quarter
Color: Green

Moon Sign: Virgo
Incense: Mulberry

---

6 Friday
Leonard's Ride (German)
Waning Moon
Moon phase: Fourth Quarter
Color: Purple

Moon Sign: Virgo
Incense: Rose

---

7 Saturday
Mayan Day of the Dead
Waning Moon
Moon phase: Fourth Quarter
Color: Blue

Moon Sign: Virgo
Moon enters Libra 10:14 am
Incense: Ivy

November ♏

8 Sunday
The Lord Mayor's Show (English)
Waning Moon
Moon phase: Fourth Quarter
Color: Amber

Moon Sign: Libra
Incense: Juniper

9 Monday
Lord Mayor's Day (British)
Waning Moon
Moon phase: Fourth Quarter
Color: Gray

Moon Sign: Libra
Moon enters Scorpio 11:02 pm
Incense: Hyssop

10 Tuesday
Martin Luther's Birthday
Waning Moon
Moon phase: Fourth Quarter
Color: Maroon

Moon Sign: Scorpio
Incense: Cinnamon

☽ Wednesday
Veterans Day
Waning Moon
New Moon 12:47 pm
Color: Topaz

Moon Sign: Scorpio
Incense: Marjoram

12 Thursday
Tesuque Feast Day (Native American)
Waxing Moon
Moon phase: First Quarter
Color: White

Moon Sign: Scorpio
Moon enters Sagittarius 10:14 am
Incense: Jasmine

13 Friday
Festival of Jupiter (Roman)
Waxing Moon
Moon phase: First Quarter
Color: Rose

Moon Sign: Sagittarius
Incense: Cypress

14 Saturday
The Little Carnival (Greek)
Waxing Moon
Moon phase: First Quarter
Color: Brown

Moon Sign: Sagittarius
Moon enters Capricorn 7:21 pm
Incense: Patchouli

15 **Sunday**
St. Leopold's Day
Waxing Moon
Moon phase: First Quarter
Color: Gold

Moon Sign: Capricorn
Incense: Marigold

16 **Monday**
St. Margaret of Scotland's Day
Waxing Moon
Moon phase: First Quarter
Color: Lavender

Moon Sign: Capricorn
Incense: Neroli

17 **Tuesday**
Queen Elizabeth's Day
Waxing Moon
Moon phase: First Quarter
Color: White

Moon Sign: Capricorn
Moon enters Aquarius 2:24 am
Incense: Bayberry

18 **Wednesday**
St. Plato's Day
Waxing Moon
Moon phase: First Quarter
Color: Yellow

Moon Sign: Aquarius
Incense: Lilac

☽ **Thursday**
Garifuna Day (Belizean)
Waxing Moon
Second Quarter 1:27 am
Color: Crimson

Moon Sign: Aquarius
Moon enters Pisces 7:21 am
Incense: Clove

20 **Friday**
Revolution Day (Mexican)
Waxing Moon
Moon phase: Second Quarter
Color: Coral

Moon Sign: Pisces
Incense: Alder

21 **Saturday**
Repentance Day (German)
Waxing Moon
Moon phase: Second Quarter
Color: Gray

Moon Sign: Pisces
Moon enters Aries 10:12 am
Incense: Sage

22 Sunday
St. Cecilia's Day
Waxing Moon
Moon phase: Second Quarter
Color: Yellow

Moon Sign: Aries
Sun enters Sagittarius 10:25 am
Incense: Frankincense

---

23 Monday
St. Clement's Day
Waxing Moon
Moon phase: Second Quarter
Color: White

Moon Sign: Aries
Moon enters Taurus 11:26 am
Incense: Clary sage

---

24 Tuesday
Feast of the Burning Lamps (Egyptian)
Waxing Moon
Moon phase: Second Quarter
Color: Gray

Moon Sign: Taurus
Incense: Basil

☻ Wednesday
St. Catherine of Alexandria's Day
Waxing Moon
Full Moon 5:44 pm
Color: White

Moon Sign: Taurus
Moon enters Gemini 12:15 pm
Incense: Honeysuckle

---

26 Thursday
Thanksgiving Day
Waning Moon
Moon phase: Third Quarter
Color: Purple

Moon Sign: Gemini
Incense: Apricot

---

27 Friday
St. Maximus' Day
Waning Moon
Moon phase: Third Quarter
Color: Pink

Moon Sign: Gemini
Moon enters Cancer 2:27 pm
Incense: Vanilla

---

28 Saturday
Day of the New Dance (Tibetan)
Waning Moon
Moon phase: Third Quarter
Color: Black

Moon Sign: Cancer
Incense: Rue

29 Sunday

Tubman's Birthday (Liberian)
Waning Moon
Moon phase: Third Quarter
Color: Orange

Moon Sign: Cancer
Moon enters Leo 7:47 pm
Incense: Hyacinth

30 Monday

St. Andrew's Day
Waning Moon
Moon phase: Third Quarter
Color: Ivory

Moon Sign: Leo
Incense: Lily

Shower Spirit Cleanse

One easy way to integrate magick into your life is to make it part of a regular daily routine, instead of trying to set aside separate time. Try adding this fast and easy ritual to your shower (if you shower in the morning, it helps to start the day off right; if you shower at night, it helps wash off anything you've picked up along the way). As you stand under the running water, visualize the droplets shining with magickal cleansing energy, washing away anything negative or unpleasant and sending it down the drain. If you want, you can say out loud:

"Water wash me clean like rain, send negativity down the drain."

– Deborah Blake

1 Tuesday
Big Tea Party (Japanese)
Waning Moon
Moon phase: Third Quarter
Color: Scarlet

Moon Sign: Leo
Incense: Geranium

2 Wednesday
Republic Day (Laotian)
Waning Moon
Moon phase: Third Quarter
Color: White

Moon Sign: Leo
Moon enters Virgo 5:09 am
Incense: Marjoram

◖ Thursday
St. Francis Xavier's Day
Waning Moon
Fourth Quarter 2:40 am
Color: Turquoise

Moon Sign: Virgo
Incense: Nutmeg

4 Friday
St. Barbara's Day
Waning Moon
Moon phase: Fourth Quarter
Color: Rose

Moon Sign: Virgo
Moon enters Libra 5:34 pm
Incense: Rose

5 Saturday
Eve of St. Nicholas' Day
Waning Moon
Moon phase: Fourth Quarter
Color: Brown

Moon Sign: Libra
Incense: Magnolia

6 Sunday
St. Nicholas' Day
Waning Moon
Moon phase: Fourth Quarter
Color: Amber

Moon Sign: Libra
Incense: Almond

7 Monday
Hanukkah begins
Waning Moon
Moon phase: Fourth Quarter
Color: White

Moon Sign: Libra
Moon enters Scorpio 6:26 am
Incense: Neroli

8   Tuesday
Feast of the Immaculate Conception   Moon Sign: Scorpio
Waning Moon   Incense: Ginger
Moon phase: Fourth Quarter
Color: Black

9   Wednesday
St. Leocadia's Day   Moon Sign: Scorpio
Waning Moon   Moon enters Sagittarius 5:25 pm
Moon phase: Fourth Quarter   Incense: Lavender
Color: Yellow

10   Thursday
Nobel Day   Moon Sign: Sagittarius
Waning Moon   Incense: Myrrh
Moon phase: Fourth Quarter
Color: Purple

☽   Friday
Pilgrimage at Tortugas   Moon Sign: Sagittarius
Waning Moon   Incense: Mint
New Moon 5:29 am
Color: Pink

12   Saturday
Fiesta of Our Lady of Guadalupe (Mexican)
Waxing Moon   Moon Sign: Sagittarius
Moon phase: First Quarter   Moon enters Capricorn 1:46 am
Color: Gray   Incense: Sandalwood

13   Sunday
St. Lucy's Day (Swedish)   Moon Sign: Capricorn
Waxing Moon   Incense: Marigold
Moon phase: First Quarter
Color: Yellow

14   Monday
Hanukkah ends   Moon Sign: Capricorn
Waxing Moon   Moon enters Aquarius 7:59 am
Moon phase: First Quarter   Incense: Hyssop
Color: Gray

15 Tuesday
Consualia (Roman)
Waxing Moon
Moon phase: First Quarter
Color: Red

Moon Sign: Aquarius
Incense: Cedar

---

16 Wednesday
Posadas (Mexican)
Waxing Moon
Moon phase: First Quarter
Color: Brown

Moon Sign: Aquarius
Moon enters Pisces 12:45 pm
Incense: Honeysuckle

---

17 Thursday
Saturnalia (Roman)
Waxing Moon
Moon phase: First Quarter
Color: White

Moon Sign: Pisces
Incense: Mulberry

◐ Friday
Feast of the Virgin of Solitude
Waxing Moon
Second Quarter 10:14 am
Color: Purple

Moon Sign: Pisces
Moon enters Aries 4:26 pm
Incense: Yarrow

---

19 Saturday
Opalia (Roman)
Waxing Moon
Moon phase: Second Quarter
Color: Black

Moon Sign: Aries
Incense: Sage

---

20 Sunday
Commerce God Festival (Japanese)
Waxing Moon
Moon phase: Second Quarter
Color: Gold

Moon Sign: Aries
Moon enters Taurus 7:13 pm
Incense: Juniper

---

21 Monday
Yule • Winter Solstice
Waxing Moon
Moon phase: Second Quarter
Color: Silver

Moon Sign: Taurus
Sun enters Capricorn 11:48 pm
Incense: Narcissus

22 Tuesday

Saints Chaeremon and Ischyrion's Day
Waxing Moon
Moon phase: Second Quarter
Color: White

Moon Sign: Taurus
Moon enters Gemini 9:31 pm
Incense: Basil

23 Wednesday

Larentalia (Roman)
Waxing Moon
Moon phase: Second Quarter
Color: Topaz

Moon Sign: Gemini
Incense: Lilac

24 Thursday

Christmas Eve
Waxing Moon
Moon phase: Second Quarter
Color: Green

Moon Sign: Gemini
Incense: Clove

☺ Friday

Christmas Day
Waxing Moon
Full Moon 6:12 am
Color: White

Moon Sign: Gemini
Moon enters Cancer 12:27 am
Incense: Vanilla

26 Saturday

Kwanzaa begins
Waning Moon
Moon phase: Third Quarter
Color: Indigo

Moon Sign: Cancer
Incense: Pine

27 Sunday

Boar's Head Supper (English)
Waning Moon
Moon phase: Third Quarter
Color: Orange

Moon Sign: Cancer
Moon enters Leo 5:31 am
Incense: Frankincense

28 Monday

Holy Innocents' Day
Waning Moon
Moon phase: Third Quarter
Color: Lavender

Moon Sign: Leo
Incense: Rosemary

29 **Tuesday**
Feast of St. Thomas à Becket
Waning Moon
Moon phase: Third Quarter
Color: Black

Moon Sign: Leo
Moon enters Virgo 1:58 pm
Incense: Cinnamon

30 **Wednesday**
Republic Day (Madagascan)
Waning Moon
Moon phase: Third Quarter
Color: White

Moon Sign: Virgo
Incense: Bay laurel

31 **Thursday**
New Year's Eve
Waning Moon
Moon phase: Third Quarter
Color: Crimson

Moon Sign: Virgo
Incense: Carnation

Talking to the Moon

Connecting with goddess is at the core of many Witchcraft practices. One of the easiest ways to do this is to simply stand outside under the light of the moon, an ancient symbol of the goddess. Witches can feel her pull most strongly during the full moon, but you can go talk to her at any stage. Simply stand where you can see the moon clearly and speak from the heart. Or you can say this:

"Goddess, I greet thee. As I stand in the light of the moon, I send thee my love and my adoration, and ask only for thy love and thy blessing in return. Goddess, shine down on me, and send me thy love and light. So mote it be."

– Deborah Blake

Fire Magic

Get Your Mojo Rising

by Tess Whitehurst

My mom always used to say that "words have usage, not meaning." In other words, language is not static, but alive and fluid. Words and their connotations are always in flux. So while, technically, "mojo" is, according to Judika Illes in *The Encyclopedia of Witchcraft*, "A talisman that enables someone, male or female, to achieve their goals and desires, whatever they may be," it has come to be used in our mainstream culture to mean (according to the New Oxford American Dictionary) general "magical power," or (according to Austin Powers and his ilk) sexual prowess and charisma. In many ways, it's similar to the way the word "charm" can be used to connote either an actual physical object *or* general attractiveness and the ability to influence people.

I like this newfangled usage of the word mojo because it describes something real. We all know if our mojo is flowing, we feel like we can achieve our goals and desires. Often this feeling of general confidence and empowerment is paired with a feeling of sexual magnetism and potency—and that's mojo! For most or all of us, it fluctuates: sometimes we've got it and sometimes we don't. When we've got it, it's great. Life is fun and the things we desire flow to us almost effortlessly. And when we haven't got it, or we've got a little less of it, a good portion of our everyday thoughts and efforts revolve around finding it and getting it back.

So, for all our sakes, I thought it'd be useful to outline some tried-and-true methods for locating and regaining our mojo, just in case it happens to stray.

Recover Stolen Mojo

Our magical power—our magnetism, or that which allows us to intentionally draw people, items, and conditions into our life experience—is very closely aligned with our sexual-

ity. As Pagans, this often isn't as much of a challenge as it is for people on some mainstream spiritual paths, but the fact remains that our culture is weird about sex. For example, our culture teaches us to compartmentalize. We get messages like *this* is sexual, *that* is not. In this instance, you should be aware of your sexual feelings, and in this one you absolutely should not—and if you don't think so, there is something wrong with you! And often, our culture also weirdly teaches us that only very narrowly prescribed sexual desires are normal and that all other sexual desires are, you name it: deviant, dirty, shameful, dangerous, evil, or any number of demeaning and disparaging things.

Believe it or not, according to authors and sex educators Dossie Easton and Catherine A. Liszt, Nazi psychologist Wilhelm Reich "theorized that the suppression of sexuality was essential to an authoritarian government. Without the imposition of antisexual morality... people would be free from shame and would trust their own sense of right and wrong. They would be unlikely to march to war... or to operate death camps." Aha! By convincing people that their natural instincts were evil, Wilhelm Reich was knowingly and almost literally stealing their mojo—and channeling it toward unthinkable atrocities. He knew that our sexuality is so closely aligned with our personal power that to alienate a whole society from their sexuality was to successfully enslave them into carrying out the Nazi's malevolent agenda.

With all that in mind, it's important to recognize that our culture has been so steeped in sexual humiliation for so long that we must be vigilant in rooting out hidden caches of power that may be hidden in our consciousness under layers of shame—and the subsequent push to establish new paradigms of sexual liberation and personal freedom. Even if we've worked on this issue before, it can be a good idea to revisit it again and again.

One way to do this is a belief clearing. In a journal or notebook, write down every limiting or negative belief you have about your own sexuality. Even if it's a thought you didn't previously think you had—something that you attributed perhaps to a parent or authority figure—if you currently notice it in your consciousness as coloring your thoughts, feelings, and decisions, write it down. For example, "Sex is dirty, one-night stands are bad, it's creepy that _____ turns me on." A good indicator that an aspect of your sexuality feels shameful to you is if you treat it as a closely guarded secret that no one—not even your closest friends and lovers—can find out.

Of course the truth is, as long as you're as safe as possible, everyone involved is an adult, you're honest with everyone, and you're not hurting anyone (against their will!), there's absolutely nothing wrong with your sexual desires and actions. So turn all these limiting beliefs around. Make a new list, and instead of "sex is dirty," write, "sex is a sacred expression of my divinity," or, "sex is a playful way to connect and express love." Instead of "one-night stands are bad," write, "as long as I'm as safe as possible, I honor myself, and I'm honest with everyone, a one-night stand could potentially be a beautiful experience," and so on.

Stay "Turned On"

Now that you've begun to recover any stolen mojo, you'll want to make a point of staying "turned on." As mentioned earlier, sexual energy is not confined to romance and the bedroom, it sprawls luxuriously throughout every aspect of your life. In other words, contrary to what many of us are fed from the time we are children, the fullness of our life experience always includes our sexual awareness. Whether we're enjoying sunlight, music, new ideas and information, poetry, the scent of baking cookies, a sunset, or hot buttered toast, our enjoyment will be more intense if we experience it the same way we do sex and attraction: with our whole body and all our senses.

Not to mention, of course, that the more sensual (i.e., connected to our senses) we are, the more magical we are. In many ways, our sixth sense might be thought of as a conscious, alert combination of all five senses, and sensuality grounds us in the cornerstone of our power: the Earth. Naturally, all of this increases our mojo, as does the fact that the more "turned on" (or inspired, awake, excited about life, present, in the moment) we are, the more attractive we are to others, and the more we naturally magnetize the life conditions we desire … And what does this sound like? That's right: mojo.

Here are just a few ideas for staying "turned on," not just in the traditional sexual sense, but also in a holistic way:

• Whenever you remember throughout the day, become conscious of your physicality. Relax any part of your body that is tense. Let your shoulders drop, and feel your belly unclench.

• If you feel bored or uninspired, do something slightly out of character to spice things up: bake a new dish for dinner, wear something unusual, dance to a new type of music, etc.

• Read erotica or watch pornography to awaken your sexual and sensual self.

• Have an honest conversation with a partner about what really turns you on.

• Eat chocolate—slowly! Don't crunch it. Let it melt in your mouth.

• Light candles and take a warm bath.

- Make a "mojo playlist"—choose songs that get you in touch with yours sensual, adventurous, confident self.
- Take little day trips that satisfy your creative self. Go to a botanical garden, a museum, or a farmers' market and bliss out on all the visual and other sensory treats.

Enjoy Your Movement

This is so simple, yet so effective. Author and feminine-power expert Rachael Jayne Groover writes, "Next time you want to turn your magnetic presence on, ask yourself, 'How can I enjoy my movement right now?'" You have to walk anyway, so why not enjoy it? My favorite moments on the dance floor have been about surrendering to the music and allowing my body move the way it wants to. Similarly, walking to walk (or standing to stand, etc.) is about surrendering to the sensual experience of the moment and of your surroundings. It's a way of opening yourself up to the magical power that flows within you and letting it flow in an enjoyable and physically pleasurable way. Talk about getting your mojo back! Conscious, enjoyable movement can help you do it instantly—and you can even do it at the grocery store. Remember to enjoy the caress of your hair on your back, your hips as they sway, your feet as they kiss the earth, the fabric on your skin, and the breeze on your neck.

Breathe Consciously

Talk about simple! This one is so simple it's almost boring. But don't be fooled, and don't gloss over it! Believe me, the benefits are immense, and intensified mojo is not the least of them. Here it is: breathe consciously. Notice your breath as it goes in and out. If you forget—and you will—and then you remember again, simply resume the practice. You don't have to force your breath to deepen, just notice it. Notice as it goes in, and notice as it goes out, and it will begin to deepen on its own. In time, you will find yourself breathing into your whole body—from the top of your head to the tips of your fingers to the tips of your toes. Where there is tension, you will breathe into it and it will begin to dissipate. Over time, your body will become deeply relaxed and receptive, your mind will be alert, your senses will be awake, and your mojo will be flowing.

Whenever I feel stagnant and uninspired, I am almost invariably neglecting to breathe this way. Once I begin again, and keep at it long enough that it turns into the norm rather than the exception, something as seemingly inane as washing the dishes can become euphoric. I revel in the scent of the dish soap, the sunlight on the water, and the warm wetness running over my hands. This goes one better than magnetizing beautiful conditions—it allows you to instantly revel in the abundance and luxury that's *already present* in every moment of your life. And like attracts like, so the more you appreciate, the more you receive. You get into a positive life momentum, and manifesting your "goals and desires, whatever they may be," becomes a way of life and a matter of course.

Take Care of Yourself

Are you treating your body like the temple that it is? Your body is your own personal doorway between the worlds: the place where form meets spirit. Simply taking the time to bathe, moisturize, and adorn your body lovingly helps nurture your sensuality, magnetism, and personal power (aka mojo). So be sure that your skin and hair are happy, and that you love the way you smell. Scents that particularly nurture mojo will be ones that awaken your own feelings of sensual pleasure and sexual attraction. These may be different for everyone, but some popular mojo-enhancing essential oils include:

Jasmine, patchouli, ylang-ylang, cedar, vanilla, cinnamon/ cassia (be very careful and use sparingly, as this oil is irritating), rose, rose geranium, verbena, and neroli.

Fashion Magic

Finally, be sure that your clothing and accessory choices are nourishing your confidence, playfulness, attractiveness, and personal power. Fortify your mojo-recovering efforts by taking the time to choose fabrics, colors, and patterns that feel good on your body and help you feel radiant when you look in the mirror and go out into the world.

For Further Study:

Deida, David. *Intimate Communion*. Deerfield Beach, FL: Health Communications, 1995.

Easton, Dossie and Janet W. Hardy. *The Ethical Slut*, 2nd Ed. Berkeley: Celestial Arts, 2009.

Groover, Rachael Jayne. *Powerful and Feminine*. Fort Collins: Deep Pacific Press, 2011.

Illes, Judika. *The Element Encyclopedia of Witchcraft*. London: Harper Element, 2005.

Broomstick Basics

by Deborah Blake

Witches and broomsticks go together like the full moon and the tide. If you ask someone to describe a typical witch (as if there really was such a thing), they might mention a pointy hat, a black cat, and in all likelihood, a broom. Many pictures of witches show them holding or riding on a broomstick, and even the most famous fictional witches—like Harry Potter and Samantha Stephens from *Bewitched* are often shown with their brooms.

So you might be interested to know that the earliest drawings of witches riding across the night sky actually had them sitting on sticks, or even farm implements like pitchforks. Still, by the time the witch-hunts were at their height, people had been warned to watch out for witches riding their brooms to forbidden sabbat gatherings, and from that time onward, witches and brooms have been tied together, for better or for worse.

Luckily for the modern witch, the broomstick is the perfect magickal tool. One of its benefits, of course, is that it is a common household item that can be found in virtually every home. You can leave your magickal broomstick out in the open, and unless you have decorated it with pentacles and other obvious symbols of witchcraft, no one can tell that you use it for anything other than cleaning.

The earliest brooms, called besoms, were made out of birch twigs that were wrapped around a stick (the handle was usually made of hazel, but other woods also worked) and tied on with willow bark or rope. Unlike today's flat brooms, made from the more flexible broomcorn, the besom was round and irregular. As a cleaning tool, they left a lot to be desired, since they left behind almost as much mess as they cleared. Nonetheless, many witches prefer to use a traditional besom for their magickal work. As with all else we use, there is no one right or wrong type of broom—it is simply a matter of choosing the one that best suits your tastes and needs.

Your Own Broom

There are two basic kinds of broom: the traditional besom mentioned above, or the more conventional modern flat broom made from broomcorn. You can make your own broom (instructions are available in books and online) fairly easily, or you can buy one already made and add your own personal touches. Like most witchcraft tools, the more of yourself you put into it the better.

How you decorate your broom depends on a number of factors. Will it be hidden or kept out in the open? And if it will be in plain sight, does it need to be able to "pass" as a regular, nonmagickal broom? Do you want a broom (or brooms) that has a particular purpose, or do you want one that can be used for any magickal work? Will it need to go with your general décor, or will it spend most of its time tucked away?

If you need to keep your magick on the down-low, there are still a number of things you can do to subtly enhance your broom. It is thought by some that early witches used brooms as a way to hide their magickal wands, by disguising them with twigs and making a besom out of them. You could do the same, taking a staff or wand and creating a broom, with any magickal symbols hidden underneath the twigs or broomcorn.

Alternatively, you could bless and consecrate the most common-seeming broom with salt and water, sage, and/

or anointing oil. (I like to use oils that are good for protection and cleansing on broomsticks.) Once consecrated, the broom will look just the same, but you will know that it is dedicated to magickal work. Just don't let anyone sweep the kitchen with it! I'm a big fan of consecrating most magickal tools, so you may want to do this step even with a broom that is clearly magickal.

If you are going to create a magickal broom that you don't need to pretend is anything else, then the sky is the limit! Brooms can be adorned with anything from dried herbs, to wood-burned or etched symbols, to dangling crystals, feathers, or ribbons. Some people use broomcorn that has been dyed so it is more colorful. Just make sure that your magickal broomstick isn't so ornate that it can't be used (unless you intend it to be purely decorative and hung on the wall); it should still be able to function as the esoteric tool that it is.

Using Your Magickal Broomstick

Broomsticks can be used in a number of different ways. Two of the most traditional are as part of a handfasting (a Pagan wedding rite) and to energetically clear a magickal space before doing a ritual.

The tradition of "jumping the broom" has been used historically in various cultures to symbolize the joining of a couple and their creation of a new household. This wasn't limited to Pagans, either. On the American frontier, when there were few formally ordained clergymen available, couples would jump over a broom in front of witnesses to signify that they were married. The practice was also used by African-American slaves, who were forbidden to marry, and carried the tradition with them from their homes far away.

These days, modern Witches often include jumping the broom as a way to honor their Pagan roots and symbolize their new start together, even if the couple has already been sharing a home. A new broom is always used for this, and some people keep the broom for only sacred work after the ceremony. Sometimes a couple will create their own special handfasting broomstick or have one crafted for them by friends or family. In this case, the broom will usually be ornamented in the colors used at the wedding, and is not expected to be anything other than a decorative treasured belonging.

"Jumping the broom" is very simple, and usually performed at or close to the end of the handfasting ritual. The broomstick is brought forward and either placed on the ground or held by two participants in the rite (hopefully only an inch or two above the floor, since no one wants to see a new couple fall flat on their faces during their own ceremony). The couple then joins hands and jumps over the broom in unison. This signals that they have officially begun their new lives together.

Using a magickal broomstick to cleanse and clear the space where a ritual will be held is almost as simple. Most people don't actually touch the broom to the ground, since you are using it to sweep energy, not dirt. The person leading the ritual (if it is a group gathering) or the individual (if it is a solitary rite) will walk around the outer edges of the circle and sweep away any negativity or unsettled energy that would interfere with the magickal working. The broom can sweep through the air right above the ground or at waist height.

Some people do this in silence, while others use some form of chant or incantation. I like to say something like:

Cleanse and clear this sacred space, and make it ready for my magickal work. I sweep away all that is negative and sweep in positive energy to help me with my ritual. So mote it be.

You can also sprinkle the broomstick with salt and water to give it an extra boost before clearing your ritual area, or waft it with a sage smudge stick. Some people use the broom as part of the actual circle casting, thus combining the cleansing with the delineation of the magickal space. If you are going to do so, you may also want to use it to dismiss the circle by walking widdershins (counterclockwise) instead of deosil (clockwise) and sweeping away the energy you originally built up to contain your magick at the beginning of the ritual.

A Magickal Cleansing Ritual

The magickal uses of a Witch's broomstick go far beyond handfastings and circle casting. Some people create unique brooms to give as housewarming gifts, or to celebrate some special occasion. They can also be used for

healing work, nightmare prevention, protection, and much more. Of course, the most basic way to use one is as part of a magickal cleansing ritual.

I like to do something I call "spiritual spring cleaning" every year. This goes beyond the usual mundane cleaning, although you will want to do that first—there is no point in trying to clear a home on an energetic/spiritual level if there are piles of dirty dishes in the sink, and dust bunnies the size of panthers under the bed!

It is a good idea to periodically cleanse the energy of the place you live, whether it is a house or an apartment. If there has been a lot of chaos or arguing, then it becomes a downright necessity. It can also be helpful if you are feeling "stuck" and having a hard time getting things accomplished. So don't just think of this as something to do in the spring; you can perform this simple ritual as often as you want or need to.

I start by doing the actual cleaning: sweep the floors (with a mundane broom, not your magickal one) or vacuum, dust, put things away where they belong, and wipe down surfaces. You want to start with a reasonably tidy space, although it doesn't have to be perfect. If you can, open a window in every room. (If you can't do that, just make sure that you mentally guide the energy you are getting rid of out of the closed windows.)

Depending on the time and oomph you have to dedicate to the task, you may want to start by going through every room with salt and water and/or a sage smudge stick. If you do this, then make sure you sprinkle the salt and water and waft the sage into every corner of every room, and around any entrances, such as doors, windows, and chimneys.

Whether or not you add that step, you will want to start by focusing your intent. For some people, this is easiest to do in a formal circle or standing in front of your altar. If there is someplace you can safely leave a candle burning while moving through your home, you can light a white candle. Otherwise simply close your eyes and visualize yourself holding your broom. See the broom sweeping away all negativity—any stale or stagnant energy, darkness and depression, leftover resentment from quarrels or disagreements, and any negative energy you might have brought in from the outside world.

If you want, you can give your broomstick a boost by dipping it in water that has been blessed and consecrated for magickal cleansing or by anointing the handle and bristles with a magickal oil containing herbs used for cleansing and protection. You can also just visualize the broom glowing with positive, cleansing energy.

Starting at the spot farthest away from your front door, move from room to room (starting at the bottom in the basement, if you have one) and sweep the room. If you are using a magickal broomstick instead of a mundane one, then don't actually touch the bristles to the floor. Walk into each room and then make your way around the entire room, paying special attention to any spot that seems particularly "off" to you.

Remember to focus as you go on your intention to sweep away all those things that you no longer want in your home. When you are done, finish up at the front door by opening the door and sweeping all that stuff outside, away from you. If you want, you can then close the door firmly behind you (with you back inside the house) and turn your broom upside down. Tap the end of the handle on the floor three times and say: *I have swept my home clear, and clear it will stay. So mote it be.*

Every Good Witch Deserves a Broom

Each of us has different magickal tools that call to us. Not every witch will have an athame or a wand, nor feel the need for one. But I highly recommend the broomstick as a magickal tool—even if we can't actually use them to fly on. I like the thought of continuing the tradition that has come down to us from those early crones who swept their homes clean with a birch twig besom and then went outside to stand under the same glowing moon we stand under. Our brooms may not be their brooms, and our magickal practices may be very different from theirs, but we are still witches, all the same. And every good witch deserves a broom.

Menopause and Magick

by Ellen Dugan

I can only please one person a day.
Today is not your day.
Tomorrow doesn't look good either.
—Familiar Saying

I realize that the title of this article may cause many readers to do a double take ... or possibly drop this book in horror. Yes indeed, you read that title correctly. This article is about menopause and magick. So why in the world am I writing about this topic? Well, because I am *living* through this right now, and honey, let me tell you, going through the stages of menopause is one intense ride.

I think of menopause as a roller coaster. You are up. Then you are down. You are happy. Then you are sad. All you can do is hang on for dear life and ride out the wild mood swings, crazy periods, insomnia, fatigue, weight gain, intensely painful breasts, night sweats, hot flashes, and my personal favorite, the "no filter." I mean *no* filter. As in none. Zip, zero, nada, the big goose egg, nothing. Whatever you think pops right out of your mouth. It's kinda scary and liberating all at the same time.

You also have the attention span of a ferret with ADD, and your memory is shot to hell. I think there are more symptoms, but I forget. Either that or I have blocked it out.

As a woman staring down the barrel of the big 5-0, I honestly thought that I had more time before the dreaded menopause phase kicked in. But after going through several brutal years of perimenopause symptoms, I wanted some answers.

Now before we go any further, I am not here to give you medical advice. What I will do is share a little of what I have gone through and what I have learned along the way in how menopause affects your magick and your abilities as a Witch.

If you are experiencing medical issues, then please go to the doctor. Use common sense and get some support. I took myself to the "lady doctor"—who happens to be a woman—this past year. I had had enough, and I wanted some answers.

So there I sat (fully dressed) on the doctor's table, and she breezed in. "Why Ellen, what brings you here today? Your well-woman visit is several months away." She smiled and took a seat.

I took a deep breath, raised one eyebrow, and asked her seriously, "Do you want the short, snarky answer or the long, complicated, and thoughtful answer?"

My doctor grinned and settled back in her chair—she knows me too well. "Oh, with you? Give me the snarky!"

"Okay," I replied in a serious tone. "I am here because I am tired of perimenopause making me its bitch."

So, long story short, once my doctor stopped giggling, we talked about some options. After hearing my complaints, she suggested that I exercise my way out of the worst of the symptoms and to up the intensity of my workouts. I had joined a gym and had just begun working with a trainer on a trial basis, so she encouraged me to hire the trainer and keep at it. She gave me a frank discussion on what I could expect weight loss-wise during menopause and what other symptoms to anticipate. Then she ordered some blood tests to figure out exactly where I sat on the perimenopause-to-menopause scale.

A day later the doctor's office called me to say "congratulations."

I clutched my chest in horror and snapped at the nurse, "Have you lost your damn mind? The *last* thing a woman just shy of fifty wants to hear from a gynecologist's office is 'congratulations.'" Once the nurse stopped shrieking with laughter (apparently she had taken bets with the other nurses as to how I would respond), she informed me that my blood count had come back.

According to the test, anything that registers 25 to 50 on the test scale meant the woman was in perimenopause. Anything over the number 50 on that scale meant the woman was officially in menopause. My blood work came back at 67.

So, congratulations! At the ripe old age of forty-nine and a half, I was in menopause. Okay, now that I had it confirmed, I actually felt better. I knew that this had been more than perimenopause. This explained so much of what I had been going through. I damn near gave myself a high five. Validation is a beautiful thing. But I also had to wonder…what did that mean for me now personally as a woman and as a Witch?

The Menopausal Witch

I don't cause emotions. I am one.
—Elphaba, *Wicked*

So, can a woman work successful magick while going through menopause? Absolutely! The first thing you need to know as a menopausal witch is that your emotions are extremely intense during this phase of life.

Let's just be honest here. The words "extremely intense" are an understatement. I think volatile, dangerous, and explosive would be more realistic. So because of this, you will need to be much more careful with your spellcraft than usual.

The good news? You will see some spectacular results with your spellcasting because of the intensity of your emotions. The bad news? You may also see some spectacular magickal screw-ups due to the intensity of those same emotions. So while going through menopause, be extra careful when you work your magick. Make sure you have a firm grip on your temper before you cast.

Nope, I am not kidding about this. The same careful lecture you might give a hormonal, young, teenage witch applies to a middle-age menopause witch as well. However, it's good to remember that, unlike a younger person, we have experience and a lifetime of acquired wisdom. So make darn sure you have yourself under control emotionally before you cast your spells. Use the knowledge that comes from years of practice as a witch and take a hard look at your honor, integrity, and your personal ethics.

My next suggestion for you is this: as long as you are in a calm mood—do the magick when you think of it. Because if you wait, chances are you will probably forget about it. Seriously. Either do it immediately or write yourself a note to work a spell later.

My husband doesn't even flinch to come home from work and see a big-ass neon Post-it note on the fridge that says "Ellen! Work Full Moon Magick Tonight!" Or one stuck to the bathroom mirror that says "Ellen! On Thursday, Work Prosperity Magick!" Keep the notes short and sweet—if you write down too much info, you will just get distracted

My next proposal is to laugh, damn it! Sister, you better find yourself a sense of humor. Honestly, we might as well laugh because it takes several years to go through the process. Take a good look around. You are not alone. This is part of life, and it is nothing to be embarrassed about.

Until you are standing there vigorously fanning yourself while sweat drips down your face in public while everyone else is either comfortable or a little cold, you have not lived. However, if there is another woman also going through the "change" in your general vicinity when a hot flash hits, you have just found a comrade.

Strangers become women united as you both stand there fanning yourself with whatever implement you can get your hands on: a pocketbook, a sales flyer, your husband's hat, a package of lunch meat, or even an exercise mat.

Don't judge me. I was desperate, and the big, red, foam mat worked! You just fold that thing in half and wave it with both arms toward your face. Sometimes menopause is funny. So you had better learn to laugh—and to roll with it.

Finally, when it comes to surviving menopause, put some of your focus onto yourself. Stop worrying so much about taking care of everyone else and concentrate on your own well-being. Now, I am not saying you should become self-absorbed during this time, but chances are your kids are adults now. Let them go about their own business and don't try to hover over them too much.

Yes, It's hard to break a habit of mothering—your grown kids, the pets, your covenmates, the partner/spouse—but while you go through the transition that is menopause, try focusing on yourself just as much as you do on your friends and family. This is the time to take some "me" time. You will probably also discover that this will lessen your stress tremendously. Think about what causes you stress. Now imagine turning that energy onto self-improvement and self-enrichment.

Explore this time of personal growth and freedom. Do something new, just for you. Take a trip, join a gym, take an art class, learn yoga, plant a garden, or start a home DIY project or two. Keep your imagination flowing and make yourself happy. Creativity is a magick all its own. Spend some time doing something creative that you love and watch your calm center return to you. Chances are if you are feeling good about yourself, then you will feel better all around.

~

Menopause is not the end. In fact, it is only the beginning of a new chapter of your life both as a woman and as a witch. This is a metamorphosis. So take a deep breath, stretch your wings, and embrace the changes in your world.

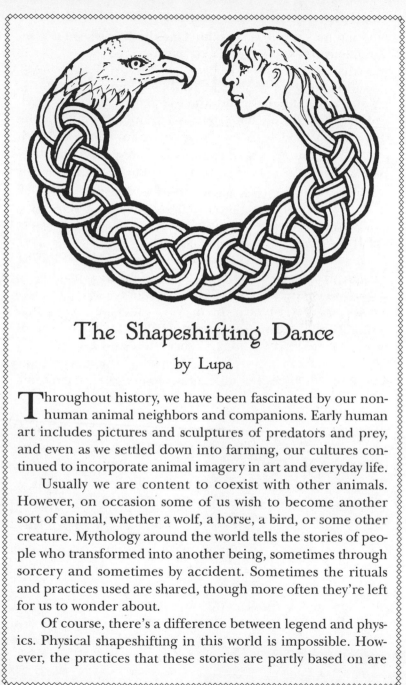

The Shapeshifting Dance

by Lupa

Throughout history, we have been fascinated by our non-human animal neighbors and companions. Early human art includes pictures and sculptures of predators and prey, and even as we settled down into farming, our cultures continued to incorporate animal imagery in art and everyday life.

Usually we are content to coexist with other animals. However, on occasion some of us wish to become another sort of animal, whether a wolf, a horse, a bird, or some other creature. Mythology around the world tells the stories of people who transformed into another being, sometimes through sorcery and sometimes by accident. Sometimes the rituals and practices used are shared, though more often they're left for us to wonder about.

Of course, there's a difference between legend and physics. Physical shapeshifting in this world is impossible. However, the practices that these stories are partly based on are still quite accessible to us today. One that I have spent years working with is the shapeshifting dance.

Dancing the Animals

We are human animals, and while we can swim passably well and may fly with the aid of technology, we're limited by the shape of our bodies. But we're great at imitation, and with practice we can move like the creatures we wish to emulate. Dancers might spread their arms out like an eagle's wings, hop like a kangaroo, or run and shake their mane out like a wild horse. (The truly creative sloth dancer could utilize a horizontal fence post or railing for the world's slowest shapeshift!)

Imitation, though, is just the first part of a shapeshifting dance. By moving like the animal we wish to "become," we are inviting its energy into ourselves. This energy may be embodied within the animal's totem (an archetypal being that embodies all the given qualities and behaviors of its species). So, for example, if I wanted to shapeshift into a gray wolf, I would ask the totem Gray Wolf to help me. I would dance like a wolf with the intent of inviting Gray Wolf to lend me some of her energy so that I could "feel" more wolflike.

This won't, of course, result in me sprouting hair, fangs, and a tail. But if all goes well, my mind and my spirit may shift to be more wolflike. When I wolf dance, I begin to see the world more as a wolf may see it, paying attention to details in the landscape that speak of "shelter" or "the presence of prey animals." I see myself as a wolf, too, and while I can't walk on all fours very well, I do try. My energy body changes to the shape of a wolf, and if I close my eyes I can see and feel the fur over my human skin. I do retain enough of my human self to not lose control—a shapeshifting dance isn't about being in a werewolf movie!

Each animal species offers unique lessons and perspectives. And my experiences with shapeshifting dance may not be the same as yours. Don't worry if you've never tried it; the rest of this article is meant to help you get started.

Pick Your Partner

The first thing you'll want to do is decide what animal you want to shapeshift into. If you already have an animal totem or guide that you've worked with before in some spiritual or magical capacity, that's a good place to start. However, if that animal chooses not to shapeshift with you, or if you're starting "from scratch," you can still find an animal to work with.

How do you go about doing that? By asking, of course! You can invite an animal you'd like to ask—even one you haven't worked with before—if you have one in mind. Otherwise, you can put out a general call for help and see who responds.

You may wish to turn the invitation into a ritual. Set up a small altar with images or other representations of the animal you wish to work with or wear clothing that reminds you of it. Then ask, either silently or out loud, "[Name of animal species], I wish to know what it is to be other than human, to wear [fur/feathers/scales/whatever is appropriate], and to see through the eyes of another. Will you help me in this endeavor to learn more about what it is to be like you?" You may feel the answer in your heart or get a vision or words in your mind.

If the animal doesn't respond, wait a few weeks, then ask again. Or if the animal declines, try asking another one. Be patient. It's best to find an animal that's a good fit. Keep in mind, too, that any animal is a possible ally in shapeshifting, not just the big impressive ones. You might even end up with an extinct or a mythological animal!

Getting to Know You Better

Before you try shapeshifting itself, get to know the animal that's helping you. Start by researching its species:

Natural history: This includes the animal's behavior and environment, what it eats, whether it lives alone or socially, how long it lives, etc.

Relationships with other species: How does this species interact with other animals? With the plants and fungi in its environment? What is its relationship like with humans?

Mythology and folklore: What sorts of stories have we told about this species? What sorts of values and messages do we attach to it as a symbol, and as a real animal?

It's good to know these sorts of facts, but you also want to spend time with the animal. Observing physical members of this species, either in the wild or in captivity, can be a great way to learn how they move and behave. If you're working with a pet species, such as a dog, cat, or goldfish, watch how your household critter interacts with its world and everyone within it. If you don't have access to the physical animals, look for books or documentaries about them.

And even if none of these are options for you, you can still work with the totem or guide of that species. One of my favorite ways to "visit" a totem is through guided meditation. There are several variations, but they generally boil down to visualizing yourself traveling through a tunnel and coming out into a wilderness area where you can meet and talk to the totem. You can discuss what you may learn from the totem or ask it to show you around its home. You can also ask what it may want as a thank-you gift for helping you with all of this.

Your First Dance

Once you feel comfortable with the animal, it's time to try your first dance! Pick a place where you have some room to dance, whether around and around, or standing or sitting in one spot. Make sure you won't be interrupted for at least an hour. If you like, ask someone you trust to be with you while you dance to make sure you don't trip and hurt yourself or feel overwhelmed—it can be a pretty intense ritual experience.

Make sure the altar dedicated to the animal is set up, including an offering for the animal if you like, and get any music that you want to dance to ready to go. Prepare whatever ritual costumes you may wish to wear; these can be as simple as a single necklace or as complicated as an entire outfit. Some people like to wear a bit of fur, feather, claw, or other piece of the physical animal as a connection, though this is not

required. Have some protein-rich food and water available for after the dance, along with a journal or recorder.

When you're ready to start, sit comfortably on the floor or in a chair. Don't worry about dancing just yet. Instead, spend a few moments focusing on your breathing, allowing yourself to relax. Let your thoughts drift by like clouds.

Next, ask the animal to join you. Say silently or out loud:

[Name of animal], I am ready for my first dance. I ask you to be my partner in this, to show me how to move like you, see through your eyes, and find the value in the world that you do. I invite you into this sacred space with me!

You may feel the animal's presence as it arrives, though if it doesn't show up immediately that's okay. Some animals prefer to use the dance itself as their entrance into the ritual.

Slowly start to move your body, just a little, still sitting down. Feel your muscles and bones and tendons, and start to move them like the animal would. How would this animal sit or lie down? What would be a relaxed position for it? How would it sleep? Spend a few moments being a quiet animal.

When you're ready, you can move more quickly and actively. You can either stay seated or get up if you feel comfortable. Think about how the animal moves from place to place, and try to move your body like it does. Don't worry about getting it "right"; remember, your body is still human and that this isn't about being the most convincing shapeshifter ever!

As you continue to move, feel the presence and energy of the animal move into your body. Visualize your energy body shifting shape from that of a human to that of the animal you're dancing. Imagine that you're seeing the world differently and notice what's more important to you. What do you want as this animal? Where would you like to go? How does it feel to be in this form?

This can be a very powerful stage in this ritual. You may find that the totem or spirit you're working with speaks to you at this point, guiding you along and keeping you focused. Don't worry about looking for signs or lessons in this experience or having some purpose to it—simply dance, and let the animal's energy flow through you.

When you're ready, slow down your dance; pull in your wings and fins, lower your tail, settle your feathers and frills. Find a comfortable place to sit or lie down and settle in to relax again. Bring your focus back to your breathing, and as you do, release the animal's energy back to it. Feel yourself becoming fully human again; if you feel "stuck," start reciting your name, address, phone number, and other "mundane" things.

Once you're fully back in your human self, thank the animal for its time and help, and give it the offering you've prepared. Even giving it the spiritual essence of the food and water you're going to eat will work, or you might promise to do a bit of environmental volunteering or make a donation to a relevant nonprofit in its honor.

Finally, once you're ready, write or record your experiences while they're still fresh in your mind. Include any observations you may have made during the dance, as well as any reflections afterward. This is also a good place to record any questions you may have for future shapeshifting dances and related work. And it allows you to revisit this first dance in the future and see how far you've come.

The Whens and Whys of Shapeshifting

You don't have to stop with just one shapeshifting experience! Here are a few occasions on which you might wish to dance with this animal again, or with another:

• Shapeshifting dance is a great way to deepen your relationship with a particular animal. The more you dance, the more you can understand what it is to be that animal and what it may have to teach you. It's also a good way to honor the animal by giving it a place in your sacred practices.

• If you ask an animal for help with a spell or other magical act, you can use shapeshifting dance to channel its energy into your magic. If you're creating a magical item, for example, you can dance around it or even carry it while you dance to let the animal's energy soak in to it. Or you and the animal can build up energy together and then release it all at once for a particular purpose.

• Some celebratory rituals, especially those of nature-based spirituality, benefit from additional wild energy. If you're celebrating a sabbat or other sacred holiday and you want it to have a more natural feel, invite the animal to join you and whoever you're celebrating with. (Just make sure it's okay to do that before the ritual starts!)

Untying the Knot

by Dallas Jennifer Cobb

This year has brought big change. After almost fifteen years of partnership with the father of my daughter, I chose to leave the relationship. Wait. This is not an article about "why" I left the relationship, but an article about "how." And how to use Pagan beliefs, principles, and practices to help you through this process.

Separation and divorce are often portrayed as angry, nasty, and painful for everyone involved. People are expected to "lawyer up" and fight their battles viciously, attacking one another in hatred and anger.

But as a Pagan, I believe that like attracts like. So, wanting to avoid negativity, I approached separation from a less acrimonious point of view. I wondered if I could consciously work through the process of dissolution knowing that separation and divorce, like autumn and winter, are normal events—part of the cycle of life. Surely Pagan beliefs, practices, and rituals could help guide the process and transform the energy of our dissolving relationship.

The magical unfolding that took place, the rapidly changing energy of the relationship, and a ton of research has taught me a lot about how to approach separation with magical intent and outlook. And I want to share some ways I approached the daunting task of "untying the knot" with my previous partner.

Tying the Knot

When we handfasted in 1999, people called it "tying the knot." Our hands were literally tied together, binding us physically, symbolic of how we were bound by love, vows, and commitment.

I chose a handfast ceremony with my community gathered to witness because it reflected my spiritual beliefs and felt more relevant than being legally married under the laws of Canada. (Incidentally, if a couple lives together for six months or has a child, they are considered "equivalent to married" under our taxation laws.)

My partner and I planned and organized the handfast. We invested our time, energy, and the resources available through our community. And we saved ourselves a lot of money.

With happy events, it's easy to plan a ritual that supports the process. Like spring, the energy is growing, the enthusiasm engaging, and the possibilities seem endless. But what do we do when a relationship starts to wane, when there is no longer happiness, and the future feels emotionally overwhelming and painful?

Untying the Knot

When loved wanes, vows are broken, and commitment is no longer desired, it feels bleak and hopeless. I have learned the importance of using structures like rites and rituals to ease me through the wheel of the year and life's ups and downs. Seeing our relationship as a cycle that was coming to completion helped me understand that I could rely on my beliefs and use ritual to get through the cycle of a personal union, including its end.

Structures can help anchor painful emotions and keep them from overwhelming us while accepting their existence, affirming their expression, and engaging their transformative energy.

When I initially proposed a conscious dissolution of our relationship, my partner was very angry and hurt, but after processing his grief, he agreed that we were better off conserving our time and money to help us on our independent paths rather than spending money on a long, drawn-out process involving lawyers.

With his agreement, I turned to conscious planning, employing magic and my Pagan foundation to help change the energy surrounding separation. I examined all the ways we were bound to one another and consciously tried to "untie the knot." While separation is difficult, there are ways to make it easier and less painful. There are also ways to save time, energy, money, and heartache.

However, while we can do so much of the personal, financial, and legal work of separation and divorce ourselves, never underestimate the magical power of a good lawyer, tax accountant, social worker, or police officer when one is needed.

Naming the Knots

We're bound to our partners in so many ways that it may take time to identify all the ways you are linked. And then there's the matter of making plans to dissolve those particular knots.

If you were legally married, you need to legally file for divorce. There are some great online resources, including the aptly titled www.untietheknot.ca, a Canadian-based resource, for doing most of the work toward an uncontested divorce yourself. For more, see www.collaborativedivorcebc.org.

If you were not legally married, then your union is considered "equivalent to spouse." In Canada, it is called a "common law" relationship. Such unions don't require legal divorce, but in many provinces and states you are required to draft and file a separation agreement, which is a document outlining how you will address the care of children and the division of joint assets and debts.

In addition to legal and financial untying, it is important to consider social and emotional untying and make plans to release each other from the family and emotional bonds that held you.

Collaborative Separation or Divorce

A collaborative separation or divorce is exactly what it sounds like—working together to dissolve the union and avoid the financial and emotional pitfalls of adversarial separation.

Professionals used in the collaborative process can include lawyers, mental health professionals, mediators, a financial specialist, and a child advocate, depending on the family's needs. A collaborative divorce process is often less time-consuming, costly, and emotionally draining than adversarial legal proceedings. In the United States and Canada, there is a growing movement of "collaborative lawyers" who believe that couples can figure out how to best dissolve their union.

I spent $700 for a collaborative lawyer and $400 for a real estate lawyer who handled the property transaction in which I bought out my ex's interest in our shared home. Almost everyone who is separated or divorced will tell you that they paid much more than $1,100 for their lawyer's services.

My ex and I were committed to resolving our union as affordably and peacefully as possible and used the well-being of our

daughter as the guide for how we would negotiate. We both used collaborative lawyers. We got a template of a separation agreement off the internet and for two months went back and forth negotiating it. We wrote a detailed and far-reaching document that addressed everything we thought needed to be resolved. When we finished, we both took a copy to our respective lawyers.

Independent legal input and oversight on a separation agreement is important. Lawyers are trained to think about the things that we don't and give sound advice. They also help you comply with your region's Family Law Act and protect your interests and the interests of any children.

Hiring a collaborative lawyer was money well spent. My lawyer reviewed the document, tightened up ambiguous wording, recommended changes, and advised me on aspects of the law that I hadn't considered, which helped me make sound, informed decisions. Following legal input, my ex and I forwarded proposed amendments to one another, and our respective lawyers helped us to find solid middle ground.

The agreement detailed the division of assets, furniture, and fixtures; the financial net equalization of our union; child custody, visitation, child-support, and financial care; and even outlined the proposed tone and method for future communication. The use of a real estate lawyer was a mere formality to ensure that the property transfer transaction was done correctly.

In my case, the collaborative lawyer worked well because my goal was a quick and fair separation. Conventional lawyers make more money if your case stretches out, which provides an incentive to fan the flames of discord. If you and your ex-partner are on speaking terms, have a conversation about using collaborative lawyers. The money you both save can be money that helps each of you move into the future.

Emotional Knots

Untying emotional knots is a long and sometimes messy process. As when winter is approaching, it is important to stock our emotional and social "larder" with supplies for the long journey ahead.

The emotional impact of separation is similar to the stages of grieving following death. Even the person who chose to end the relationship has do deal with loss, grief, and pain. Emotions can be huge and scary, so put supports in place. I chose to process emotions privately and not air dirty laundry in public. I used a therapist who provided perspective and guided me in providing emotional care for myself and my daughter. My mother and her partner acted as sage counsel to check out my big decisions. I turned to my closest allies to practice strong cleansing, protection, and blessings magic, and I undertook a lot of solitary practices to help steer myself (and my daughter) into the future.

I tried to communicate with my ex in a clear, straightforward manner and specifically focused on our legal and financial processes, our daughter and her best care, and the practical details of moving and dividing. When he lapsed into acting out his emotions, trying to badger me with anger, blame, or bullying, I carefully broke off the conversation. I chose not to delve into the negative with him, or about him, believing that like attracts like.

In our fifteen years together, we fulfilled the purposes of our union: we loved one another, created our daughter together, moved to the country and built a home, and supported one another through many difficult life experiences. With these tasks complete, our purpose—and our union—was complete.

My closest friends supported me strongly throughout the process, spending time in ritual clearing old, stagnant energy, and helping to welcome, envision, and enliven my new life. These women helped me grieve, honored my feelings, and showered me with love, affirmation, and affection. They sowed the seeds of new life in me as I came through the winter of grieving and letting go.

When I bought my ex out of our shared home, my friends helped to ritualistically clear, cleanse, and bless the house. Throwing doors open, we moved through each room, smudging away the old energy, clearing the final bits of his property, and ringing a small bell to clear the vibrations of the past from the premises. I wept through the entire process, overwhelmed with feeling. And these women held me.

Magical talismans from my altar were then placed on the feast table and charged with love and merriment. Later, people placed these objects throughout my home, energizing the new life my daughter and I were starting. The objects remain where they were placed, and when I see them, I'm affirmed by the energy of love and merriment.

Untying the Knot Ritual

A ritual provides a structure to consciously work toward changing the energy that needs to change. Untying the knot is useful for symbolically loosening the binds that held you together and creating space for letting go of anger, hurt, expectations, and resentments as the relationship ends. The blessings offers a chance to create a vision of a future separate and apart, and affirms the people leaving the relationship. Blessed and empowered they leave the circle to start life anew on a fresh path.

This ritual can be adapted for a group of any size. You could have a large group such as those who witnessed your handfasting, a smaller group consisting of your ritual circle or coven, or conduct the ritual with just an officiant you and your ex. In fact, this ritual can be done alone, without your previous partner, and still be highly effective. Don't get too hung up on the format. Focus on the process of magic—transforming or changing the energy.

Prepare an altar. Use the handfasting rope if you have it, otherwise take a length of rope and tie many knots in it, visualizing the ways you are bound to your partner. This work can be done in

advance by the couple or by one person. With each knot, know the ways you're tied.

For endings and beginnings use a black candle and two white candles, one for each person. Prepare blessing oil in advance.

The ritual is one of transformation, dissolving the partnership, blessing each individual.

A sacred circle is cast:
Come together and circle round,
In circle's center safety be found.

The couple moves to the center
We encircle this couple in sacred space,
And work strong magic in this place.

Call in the directions clockwise:
From the North this couple received nurturing.
From the East, delight and joy together.
From the South, this couple received passion.
And from West their fluid feelings.

Then stand here at the center in spirit.

We gather to witness the end and new beginning, as _____ *and* _____ *are untying the knot. This rope represents the many ways they have been bound together.*

Light the black candle.
We illuminate the gifts of this relationship.

Light the two white candles.
We illuminate the two strong souls who grew together.

Knotted rope is handed over to the couple who hold it together. The couple unties each knot, saying aloud what they are dissolving: Commitment, monogamy, shared banks accounts, cohabiting…whatever is relevant to them.

We witness your untying.

The priestess takes the rope, then extinguishes the black candle. The two are separated, anointed with blessing oil, and handed a flickering white candle.

We bless you in your choice to walk apart.
Your spirit is yours to guard.

Join the circle.
The two people ease into the circle.
Close the circle counterclockwise:

Bless these two as they journey on:
West bless their clarity and deep resolve
South bless their strong spirits
East bless their conscious thought and choice
North bless their firm foundations

May you walk in peace, and meet in peace, as you go your separate ways.

The circle is open, but never broken.
Merry meet, and merry part, and merry meet again.

Each person walks away in a different direction, on their own. The priestess takes the black candle to bury, the individuals extinguish and take their white candles home.

Nine Woods in the Fire Go ...

by Ellen Coutts Waff

Folklore and folk rhymes come down to us as a way to remember important practices; things folks would have grown up knowing in the past. Two of these mnemonic devices are the Tree Ogam and the Wiccan Rede.

"Nine woods in the fire go" begins the Tree Song within the Wiccan Rede, by Lady Gwen Thompson in 1970. Of the twenty sacred woods found in the ancient Druidic Tree Alphabet, or Tree Ogam, the Rede presents us with but nine: Birch, Oak, Rowan, Willow, Hawthorn, Hazel, Apple, Grape, Fir, and Elder." But that adds up to ten! The last, Elder, is *not* to be burned: "Elder be ye Lady's tree, burn it not or cursed ye'll be!" Gwen Thompson said that her grandmother Parsons had taught her these folk wisdoms.

The Tree Ogam manuscripts from the sixth century are written in Gaelic. What follows is a rundown of these special trees in as original form as possible. Where applicable, the source of the translated lines follow in parentheses.

Elder, or Elder Mother, is revered and respected, as she is the Cailleach, or Great Hag, eldest and most mysterious of the gods. Elder in the Tree Ogam is *Ruis*, the red of strength, passion, of the redness of the fire upon Fionn's brow. That intensity of anger is best not brought down upon any human. Do not tempt the wrath of the Elder! Another tree song says: "Make a fire of Elder tree, Death within your house will be." In versions on the "A Walk Around Britain" website, the folk verse claims: "Green Elder logs it is a crime for any man to sell." Dangerous stuff, indeed!

Birch is the first of the burnable woods mentioned in the Rede. Birch is always the first: the first tree of the Tree Ogam, and the very first tree to colonize Northern Europe after the retreat of the ice 10,000 years ago. (Simmons, Ian, and Michael Tooley. *The Environment in British Prehistory*. Cornell, 1981.)

"Birch in the fire goes to represent what the Lady knows." Birch is supple, bearing delicate, spring-green leaves, a perfect icon for the Lady. Another "Firewood Poem" states that "Birch and Fir logs burn too fast, Blaze up bright and do not last." (Congreve, Celia, "The Times," 1930.) The Lady's knowledge then, must be seized and held, lest it be quickly consumed.

Fir, in the Rede, is noted as evergreen: representative of immortality. Erynn Rowan Laurie, in her book *Ogam: Weaving Word Wisdom*, names Fir, *Ailm*, meaning initiation, where birth and death are one, creating an epiphany of the human spirit becoming immortal, but only for a moment. Here Fir and Birch are linked in the birth/rebirth moment and also linked in their quick flash of fire.

"**Oak** in the forest towers with might, in the fire it brings the God's insight," states the Rede. According to the Firewood Poem, "Oak logs will warm you well, If they're old and dry." Oak has ever been associated with strength, royalty, and the God. It was revered throughout the ancient world, gateway to sacred groves everywhere, as it is a door into other worlds. The very word for Oak in the root Indo-European language is *Duir*, door or gateway. It is the basis of the word Druid, man of the Oak. Brehon Law, the legal system of the Celtic peoples, names Oak a Chieftain Tree.

"**Rowan** is a tree of power causing life and magic to flower." In the Tree Ogam, the word for Rowan is *Lus*, which is "flame," "shining" (Laurie), and also the Gaelic word for "herb." Bridghe is the Goddess associated with Rowan. She is the sacred flame and the patron of poetry, smithcraft, and healing. Since a poet's inspired words are equated with flames, poetry is magic, transformative. Herbs heal by helping the body transform sickness into wholeness, supporting life. True magic.

"**Willows** at the waterside stand, ready to help us to the Summerland." Willows do love to have their "feet in the water," as they say. Willow is not good to burn. Its flexible withies are best used for basket-making, hence the connection to the Summerland: Willow was used to weave coffins in old times (Laurie). The ogam for willow is *Saille*. The tune "Down By the Sally Gardens" refers to a willow grove. The color of the leaves, leaf-backs, and possibly the bark was considered "the hue of the lifeless" (Laurie). The tree branches and withies can be heard whispering messages from the dead in the wind. No other firewood poem mentions willow.

"**Hawthorn** is burned to purify, and to draw faeries to your eye." Hawthorn has another name: "May." In this guise, it tells of the arrival of true Beltaine, May Day. In Ireland, Hawthorn is known to mark Fairy mounds; it is the tree of the *Sidhe*. There are countless tales of foolish men attempting to cut or move thorn bushes, and the bush would either move back or grow again overnight. If the fools succeeded, they were likely to be visited by death or ill-luck within a fortnight. (Lenihan,

Eddie. *Meeting the Other Crowd: Fairy Stories of Hidden Ireland.* Tarcher: New York, 2003.) Dew from a thornbush allows one sight of the fairies, if the eyes are bathed in it on Beltaine morning. The Firewood Poems both mention Hawthorn: it "bakes the sweetest bread" in Ireland, and logs are "good to last, if cut in the fall" ("A Walk Around Britain"). The thorns were reputedly used by the Druids to "focus malevolent intent," but it was also planted near doors to ward off evil. (Laurie) The female-smelling frothy blooms are allowed indoors *only on Beltaine* to ensure good luck and protection for the agricultural year (Laurie). The ogam for Hawthorn is *h-Uath* which means "terror!"

"**Hazel**, the tree of wisdom and learning, adds its strength to the bright fire burning." Hazel is not mentioned in any other firewood poem. The ogam word is *Coll*. Hazel appreciates wet feet like willow. The archtypical story about Hazel is that of the Salmon of Wisdom swimming in Fec's pool, eating the hazelnuts of Wisdom as they drop into the still water. Strength comes from gaining knowledge gradually and using it wisely. This kind of wisdom is found only in nature. The five streams flowing from Fec's pool are those of the five senses, to be employed in finding and utilizing that Wisdom.

"White are the flowers of **Apple** tree, that brings us fruits of fertility." To humankind, Apple speaks of domesticity and husbandry. She provides food for body and soul. *Ceirt* or *Quert* is the ogam. All fruit trees have evolved from the rose family, providing both beauty and scent: "Pear logs and apple logs, they will scent your room; cherry logs across the dogs smell like flowers in bloom." "Apple logs will fill your room/ With an incense like perfume" ("A Walk Around Britain"). Fruitwood fires are the best, but fruit orchards in bloom are without peer among beauties! When pears and apples are cut across the fruit, a pentagram is revealed, a lovely reminder of the five-petaled spring blossom birthing autumnal fruit. The apple is associated with the Summerland, as in Avalon, Isle of Apples, and Emain Abhlach, the Irish Realm of Apples. Pleasant places, no doubt.

"**Grapes** grow upon the vine, giving us both joy and wine." Perhaps the joy comes as a result of imbibing the wine? The grape and its product produce pleasure, joy of a sort, but also drunkenness. Wine both helps and hinders communication between individuals. This "tree" which is not a tree is one to be wary of. *Muin* is the ogam.

～

Helpful rhymed verses like these, often termed "runes" allow us to make informed choices with the aid of elder knowledge. "Witness hereby the ancientry of Oak, and Ash, and Thorn" sings Kipling in "Tree Song." We sing along.

The Nine Woods/Wiccan Rede (excerpts)

Nine woods in the fire go, burn them fast or burn them slow.

Birch in the fire goes to represent what the Lady knows.

Oak in the forest towers with might, in the fire it brings the Gods' insight.

Rowan is a tree of power, causing life and magic to flower.

Willows at the waterside stand, ready to help us to the Summerland.

Hawthorn is burned to purify, and to draw fairies to your eye.

Hazel, the tree of wisdom and learning, adds its strength to the bright fire burning.

White are the flowers of Apple tree that brings us fruits of fertility.

Grapes grow upon the vine, giving us both joy and wine.

Fir does mark the evergreen, to represent immortality unseen.

Elder be the Lady's tree, burn it not or cursed ye'll be!

The Blessed Bee

by Natalie Zaman

Have you ever been "as busy as a bee?" Is your home a "hive" of activity? Have you ever felt like a drone? Or a tireless queen? Assigning animal traits to human behavior is a conceit humans have practiced since we've had the power of language. We've "been as the bee" for millennia.

Bees have been feeding, curing, and lighting our lives with their honey and comb for at least 7,000 years if Spanish cave paintings of Stone Age apiarists are to be believed. On top of this, a bond of a divine nature also exists. Carvings in Aegean tombs show bees escorting departed souls to the underworld. Aphrodite's handmaidens, her "Melissas" (whose name literally translates to "honeybee"), used the bee as their personal emblem. And it is speculated that the original beehive hairdo can be found on the Venus of Willendorf—her rigid "cap" might just be a beehive. Many cultures have connected man to bee, but at some point guardian, nymph, and Mother Goddess melted into obscurity as the practical was sundered from the spiritual. Bees were kept for produce, and prayer was taken out of the apiary. Perhaps, at last, it is time to return to the old ways.

In recent years, a disturbing phenomenon has decimated the world's bee population: Colony Collapse Disorder. Worker bees abandon their hives, leaving their queen and drones behind to perish. Scattered and alone, they die as well. No one knows exactly why this is happening, though parasites and pesticides have been named as potential causes, so as of now there is no solution. Scientific studies have also theorized that if the bee population disappears—specifically honeybees and bumblebees, the species' chief pollinators—the human race will inevitably follow.

The time is right for us to renew our connection to the blessed bee—in both the spiritual and the mundane. Use ritual to bring the magical qualities of these marvelous creatures into your life. By adding a bit of practical craft, perhaps we can help restore the bee to its proper and needed place in the spiral dance. In helping the bees, we help ourselves.

Drone, Worker, Queen
Crafting Gratitude Beeswax Candles

Bumblebees and honeybees are very different creatures, but the order of their communities is similar. Workers go out, collect pollen, and produce honey; drones mate with the queen, who lays eggs. This structure ensures that each bee has a role to play, ensuring the continued survival of the colony.

Unlike bees, we humans assume many roles throughout our lives and often, we get to choose which parts and when we play them. There are times when being a "worker bee"—having a specific job to do—is comforting. A niche-purpose allows a person to focus on the task at hand, unfettered and free of the distraction of outside ambitions. Conversely, being the source of creation, the center of everything, can be exhilarating—though that position often comes with great responsibility. There are times when any role can weigh heavily. A bee blessing can help with this challenge.

To imbibe the energy of the Queen Bee and her Court, craft candles of beeswax infused with honey and amber to aid with vitality and endurance. Burn one of these candles to encourage you to work to your best potential. And as positive change begins and ends with gratitude, express thanks—for the support of others, for your abilities, and for the opportunity of the experience.

You will need:

Sheets of honeycomb-pressed beeswax. These can be purchased at a craft store, but you can try to buy beeswax and related products from a local apiary. Doing this supports a local business while also assisting with bee preservation. Beeswax sheets come in different lengths, thicknesses, and colors. Height and breadth do not matter—make your candles in sizes that please you, but do use beeswax in its natural, undyed state (Use dyed wax when making candles for specific intentions).

Candle wicks

Amber chips or small tumbled stones. Amber's golden color is reminiscent of honey and its qualities of vitality and endurance add vital life-force energy to this spellwork.

Honey (again, locally produced if possible)

Hair dryer

To make the candle, unroll a sheet of beeswax so that it lays flat on your workspace.

Place a candle wick at one end of the sheet so that the end of the wick lines up with the edge of what will be the bottom of the candle. The opposite end of the wick should extend past the other edge of the wax sheet. Press the wick into the wax with your finger to secure it in place.

Next, fit the amber chips into random cells of the beeswax. As you place each piece, visualize the life force contained in the amber becoming a part of the candle.

Drip three drops of honey into three different cells: one near the wick, one in the middle of the sheet, and one near the bottom. With each drop, picture the honey's healing and nourishing qualities melting into the wax. Now you're ready to roll.

Being careful to keep the top and bottom of the candle even, and starting at the wick end, roll up the beeswax sheet with a tight hand. (When you're finished, the wick should be in the center of the candle.) As the candle forms, say this mantra aloud or to yourself:

Sweetness and light,
Be in all that I do,
And in all that I be.

Finish rolling up the candle, then use a hair dryer to soften the wax of the exposed edge. (You can also hold the candle horizontally at a safe distance over a heat source such as a lit candle). Press the edge down to seal it. If the wax is stubborn and unravels, secure it by tying it with a piece of yarn or ribbon until it is time to light it.

Burn a Queen Bee and Court candle when you find yourself unhappy with a task you must complete, feel overburdened with responsibility, or need a reminder of all of the positive aspects of your life. Repeat the mantra each time you light the candle.

When all of the beeswax is melted away, release the amber chips or stones into nature, repeating the mantra one last time, and end with a statement of gratitude:

Thank you, Blessed Bee!

The Hive

Build a Bee Spirit House

For a bee colony, hive is home. And while you probably don't want a single bee, let alone a colony in your home, you can welcome them in spirit (and invite some live bees into your neighborhood) with a little help from some Eastern philosophy.

Wander through the streets of Thailand and you're sure to see a Spirit House—a shrine in miniature made of wood, metal, or stone and decorated with mirror mosaics and precious gems. These tiny temples are temporary dwellings for transient spirits wandering the earth. The house and offerings left inside and around it are meant to encourage those who have passed on to stop for a while and bestow blessings of good fortune.

Solitary bees, victims of Colony Collapse Disorder, or travelers looking for food to bring back to the their colonies (honeybees can travel hundreds of miles to gather pollen) have a better chance of survival if they can find temporary shelter. Welcome bees in body and spirit by crafting and dedicating a Hive Spirit House—a fitting tribute for this former escort of departed souls. You will need:

Sandpaper

A piece of wood (be sure to use untreated lumber) approximately 4 inches wide by 4 inches deep, and 18 to 24 inches long (This will become the foundation of the house.)

A drill with different sized bits

Two 6-inch-square, flat pieces of wood (also untreated) to form a
triangular, pitched roof (**Note:** You can use a larger piece of
wood for the foundation. Just be sure to make a roof that is
proportionately larger because you want overhanging eaves.)
Hot glue gun
Broken bits of mirror, plates, and/or chips or tumbled stones (Use
onyx for protection, amber for vitality and health, and jade or
malachite for safe journeys—all blessings traveling bees need.)
Hook and weatherproof cord for hanging

 While you are making your Hive Spirit House, keep your purpose in mind—to attract the bee spirit and bring its energy to
your life and offer live bees protection.

 Before you begin construction, sand down all the wood. This
will help prevent splinters. Additionally, any embellishments you
add will adhere better to a rough surface.

Next, prepare the foundation by drilling holes into one side of the long piece of wood, being careful not to pass the drill completely through it. Vary the size of the holes; what constitutes a snug, "just-right" hole will differ from bee to bee.

Assemble the roof before attaching it to the foundation. This part of the Hive Spirit House is not merely decorative; it will protect future occupants from predators, sun, and inclement weather. Line up the two flat pieces of wood edge to edge so that they form a triangle. Fix the pieces together with a few drops of hot glue.

Center the roof over the foundation and attach it with more hot glue.

Decorate the roof and sides of the Hive Spirit House using the tiles and stones. To add to your intentions, make symbolic patterns such as pentacles, spiral patterns, goddesses, or even the shape of the bee itself. Attach the embellishments to the wood with hot glue. Do not varnish, treat, or water-seal the house; you don't want anything to seep into the wood and affect the bees staying there.

Attach a hook to the back of the house (be careful not to interfere with the holes in the front) and use the cord to hang it up.

Where you put your Hive Spirit House is important. Do not place it in a shared living space like the common area of an apartment complex—you don't want the bees to sting anyone, and you never know who might have an allergy. Install the Hive Spirit House at a little distance from your home—a tree or post in the corner of a yard where it's likely to catch the morning sun is a good place. Call to the spirit of the bees when you are ready to hang their new home:

We were bound together long ago,
Let it once again be so.
This message to the bees I send:
Welcome, golden, winged friends.

A last and essential element of the Spirit House is a daily offering. For bees, nothing is better than flowers and water. Leave a shallow dish of water near your Hive Spirit House, or if you can, place the house near a water source like a pond or stream. Like all living creatures, it is important for bees to keep hydrated. Dysentery is a common ailment that plagues many apiaries.

Do some research to find out which plants are attractive and beneficial to bees in your area. Plan your garden to bloom continuously—some plants bloom only in the spring, some in the fall, and others throughout the summer. Leave the flowers in place until they are brown (naturally, as you should avoid using herbicides and pesticides), then prune them to allow as much access to the blooms as possible. Do NOT include any yellow plants or other decorations. Aggressive species such as yellow jackets and ground bees are attracted to the color yellow.

A constant and colorful food supply planted around your Hive Spirit House, in the ground or in pots, will encourage pollination and honey production. Such a garden will also attract butterflies and hummingbirds when the weather is right.

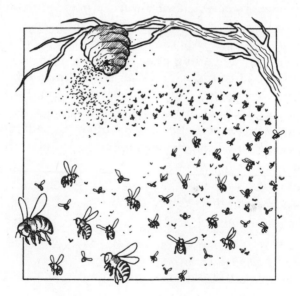

The Swarm Is Normal

The "Change Is Good" Ritual

A swarm of bees. Those four words can conjure up a frightening image: a dense, black droning cloud bent on destruction. However, nothing could be farther from the truth. Swarming occurs when a newly created queen bee leaves her hive, taking enough drones and worker bees with her to start a new colony. This expansion and diversification, which bees do instinctually when a queen reaches middle age, ensures survival. Beekeepers try to rein in this instinct to maintain order and regulate honey production, but it can't always be prevented. Nature finds a way.

Sometimes, change is inevitable—and while it can be uncomfortable, it is necessary for growth and evolution, and this is just as true for humans as it is for bees. Revive our ancient connection to the bee and ease into change by "becoming the bee" in a ritual that can be done almost anywhere, and requires only your own breath and a few flowers.

Instructions: Go out into nature where you will be able to collect wildflowers (or use hothouse flowers if you are doing the ritual at a time of year when wildflowers are not available). Try to select plants that visibly have pollen on them.

Find a quiet place—where you can be alone if possible—and think about the impending change coming your way. Perhaps you're in the midst of it. Are you afraid? Exhilarated? Examine your feelings. Speak out loud about them if you can. Take as much time as you need to vent them out.

Shake the pollen from the flowers into your palm or hold the flowers out in front of you. Speak this mantra aloud or to yourself:

The time has come
For me to swarm.
Change is coming,
And not to my harm.
I let go of care.
I fly on the wind.
I'm ready to begin again!
So mote it bee!

When you finish speaking, take a deep breath and blow the pollen out into the air. Picture your anxiety and fear about the change floating away with the tiny particles. As they disappear, feel your fear transforming back into pure energy, an increasing, brightening light. When all negative association is gone, visualize the light stretching out in all directions—you are the bee, pollinating positivity so that it will spread and grow.

Use this ritual to help you get through challenging changes. Even if the change is something you're excited about, perform this ritual to center and ground, creating an aura of peace and contentment, a quiet before the swarm.

~

There is an abundance of websites and books and shops that promote the benefits of bee products: beeswax as a moisturizer, royal jelly as a super food, and countless recipes that blend honey with herbs and spices to create healing elixirs. There seems to be no malady that honey can't cure, or at least help ease the symptoms.

Before you use bee-based remedies, always seek professional medical advice. In addition to any potential effects and side effects of bee products, it is important to know if you have any allergies (also essential if you keep a bee box near your home). Be especially careful with children under three, the elderly, and anyone who has a compromised immune system. (Raw honey contains different bacteria that could prove dangerous to certain people.)

If you have the time and inclination, you may consider keeping bees. Print and electronic resources on this topic are abundant—and a good place to start. However, before you acquire your own swarm, think about volunteering and apprenticing for a master apiarist. Hands-on experience and the passing of knowledge from one person to another is a bee-utiful thing.

May your bee-blessings abound!

Honoring Trickster

by Sybil Fogg

When I was pregnant with my fifth child, my husband and I went shopping for something special to mark his entrance into the world. Since we were well equipped with all the necessary items, clothing, and even many toys, it was difficult to find something unique. But we liked to welcome each child with something special to symbolize that they are an individual, even in our large family. Close to his birth, we stumbled on a little fox rattle and found a matching swaddling blanket, and Fox became Theo's emblem. I wasn't certain if Fox would have much influence over his life, and beyond thinking that the little red fox rattle was a cute toy, I didn't about it much until three years later when my children and I were attacked by a rabid fox while in a playground at a state park. The fox went after Theo and clamped on to his hand. My other children were up on the playground equipment, out of harm's way. When I picked up my son, the fox would not let go and a struggle ensued, prompting the rest of my family to jump down to defend their little brother. After a bit of a wild chase around the park, we managed to hide in a bathroom until help arrived. Thankfully, my other children escaped harm, but Theo and I suffered bites and scratches. This, of course, resulted in a series of rabies vaccines and a hospital stay for my son, as the fox broke a small bone in his hand and there was a concern about infection. Up until then, I had always found foxes fascinating, somewhat cute, and not the least bit physically dangerous. As the medieval Reynard the Fox managed to outwit his adversaries, I generally viewed the fox as a trickster, relying on his wits more than his brawn to get out of scrapes. After the incident with the fox, I began researching tricksters.

Reynard the Fox was the trickster of medieval Europe. Reynard was (like many tricksters) physically weak, but long on charm and brains, using his charisma and slick talk to wriggle his way out of trouble. Many stories feature the exploits of Reynard the Fox, one being how he went into partnership with Bruin the Bear mainly to liberate a beehive full of honey from the bear.

After thinking about how to go about it, Reynard informs Bruin that he must go on a trip to be godfather to the child of one of his good friends.

So he starts off and after a while, turns back and hits up the beehive full of honey. Upon returning to Bruin, the bear asks Reynard what the child had been named. Reynard without thinking, states, "Just-Begun."

After some time passes, Reynard wants more honey and tells Bruin that he must go to another christening. Upon return, he tells Bruin, the child's name is "Half-Eaten."

On the third "trip," Reynard professes that the child was named, "All-Gone."

Naturally, Bruin decides he would like some of his honey and offers to share it with Reynard. When they arrive at the beehive, Bruin sees that the honey is all gone and turns to Reynard, stating, "Just-Begun, Half-Eaten, All-Gone. So that is what you meant. You have eaten my honey."

Reynard denies this and suggests that Bruin must have eaten it in his sleep. To prove his point, he decides they must take a nap with the assertion that the sun will "sweat" the honey out of the culprit.

Bruin agrees and they lie down and soon Bruin is asleep. Reynard takes up some honey left in the beehive and smears it on Bruin. Upon Bruin's waking, Reynard points out the honey and confirms his argument.[1]

The American counterpart to Fox is **Coyote**. He is popular amongst Pagans who delve into Native American traditions and is probably familiar to most people. Of the many different Coyote legends spanning the range of Native people in the Americas, some include creation myths, how-to stories, and moral fables. A good source of Coyote legends can be found on the Native Languages of the Americas site.

Along the line of well-known tricksters is the shapeshifting **Loki**, a Norse God (or giant, depending on the source), often called the god of strife because of all of the trouble he causes. In most of Loki's myths, he causes trouble and then sets things right, a pattern that continued until he accidently caused the death of Odin's son Baldur, and was sentenced to an eternal punishment. For more about Loki, a search of Norse mythology books will render a nice selection of titles.

Tricksters are not limited to Western mythology. They also make their appearances in the Eastern traditions. One such god is **Sun Wukong**, the Monkey king who always felt

1 Joseph Jacobs, *European Folk and Fairy Tales*. New York: G. P.
  Putnam's Sons, 1916.

slighted by the rest of the Chinese pantheon, mainly because he feared death and desired the longevity afforded to other gods. He eventually managed to achieve this goal by devouring the peaches of immortality while ransacking the palaces of heaven. This stunt resulted in an ongoing battle that lasted longer than the gods of heaven expected, causing the Jade Emperor to call in Buddha for assistance, who eventually trapped Sun Wukong under a mountain for five hundred years.[2]

Sun Wukong is often associated with the size-shifting Hindu god, Hanuman. **Hanuman** is one of the most popular gods in the Hindu pantheon. He is worshiped as a symbol of devotion, vigor, and determination. Hanuman appears in the ancient Indian text the *Ramayana* as Lord Rama's devoted partner. Hanuman is best known for leading a monkey army to defeat the demon king, Ravana who had kidnapped Rama's wife Sita. In the battle, Hanuman managed to burn Ravana's city to the ground using trickery.

When Hanuman scouted Ravana's home to find Sita, he was captured by the evil king. To punish Hanuman, Ravana had his people set fire to the monkey god's tale. By this point, Hanuman had had enough of Ravana's cruel tricks, so he grew to an enormous size, swishing his tail back and forth until he managed to set fire to all that Ravana cared for. Hanuman's part in the *Ramayana* teaches us to face our trials with aplomb and work to conquer obstacles of any size. Perhaps a more appropriate trickster from the Hindu pantheon would be Krishna, the butter thief.

Krishna is the eighth incarnation of the god Vishnu. A playful and flirtatious god, Krishna is often associated with theft, first of ghee (Indian butter) when he was a child and later a thief of hearts.

---

2 http://www.pantheon.org/articles/s/sun_wu-kung.html

The Japanese **Bake-danuki** is a big-bellied, well-endowed, sake-drinking mischievous god depicted in statuary meant for good luck. These creatures are a personified version of the Japanese raccoonlike dog, the danuki and are similar to the Japanese and Chinese fox lore in which there is much information to be had about these animals' abilities to perform magic, shape shift, cause mischief, and possess people. Tricksters are not simply fools or troublemakers. They tend to be nonconformists who like to shake things up. Much like a fox holds a separate line in the Canidae family (the *vulpini*), tricksters are often on the outside of society. Lewis Hyde put it best when he pointed out that "trickster is a boundary crosser,"[3] pointing out that tricksters will cross boundaries and break societal rules. They often are capable of shifting shape physically and will blur the boundaries

---

3 Hyde, Lewis, *Trickster Makes this World: Mischief, Myth, and Art* (Farrar, Straus and Giroux (August 17, 2010)p.7

of what is right and wrong, moral and immoral often with seemingly little reasoning.

That is certainly what if felt like three years ago when my son and I crossed Fox. When asked why he did not run when the fox approached, Theo said he thought it was a cat or small dog and did not realize it was a wild animal. Foxes do have feline qualities. They are smaller than most dogs, and most certainly foxes, coyotes, and wolves and have lush coats and full tails giving them an alluring appearance. Gray foxes are capable of climbing trees, a trait not often associated with others of its species. They are known for being wily and tricky, capable of sneaking through farms at night and stealing chickens or chasing cats. They slink through the shadows as if moving through the thin veil between our world and another, or maybe simply the wild and the domesticated.

We visited a wild animal park not long after the attack so my children could see foxes that are not sick. The gray fox there was tame and ran right up to the fence. I thought Theo would be frightened, but he held his hand out, stronger from his previous encounter. Theo still has the scars that show he was marked by Trickster and we have all decided that there is much to learn from Fox. In fact, we can all learn something about stepping beyond the boundaries of conformity on occasion.

Ritual to Honor Trickster

There are many ways to honor Trickster in our lives. It can be attending a rally to stand up for what you believe in—even if that is not the status quo. It can mean taking a chance on something that might not pan out. One could take a stand on their Facebook wall that will certainly spark a debate. It could mean challenging oneself to try a hobby that might seem off the wall to others. Or it could simply mean playing a good-old harmless practical joke on a family member or friend. I once got a long laugh out of supergluing quarters to the entryway floor. Each of my children tried in vain to hoist them up, but didn't want to ask for help for fear that they might have to share.

Here is a short ritual to honor your Trickster of choice. The best time is a Tuesday during a New Moon in Leo.

Tools Needed:

Yellow candle

Quarter candles, appropriately colored and anointed if need be

High John (for confidence) anointing oil

Charcoal block and incense burner

The following herbs to be burned:

> Clove for stimulation
>
> Fennel for vitality
>
> Ginseng for rejuvenation

A piece of paper with what aspect of (or which) Trickster you wish to honor written out clearly. This may take some time to produce. This step is necessary to complete before the ritual because Trickster cannot always be trusted, and it is not wise to leave it up to the elements to make this choice for you. For the first invocation, you may want to simply ask Trickster to plant the seed of playfulness or ability to step off the well-worn path to find your own journey.

A vessel in which to place burning paper

A cup or glass of water in case you need to put out flames

An offering for when you close the ritual. This will take a bit of research to discover what libation each Trickster prefers. For example, eggs are suitable for Fox, ale for Loki, and sake for Bake-danuki.

Instructions: Set up your space. Place the vessel to hold burning paper between where you will sit and the yellow candle.

Call the quarters and cast the circle as you normally do.

Anoint the candle and place it in a holder.

Light the charcoal block and sprinkle the herbs on the charcoal.

Place your paper in front of you and light the candle.

Read out what or who you are invoking.

Spend some time contemplating walking the boundary. I like to imagine I am walking in a circle around the boundary and issue that I know will be challenging because I will have to break the status quo to find any satisfaction.

When you are ready, imagine that you are stepping over the line.

Light the paper from the candle and drop it in the prepared vessel. *So mote it be.*

Allow the candle to burn down.

Offer your libation.

Close the circle and thank the quarters.

～

A trickster doesn't just play tricks or behave in an unconventional manner. They also challenge the norms that we live by and allow us to develop new ideas and experiences. They can bring a deeper understanding to our magical workings as well. Trickster is not afraid to keep trying new things as even when he fails, he returns to try again. A lesson we can all use.

The Element of Surprise and Drama in Ritual

by Mickie Mueller

Throughout history, temple priests and priestesses used ancient technology to add elements of drama to their rituals. They heated water in giant cauldrons that magically caused the temple doors to open using hydraulics and designed entire temples around the rising of the sun and moon on specific days. The first coin-operated machines were actually made as a seemingly magical way to dispense blessed holy water. They were more than just spiritual leaders—they were entertainers! They knew these displays would enhance the participant's experience, adding mystery and excitement for everyone involved. Of course back in those days, the priests would claim these tricks as being magic actually perpetrated by the gods. Even though today most people have a basic understanding of how these things work, we can still work the element of surprise into our rituals to add to the effect, not to fool anyone, but to create drama. And quite frankly, it's fun.

Here are some great dramatic ritual elements that I've actually used in coven gatherings and public rituals to the delight of the people in attendance. When you add elements of surprise, it can be very powerful and memorable.

Add Drama to Petition Magic

When I was younger I was entranced by Harry Houdini and loved stage magic. I even did a short magic show for my middle-school talent show. While looking for a new idea for a coven I was working with, I got this great idea to use magician's flash paper for the petitions in the ritual. I popped on the internet and found a little pack of reasonably priced 2-by-3-inch flash paper from a stage-magician supply shop. Flash paper is how magicians make flames seem to appear from their fingertips; it doesn't burn like regular paper—it bursts into a big flash!

When working with flash paper, there are a couple of important things to remember: keep it very dry, and don't dangle long hair or sleeves near it (just like when working with candles). To make it more fun for everyone, I did not let my coven in on the secret. I kept the flash paper in a small zipper plastic bag and placed that inside of an organza bag to place on the altar to protect it against humidity. When it came to the point in the ritual to write our petitions, I handed out the paper and pens and everyone wrote down something they wanted to banish from their lives. I had everyone pull back their sleeves to allow the energy to flow down their arms into the paper (and to make sure no one's sleeves were too close to the flame!). One by one we went around the circle and as each person touched their petition to the flame they gasped, laughed, and watched their obstacles not just burn up, but flash into oblivion! It was wonderful! I even sent some flash paper home with some of them for future use.

∾

I was teaching a year-long series of classes with closing rituals at a local New Age shop and I was always trying to come up with ways to keep the rituals fresh. One of the challenges was that we couldn't burn candles due to their insurance, so I used electric candles for the rituals, but there was no way to burn petitions, so I had to get creative. Again, I searched online and discovered dissolving paper! It's nontoxic and safe for the environment—and I was fascinated by the idea of dissolving your petition—so I ordered a pack. Again, much like the flash paper, keep this stuff very dry. It comes in 8½ × 11-inch sheets, so I cut them up into twelve pieces (about 2 × 3-inch slips). At our ritual, I was careful not to pass out the paper to everyone until right before we were ready to make our petitions. I didn't want any sweaty hands to give my trick away.

In the middle of the table, I placed a large, clear glass container full of water so that everyone would be able to clearly see the effect. I asked everyone to write down regrets from the previous year, and I assured them that no one would see them or read them aloud. We used a clearing chant to push the emotions from the event into the petition and then we all simultaneously cast our petitions into the water. I stirred with a wand—and the petitions just vanished! Several participants said they had a brief moment of panic they thought their regrets would be visible as the paper went into the water, but that seeing the paper vanish was a perfect feeling of relief—and they felt that the regret was totally gone for good. It was a very powerful ritual for us all. We poured the water onto the earth for the energy to be absorbed and neutralized. The manufacturers say that if you print on this paper with a laser printer, the paper dissolves but the letters float around in the water. I haven't tried that yet. Perhaps you could print a pentagram or other magical symbols on the paper before casting your petition into the water!

Messages from Spirit

Many of us remember making invisible ink when we were kids, but did you ever think of including it as ritual tool? I use parchment-colored paper from the office-supply store,

but any paper will do. Cut the paper into strips (about 2 × 4 inches each). In case you didn't know, the secret recipe for invisible ink is lemon juice. You can write with it using a cotton swab, paintbrush, or even a calligraphic dip pen if you want to get really fancy. Using lemon juice as your ink, write one positive affirmation about the future on each piece of paper. I like to make enough for everyone and then do five more so there are lots of choices. Place these in a bowl or cauldron on the altar. During the ritual, each person chooses one at random. Then they can take turns holding the paper carefully over a candle and watching as the heat makes the message appear as mystical brown text and offer guidance for future endeavors. Even if you remember this trick from childhood, adding it to a ritual offers a really unique ritual experience and awakens your inner child.

Cakes and Ale, Blessings of Magic

The magical communion that we witches know as cakes and ale offers several opportunities to add some drama and flash to your ritual. Here is one interesting idea to magically change white wine into red wine. Okay, technically if you're a wine connoisseur you're not going literally turn a Pinot Grigio into a Shiraz, but the appearance of pouring a white wine into a chalice that mysteriously turns red before your eyes is a pretty cool trick! Simply put three or four drops of red food coloring into your empty chalice several days before the ritual. The liquid will evaporate, leaving the dry food coloring in the bottom of the chalice. With all the items on the altar and the candlelight, that little dot of red isn't noticeable. When you are ready for your cakes and ale, open a bottle of white wine and during the blessing, talk about the power of transformation from one form to another and the connection of generative power of the ocean and the life blood of the Goddess. Then as you pour from the bottle, make sure that your group can see the wine entering the chalice so that they can see it turn red. It's very simple but makes a great presentation and magical lesson!

As for cakes, there is the traditional magical Irish bread called Barmbrack that has small tokens baked inside. The token you discover is the prediction for the upcoming year. People also have added special charms attached to ribbons beneath the icing on wedding cakes for their attendants to pull and divine their future through the symbolism. You could also do something similar with ritual cakes. Little metal charms are available at your local craft store, so you could choose charms for different symbolism—a key for opportunity or the goddess Hecate, or an acorn for prosperity or the god Cernunnos. You could bake them into individual cakes, scones, or even cookies. Whatever you do, make sure that you let your ritual companions in on the fact that there are charms inside the cakes—having someone break a tooth or choke during ritual would not be very magical at all.

≈

I hope these ideas spark your imagination. What other ideas can you come up with to add drama and surprise to your next group ritual? Using some of these ideas can make your magical circle memorable and remind us of a time when we recognized that the world was a magical place every day.

Water Magic

Dream Magick
for Night and Day

by Melanie Marquis

Much of our lives are spent in sleep, a time when the subconscious mind reigns supreme. That subconscious mind knows a lot of stuff that the conscious mind doesn't, and your dreams are a key to accessing this hidden knowledge and insight. The magick of dreams takes many forms, from divination based on dream interpretation to prophetic dreams that inspire new religions, new inventions, and more. Through dreams, we become aware of our deepest desires, our deepest fears, and our deepest wisdom. Combine that wisdom with a heavy dose of magickal intention, and amazing things become possible.

Sometimes our typical magick just doesn't do the trick, for instance, when our goals are far-fetched or the focus of our magick is far away. Spells that face such barriers often perform better when cast with dream magick. Dream magick can be useful for achieving many spellcasting goals, it's a useful form of divination, and it's even an excellent way to build magickal skills and abilities. Want to try a little dream magick of your own? Let's take a look at some traditional magick for inducing prophetic dreams, then we'll talk about lucid dreaming, "sleepcasting," and the art of daydreaming as an act of magick.

Dream Magick Traditions

European and American folk traditions abound with spells to dream about one's future destiny. Many such spells were focused on an ever-popular topic—love! There are spells to dream about whether or not true love will be

found, spells to dream about whether or not marriage is in the forecast, and spells to dream about what sort of person your future lover will be. One traditional spell calls for a pill to be made of a mixture of nutmeg, walnut, hazelnut, butter, and sugar. The pill is eaten before bed in order to induce dreams regarding the fortunes of your future lover. Dreams of thunder and lightning indicate the lover will be a traveler, while dreams of gold indicate that the lover will be especially wealthy. If the dream is noisy, it indicates the future lover will find a profession in a trade or craft. Another custom used to incite dreams to reveal your next sweetheart requires bay leaves to be placed on or under the pillow—and the future lover's face will appear in the dream. A different spell suggests carrying two pieces of lemon peel around all day, then rubbing the peels on the bedposts at night. This is believed to induce within the dream a vision of the future lover carrying a lemon in each hand.

Of course, not all traditional dream magick was focused on love. For the Pennsylvania Dutch, one charm to induce dreams of the future involved walking backwards through the front door on Halloween night, collecting a bit of grass or dirt, then retreating inside to wrap the dirt or grass in a piece of paper. The bundle was then placed under the pillow and slept on—and prophetic dreams would soon ensue. In Jewish magick tradition, though not at all sanctioned by the religion, one dream-magick procedure recommended lying over a grave and beseeching the dead to appear in a dream to answer any questions put forth. One early nineteenth-century text describes a formula for oracular dreaming used by ceremonial magicians: An image of an angel, named for the sun, is drawn on a piece of paper. Upon the angel is drawn a picture of one's self, and on this self, the name of what the person wishes to dream about is written. The paper is slept on, and whatever is therein indicated will appear in the dream.

Lucid Dreaming and Sleepcasting

"Lucid dreaming" is the term used to describe the phenomenon of becoming consciously aware during sleep, realizing that you're in the midst of a dream. With this awareness comes a wide range of possibilities, from astral travel to "sleepcasting"—performing magick in the dream world to affect the real world. The first step to lucid dreaming is becoming more intimate with your dream self and more involved with your dream time. An easy way to get started is to make an earnest attempt to remember your dreams. Get plenty of rest and eat right, but don't eat too soon before bedtime. Tell yourself that you intend to remember your dreams and that you intend to write them down when you awaken. Whether or not you remember your dream, make a note about it. With a little diligence and practice, you'll start remembering more and more of your dreams. Once you're doing that, work on becoming consciously aware during the dream, achieving a lucid state. Some people try to look at their hands when they're dreaming, because for some reason seeing your own body clues in the psyche that you are indeed still conscious and can freely think and act. I find it helps if I draw a glyph on the back of just one of my hands, a customized symbol designed to reflect whatever I wish to do in my dream time. Then when I'm dreaming, I will catch a glimpse of the symbol, and that will remind me that I am the one in control. Scent can also work exceptionally well for this purpose. Try blending some essential oils (jasmine, coconut, or myrrh are good choices), then anoint your temples just

before you go to sleep. Place a drop or two under your nose, as well. The scent can follow you into your dreams and remind you of your conscious awareness.

Once you reach the point where within your dreams you're aware of the fact that you're indeed dreaming, you can do all sorts of fun dream magick. If you'd like to try a little "sleepcasting," write down your magickal intention on a piece of paper, then sleep with this under your pillow. As you drift off to sleep, focus on that intention, and think about what your spell will be doing on the energetic plane—the "as above" component. In your dream, if you're lucky enough to enter a lucid state, focus again on your intention, gather needed resources or visit the place where your spell is to take effect. If you're not able to become aware while dreaming, don't worry—the simple act of writing down your goal, focusing on it before bedtime, and charging it with dreamy energies as you slumber will still go a long way toward helping accomplish your magickal wish.

Daydream Magick

Dream magick doesn't have to be kept in the dark. Daydreaming, fun and relaxing as it is, can also serve as an excellent way to practice and improve magickal skills. Dreaming in the light of day while fully awake, letting your thoughts drift into imagination and fantasy, refreshes the spirit and focuses the mind. When we're anxious, we're not able to cast magick very well, and daydreaming can soothe the nerves during or after a long and stressful day. Daydreaming also provides ideas for magick, inviting us to allow our hearts to reveal to us our truest, most secret desires. The most significant way daydreaming helps with magick, however, is in the dreaming itself. When we cast a spell, we often create a mental image of our magickal goal, and then we charge this image with emotional energy and intention. We do much the same thing when we daydream, letting our emotions mingle with our thoughts to create extraordinary visions of the reality we wish would come to be. The only difference is that we usually don't daydream intentionally; it's something that just happens, often when we should be focusing on something else! Daydreaming intentionally is a whole new animal. Try setting aside five to fifteen minutes each day to let your mind drift off into fantasy. Let the daydream become detailed and vivid, and allow it to carry on for a bit. Focus on making the image as clear as possible, and be sure your emotions are intense. When you've reached the end of the daydream, project your intention to make that dream a reality. By practicing daydreaming intentionally, you'll have a great new way to relax, recharge, and practice the mental and emotional discipline and artistry required for excellent magick.

Dream On

Our lives are often hectic, and many of us run around most of the time on little to no sleep. Dreaming is important, and if we don't make it a priority, our bodies, our sanity, and our magick can suffer. You know many ways to give dream magick (or daydream magick) a try, and you're bound to come up with many other methods as you start experimenting. Keep it fun, keep it fresh, and keep it adventurous. But also keep it relaxing. With the excitement that successful dream magick can bring, you might just discover a greater need and more opportunity to make dreaming a daily priority!

Wedding as Ritual

by Lisa Mc Sherry

Creating your own wedding can be incredibly complicated, confusing, and frustrating. That said, any "wonderful wedding" experience does not happen without a lot of careful planning, and the rewards for creating your own can be immense.

This article presumes that you want to create a wedding ceremony that honors or in some way incorporates the Divine, but not in a way that feels typical (aka, "traditional"). So, let's start with the basics: What makes a good ritual? At its most basic, a good ritual brings together the participants in a way that feels good, shares that positive energy all around, all the while accomplishing a stated purpose. I believe that by keeping this general definition in mind, you can create a wonderfully inclusive and special ritual to celebrate your relationship's transition to a new level.

You'll want to start planning your ritual as far in advance as possible, as having more time to pull all the pieces together will greatly reduce your stress.

Starting Points

Let's start at the beginning. When do you want your ritual? As with traditional weddings, timing is a core factor that influences many other decisions. In thinking about the date, consider whether you want to hold the ritual on or near a sabbat, a day sacred to your Deity, or one linked to marriage. Ostara, Beltane, and Litha all have positive associations for relationships, and I think Mabon and Yule would work as well, although you'd be stretching the symbolism a bit. Deities associated with marriage might include Hera, Juno, Aphrodite, Venus, Demeter, Janus, Freya, Freyr, Frigg, Yue-Lao, Bes, Hathor, Hymen, Kamedeva, Innana, Oshun, and Sjofn. They all have days of particular importance, and a little research can produce a nice list of potential wedding dates.

Once you've decided when, you'll want to choose where. The specific location is important, of course, but stay big picture for a moment: indoors or out? By temperament, we tend to prefer to worship in nature, but this may not be practical. Are any of your guests elderly or have special needs that make anything other than a smooth surface unusable? What is the typical weather around your chosen date, and how does it affect your planning? My fiancé and I wanted to hold our ritual on Beltane, which in the Seattle area is as likely to have heavy rain or sleet as sun. In addition, we both have elderly relatives who are not very mobile under the best of circumstances. In the end, we chose to have our ceremony indoors, but in a venue with a panoramic view overlooking Lake Washington to bring a strong sense of nature into the ritual. A friend held her ritual outdoors, but in a large park shelter in case of bad weather. Another friend held his ceremony in a civic building against tall windows that opened on to a splendid public garden. Selecting a date and finding a location are two of the biggest and most time-consuming decisions you'll have to make, and I believe you can't get them done soon enough.

Creating the Ritual

Having the timing and location decided will influence the style and format of your ritual. While not impossible, it feels dissonant to do an elaborate ritual with fifteen props and readings in the middle of a simple stone circle or field. Allow your surroundings to influence your ritual, and you'll start the energy flowing in a positive direction. Similarly, decide early on how obviously nontraditional you want your ritual to appear. Personally, I felt that we were inviting people from diverse backgrounds (including my fiancé's devout Presbyterian parents, my atheist father, and Pagan friends) and creating a comfortable atmosphere for all of them was a very important component.

One note, I do not recommend using your wedding ceremony as a "coming out" statement. People don't expect weddings to include possibly painful surprises, so it's far more respectful (and safer) to let loved ones know beforehand. A friend, the daughter of strict Catholics, sent Pagan-themed invitations, used the word "handfasting" instead of "wedding" and called her parents after they received the invita-

tion. While they were very unhappy about her choice, she was straightforward and told them "I will understand if you choose not to attend, but this is my wedding." (They chose to come, and they had a great time.) So be prepared to have honest conversations before the wedding if you want to be obvious about your spirituality.

Start tracking the symbols you feel support your theme. Some people avoid fertility images (eggs, rabbits, etc.) while others feel they are a necessary component. What energies do you and your partner want to bring into your new relationship? Wealth? Abundance? Joy? Use images from shared moments of your time together. Feel free to be funny or silly and even incorporate inside jokes. For us, the images of flying pigs were part of a long-standing joke, so we used them in various ways. Also, I met him when he was leading a D&D game, so our wedding cake "topper" was two minis, hand-painted by us, of a witch and a paladin.

One often-debated detail that varies greatly is the length of the ceremony. Based on my decades of ritual work, I would say that anything less than twenty minutes will feel too short to your guests, and if it goes longer than forty-five minutes, they will start to lose focus. A thirty-minute ritual is enough to have opening music leading to a processional, a greeting from the officiant, quarter calls (if you have them), three readings, a speech by the officiant, an exchange of vows and rings, some kind of symbolic unifying moment, a kiss, and the recessional.

We felt that we needed to call a circle to make our ritual sacred, but didn't need to get more obviously Pagan than that. We each took turns greeting the quarters, and worded them in a way that felt biblical (we were inspired by the "Song of Songs"), but were entirely our own.

His

I went to the east, to the crèche of the dawn,
and I heard my beloved calling my name.
Her voice was the singing of birds in the morning.

I went to the south, to the strike of noon,
and a great light appeared;
I saw my beloved clearly.
Her spirit was a bright flame that guided me home.

I went to the west, to the respite of evening,
and I found my beloved waiting for me by a cool river.
I took her hand and in it placed my heart.

I went to the north, to the home of midnight, and I made a place
for my beloved and I to put down roots.
Her grace is the willow, which weathers adversity and returns
stronger than before.

Hers

I went to the east, to the cradle of beginnings,
and I called out for my beloved,
and he answered.
His voice was the touch of a spring breeze.

I went to the south, to the bosom of passion,
and a great light appeared;
I saw my beloved clearly.
His spirit was the light of the sun itself, warming my path.

I went to the west, to the seat of emotions,
and I found my beloved waiting for me by a deep well.
I took his heart and gave him my own in exchange.

I went to the north, to the throne of abundance, and I found the
place where my beloved awaited me.
His strength is the oak, with deep strong roots, unshakable in the
face of adversity.

For those in the know, this was clearly a circle casting based on the four elements and in a typically Wiccan framework. For others, it was simply lovely poetry. (I later overheard my father telling my mother-in-law that he thought we'd borrowed from Kahlil Gibran, only to have her tell him that it was from the Bible. Success!)

We chose three readings that had great meaning for us and had other people read them. This allowed us to honor people who are special to us and gave us a bit of a break out of the limelight. Shakespeare is a wonderful resource, as are more modern poets. A Google search for "love poems" will give you a huge collection to choose from.

By the way, the only way to know how long the ritual will take is to rehearse it, complete with props. You don't need to read the actual words out loud (if you want to keep your vows private, for example), but you should substitute something similar in length. You can estimate length by planning for about a minute for each 100 words spoken, but nothing beats having a rehearsal—so make sure you schedule one.

Writing Your Vows

Your vows are the heart of the ritual, the sacred intention you make public, the binding you will voluntarily take upon yourself. They are also damn hard to write. Here are a few things you can do to make the process easier and the final results better. First, you both need to be involved—this is crucial—and decide whether you are writing them separately or working together on one set. Will you want to share them with each other before the ceremony? You will want to agree on a basic format and tone. Should it be lighthearted or deeply romantic? Completely original or borrowed from other sources? Finally, you'll want to agree on the structure: just vows, or perhaps a bit of a story to start?

It might be a good idea to schedule a date to talk about your vows. My fiancé and I enjoyed talking about our relationship and what marriage means to us both. Discussing the merits of traditional vows versus writing our own helped clarify what we were looking to say and hear.

A wedding is a performance, so remember your audience. Your vows cannot be so cryptic or salacious that people are confused or uncomfortable. Reading your vows out loud (to a mirror if not to another person) will help smooth your delivery, catch the places you might stumble, and let you hear the words that may not sound quite right when no longer confined to your head. When in doubt, be plain; the audience always loves genuine feeling.

Setting a deadline well in advance of your ritual for sitting down with your drafts and talking them through is a good idea. You don't need to share the exact words, but you'll want to check in with each other. If nothing else, make sure both of your vows are similar in tone and length.

Expect the Unexpected

Be flexible and allow for things to go wrong. A couple with a romantic dynamic of the knight and his lady found a gorgeous location in a local park, complete with a medieval-style stone tower and grove of oak trees surrounded by an acre of flowers. Two weeks before their wedding, a hurricane blew through and completely destroyed the area, uprooting the trees and destroying the flowers. They volunteered to be a part of the cleanup crew and were rewarded by being given an alternate location near that stone tower. It wasn't ideal, but their wedding pictures are amazing, and you'd never know that they had to improvise at the last minute. More importantly, they are still together a decade later.

∽

Creating your own wedding, especially one incorporating nontraditional beliefs, can be overwhelming, but doing so gives you the opportunity to make sure your guests *understand why they were there in the first place*—a point that can easily be lost in some traditional ceremonies. Crafting your own ritual can bring you the certain knowledge that what you and your partner have created is the perfect expression of your beliefs, your love for one another, manifested within the positive energy that any good ritual brings.

Sympathetic Magic
in Shirley Jackson's "We Have
Always Lived in the Castle"

by Shawna Galvin

As Mary Katherine Blackwood, or Merricat, the main character and narrator of Shirley Jackson's *We Have Always Lived in the Castle,* we see and hear about her various rituals. Her behavior sparked my interest and led me to discover sympathetic magic. In my findings, it made me wonder if many people practice sympathetic magic without knowing what it is.

It seems there is no single definition of sympathetic magic. Perhaps the most concrete explanation comes from social anthropologist Sir James George Frazer (1854–1941). In his 1922 book *The Golden Bough,* sympathetic magic is based on the assumption that a person or thing can be supernaturally affected through its name or an object representing it.

Within the story, Jackson weaves in sympathetic magic without saying what "it" is. Sympathetic magic can include superstition, ritual, spirituality, affirmations, visualization, and the use of good-luck charms. Before we see Merricat using sympathetic magic, she begins the story by introducing herself as Katherine Blackwood, who is eighteen years old and lives with her older sister Constance. She then goes on to say:

"I have often thought that with any luck at all, I could have been born a werewolf, because the two middle fingers on my hands are the same length, but I have had to be content with what I had."

Werewolves are not mentioned again. It could be that Merricat wished herself a werewolf because mythical Irish werewolf legends are shapeshifters who are protectors of children and the lost and wounded, which might translate into a sympathetic werewolf entity. As the story progresses, this theory makes sense.

Merricat likes her older sister Constance and says in a blunt manner: "Everyone else in my family is dead." This presents a greater mystery that lends to the manner in which she protects what is left of the family. As the story moves, we continue to follow Merricat and learn that her family—all but her older sister Constance, Uncle Julian (who perishes later in the story), and her black cat Jonas—had been poisoned by arsenic placed in the sugar bowl, which the deceased family members sprinkled on their berries and consumed one day at a meal.

The Blackwoods live in seclusion, except for Merricat who ventures into town twice a week to do errands. Local villagers do not like the family, and they mock Merricat whenever she is in town. She shields both her feelings and the Blackwood property through aspects of sympathetic magic.

For example, Merricat recalls the last time she brought home library books, which have been overdue since the family's deaths six years earlier—meaning Merricat was twelve when they all perished. Although she is fond of her home, Merricat tells how she despises her small town and its inhabitants by describing a "fine April morning" when she came out of the library, "the sun was shining and the false glorious promises of spring were everywhere, showing oddly through the village grime."

Merricat goes on to wish that she could walk home across the sky instead of passing through the village, which many can relate to. For instance, wishing for a direct bridge or road to take us to our destination so we can by pass the obstacles. In her case, the obstacles were the cruel villagers.

This passage shows how Merricat used visualizations to help her get through each obstacle she faces when going in and out of town. Many can relate to wishing to be somewhere else or imagining a bridge across the sky, yet, she builds on her techniques as the story progresses.

Next, Merricat looks back on how she stopped at Stella's coffee shop each week to demonstrate her pride while ignoring locals who taunted her and said unkind things about her family while she sat at the counter. "I put my hands quietly in my lap, I am living on the moon, I told myself. I have a little house all by myself on the moon." These affirmations are techniques she used to deal with adversity in the village. From there, she turned to superstition, a more common ritual of sympathetic magic as she reminisced about walking past Stella's. Merricat remembered a crack in the sidewalk and how it looked like a finger pointing. To her, the crack had always been there. She thought about how she used to carefully roller skate across that crack because touching it could "break our mother's back."

Merricat used several forms of sympathetic magic to turn her dreaded weekly trips into a game. We experience her ups and downs as she attempts to ward off the villagers' wicked words. At the end of recounting this trip to town, Merricat tells how she sort of teleported herself away when walking back home and was teased by a few children: "I was pretending that I did not speak their language; on the moon we spoke a soft liquid tongue, and sang in the starlight, looking down on the dead dried world; I was almost past the fence." Maybe her affirmations and visualizations were the closest she could come to saying a prayer to get through these obstacles.

~

Many believe that sympathetic magic can include prayer. When I was younger, my religious upbringing in a Roman Catholic family was full of ritual, ceremony, and prayer. I learned to believe in spirits, both good and evil, and that my religion could protect me from the latter. The use of objects such as the rosary and religious medallions with engravings of saints were used for protection, forgiveness, and healing. Now, two main prayers stay with me: "Our Father," and my favorite, "The Hail Mary," which I find myself chanting often—perhaps like a mantra.

Another way to relate to sympathetic magic is through healing energy practices such as Reiki (*Rei*—spiritual wisdom, *Ki*—life force), an ancient Japanese healing technique done by the laying on, or near, of hands. Reiki uses elements such as visualization, affirmations, prayer, sending healing energy, and positive thoughts, and it is performed with love and good intentions. On a family trip not long ago, I visualized a white light surrounding the plane, my family, and the people on board. I imagined angels or protective spirits sitting on the wings, which helped me feel better about traveling.

~

Throughout the story, there are hints of more sinister things that had taken place before the deaths of her family members. The reader is never really sure exactly what came before, but Merricat sheds a light on darker happenings within the family dynamics prior to their deaths. Within these implications, Merricat's will to do what she can to uphold what is left of her family and their property becomes more evident, such as the ritual of burying objects that are symbolic to her.

A powerful passage in *We Have Always Lived in the Castle* that reveals Merricat's sympathetic magic rituals is in chapter three when she reveals how she would examine her safeguards on Sunday mornings. She'd buried a "box of silver dollars by the creek, and a doll buried in the long field, and a book nailed to the tree in the pine woods." Merricat believed as long as they were where she had put them, then no one could get in to harm what was left of her family. She says she'd always buried things—the same way she always remembered the crack being in the sidewalk. It seems that her rituals and beliefs had forever been part of her life. She talked about how she once quartered the long field and buried something in each quarter to make the grass grow higher as she grew taller, so she would always be able to hide there. "I once buried six blue marbles in the creek bed to make the river beyond run dry."

Merricat continues to talk about burying items and how her sister Constance encouraged it by giving her treasure to bury when she was small, such as a penny or a ribbon. She even buried all of her baby teeth and hoped they would grow as dragons.

"All our land was enriched with my treasures buried in it, thickly inhabited just below the surface with my marbles and my teeth and my colored stones, all perhaps turned to jewels by now, held together under the ground in a powerful taut web which never loosened, but held fast to guard us."

Merricat's use of sympathetic magic includes belief in a mystical influence through these objects. She believes in human control of supernatural agencies or forces of nature, such as trying "to make the grass grow higher."

$\sim$

Jackson's story led me to explore other purposes and information about sympathetic magic. Its uses and beliefs can vary from person to person and may not be defined at all for many.

In essence, sympathetic magic is natural, easy to do, and often self-made. There is freedom and opportunity to conjure one's own magic and beliefs. Merricat's character made me think about some of the ways I'd been practicing sympathetic magic without prior knowledge of the term.

I own jewelry that was both given to me and inherited from my mother and grandmother, who have both passed on. There are particular pieces I wear on certain occasions and others I wear every day to keep their energy close to me, or for good luck. Other times I wear a specific stone, such as moonstone or amethyst for protection, positive energy, and even healing purposes. It is as though sympathetic magic is part of a natural belief system that can help navigate through mysteries and ideas about life, and perhaps even help get through challenging times.

Keeping memories of deceased friends and loved ones alive through personal possessions they left behind reveals other aspects of sympathetic magic; this is what Frazer called the "Law of Contagion," where objects that were once in contact with each other—such as a pair of gloves once worn by someone who passed on—continue to act on each other at a distance after the physical contact as been severed. Perhaps these objects are a bit like magic, maybe just for a memory, or hope that there is some energy and enchantment left in them.

Magic is sometimes viewed with suspicion—and practiced in isolation and secrecy—because it involves mystical elements or powers. When used for higher good, most believe that magic is intended for spiritual growth and enlightenment.

Faith in spirit guides is another way sympathetic magic might be viewed. My Uncle George, a Vietnam veteran was a guardian of mine in human form, and I believe he remains so in spirit. Most of my family members have passed on from illnesses, and I often pray to them, call on them to guide and protect me, or just feel their presence. Other times, I dream about them and write poetry or stories about them. This may be a form of sympathetic magic, because I believe they watch over and guide me.

Sympathetic magic is wide open for interpretation, but overall it seems to be a way to summon supernatural forces and entities for protection. Some people believe they can summon spirit messages through clairvoyant abilities. For example, those who claim to talk with spirits and pass on messages from them to others. This conviction helps them feel they are protected, influenced, and perhaps even being warned.

Merricat exhibits traces of having psychic abilities in the middle of the story. She repeats that "a change is coming" several times. This not only gives the reader a sense of foreshadowing, but also of Merricat's intuitive premonition. Soon, their long-lost, greedy cousin Charles appears on the Blackwood property and tries to take over. When he finds silver dollars that Merricat buried and witnesses some of her other rituals, he calls her a "crazy kid." Merricat views Charles as a ghost-demon, and we see her use a darker side of sympathetic magic as she wishes harm on those who harm her, and in extreme instances, acts on them.

Overall, Merricat may be an unreliable character, but the things she does—a sort of sympathetic magic witchcraft—are all to safeguard the Blackwood house and most of all herself, her sister, and the cat. Although Merricat seems to have good aims, more established practices might include defending and protecting against negative forces through sage smudging, visualizing white light, prayer, and refusing bad energy.

There is an overarching sense that Merricat may have been hurt both violently and emotionally in her past. She is a troubled young woman, and it is what we do not know about her or her history that makes one sympathize with her in this cruel situation she lives in. In some cases, her actions might be argued as self-defense. Other realms and practices of magic are woven into the events in this story and can be examined further.

Jackson suggests other magical elements such as spells, shapeshifting, and voodoo. The magic in this story stands on its own. It "just is" and doesn't "tell" everything, leaving plenty for the reader to interpret, imagine, and decide, and that is the true magic of *We Have Always Lived in the Castle*.

~

What some might take away from this journey into sympathetic magic is that it's a way of becoming more aware. It can be a reminder of how every thought and action is significant and connects to all things. Sympathetic magic is a way to repel or reject negativity in one's life and can help focus on spirituality, no matter what belief system a person holds. Sympathetic magic may be a means to help become more centered and grounded. It's a way to create and use positive energy and to pass it on.

A Stitch in Magic

by Charlie Rainbow Wolf

The deeper we get into our magical lifestyle, the more we realize that everything is intertwined. This allows us to delve even further into our beliefs and start to connect the mundane with the magical on many levels. For me, my favorites are gardening, cooking, and knitting.

Knitting—or crochet, or any other type of needlework—isn't just making an article when it is approached from a magical perspective. The number of stitches, the colors used, the patterns interwoven—they can all be chosen to mean something. This creates an even stronger bond between us, the item we are making, and the person for whom the item is being made.

When we create a piece of needlework, we put our own energies into it. We each have an energy field, an aura, and when we work with our hands, we are moving our energy field to manipulate the yarn or thread to create a stitch. That stitch then holds a residue of the energy that we used to create it. Psychometrists work with this type of vibration all the time. By holding something that belonged to a person, a psychometrist can read the energy signature on that item and tell you about the person that owned it.

It's not just about what we put into the item with our manual creativity. We can take it much farther than that. For a start, the colors can tell a story. Red speaks of passion, warmth, and vitality, while pink's message is of love and devotion. Greens are healing and blues cooling, while yellows are uplifting and communicative, and oranges are encouraging and protective. Purple is a very high spiritual color, white brings purity, and black brings grounding. Of course, people are always going to have a favorite color, or one that is associated with them. Embellishments for the item being made for them can always consist of complementary colors, each contributing their own color-encoded message.

The numbers are important when including magic in needlework, too. Every number means something. Ones symbolize new beginnings; it's not hard to see that one! Twos represent the duality in all things, which often comes with a choice. Threes indicate union, where things are starting to come together. Fours relate to foundations—the four corners of the earth, the four seasons, the stability of what we know. Fives bring with them changes, and often growing pains. They represent the realm of manifestation. Sixes have no real balance; they are three twos, or two threes, but have no real stability of their own. In numerology, sixes are a positive number and indicate a kind and loving nature, but there is not much strength or stamina here. Sevens are considered to be very magical indeed. There are mystical tales about someone being the seventh son of the seventh son, we talk about the Seven Wonders of the World, we hear about seventh heaven. Eights are very karmic. The symbol for infinity—sometimes called the lemniscate—is a number eight lying on its side. Eights, like fours, relate to foundations, but eights are not as rigid as fours. Eights also bridge the gap between the magical world and the material one. Nines are very mathematically unique; the three threes that multiply to make the nine create a geometric triangle. The energy of the number nine is humanitarian and forgiving.

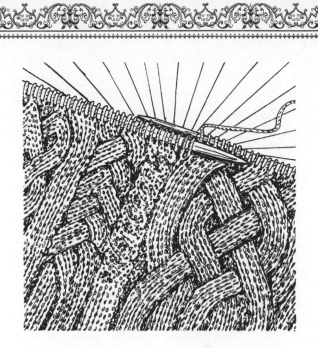

Using the above paragraph as a rough guide, it is easy to see that we can work the magic of numbers into most patterns. I enjoy working with stitch repeats, trying to get as many different combinations as I can into the piece being created so that I can include as much math-magic in it as possible. Planning the size and shape of the item to be made in this way can be fun, although somewhat challenging! That's usually not the end of the journey, though.

Once the size and shape have been determined, it's time to start working with individual stitches. These can be just blocks of color, random changes every so many rows or so many repeats, or they can be meaningful in and of themselves. Aran knitting has a very rich history of stitch patterns, with such wonderful names as "fivefold braid," "wheatsheaf," "tree of life," "blackberry stitch," "coin stitch," "moss stitch," and more. It's been said that these patterns were once a closely guarded secret, preserved and passed from generation to generation. Each of these pattern combinations was unique, so that the wearer of the garment could be identified by those who knew how to interpret the patterns.[1] It doesn't take much of a stretch of the imagination to see how these can be planned into the needlework to convey messages of their own. A lap blanket for someone on hard times might include the wheatsheaf stitch, the blackberry stitch, and the coin stitch to wish the recipient enough to eat and a coin to spend. The tree of life might be worked on a prayer shawl for someone recuperating from an illness, so that they might be reflections of the prayers for recovery and longevity.

Even when working with color, numerical values can be important. It's very easy to use graph paper to design stitch patterns. Traditional Fair Isle, or stranded work, uses this method. Like the cabled patterns, there are popular Fair Isle patterns that have stood the test of time, including trees, diamonds, and snowflakes. The beauty of designing from scratch is that it is possible to include anything in the pattern. Names, dates, planetary symbols, runestaves, and more frivolous—but equally magical—items can be drawn on graph paper and used in the construction of a needlework item.

Both the traveling cable stitches and the stranded colored stitches take a bit of patience to design, because we're working with multiple sets of numbers. Try to get numbers that are divisible by many factors. For example, a pattern worked over 28 rows can be divisible by 2, 4, 7, and 14. That means that another

---

1 Hollingsworth, Shelagh. *The Complete Book of Traditional Aran Knitting.* London, England: B. T. Batsford, 1982.

pattern worked over four rows would fit seven times in one pattern repeat, or that a pattern worked over 14 rows would fit twice over three pattern repeats. It sounds complicated, yes, but once you start working with it, it gets highly addictive!

Knitting and crochet are not the only ways that we can create magic in our needlework. The numbers and colors can be incorporated in pieces of embroidery, crewel work, beadwork, or cross-stitch. I once had a friend who made little framed cross-stitch caricatures for all her friends. Yes, they were whimsical and fun, but she also used the math-magic and the colors to enhance the piece, so that the recipient was given a truly unique work of art.

~

The magic doesn't stop when the piece is finished and with its new owner. I still use my mother's knitting needles, the ones on which she knit me a cape when I was eight years old. Every time I cast on a project, I feel her energy close, her hands holding mine as I manipulate the wool into a garment to give to a loved one, or a toy to share with a child.

All things are in all things, and the more magical our lives become, the more we realize that everything is connected. The energy that we put into making something stays with it long after it is complete. Whether it is yarn work or thread work, whether it is a garment to be worn or a decorative item to be displayed, the finished piece is a lingering reminder of the affection that we put into every stitch. With a little focus, we can turn this into a powerful prayer that has the potential to continue sharing the gift of love, long after we have departed.

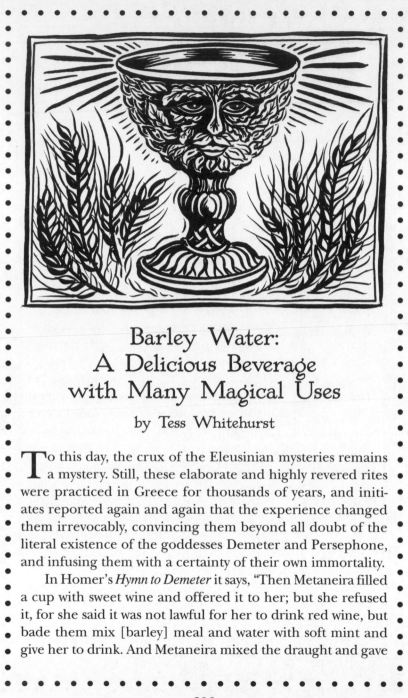

Barley Water:
A Delicious Beverage
with Many Magical Uses

by Tess Whitehurst

To this day, the crux of the Eleusinian mysteries remains a mystery. Still, these elaborate and highly revered rites were practiced in Greece for thousands of years, and initiates reported again and again that the experience changed them irrevocably, convincing them beyond all doubt of the literal existence of the goddesses Demeter and Persephone, and infusing them with a certainty of their own immortality.

In Homer's *Hymn to Demeter* it says, "Then Metaneira filled a cup with sweet wine and offered it to her; but she refused it, for she said it was not lawful for her to drink red wine, but bade them mix [barley] meal and water with soft mint and give her to drink. And Metaneira mixed the draught and gave it to the goddess as she bade. So the great queen [Demeter] received it to observe the sacrament." Historians believe that ancient Greeks would have recognized this immediately as one of the most essential practices of the Eleusinian mysteries: the abstinence from wine, and the drinking of a very specifically prepared barley water and mint potion, known as *kykeon*. (Interestingly, some renowned experts, such as chemist Albert Hoffman and mythologist Carl Kerényi, have hypothesized that the barley used for the mysteries helped cause intense spiritual experiences because it was riddled with ergot, the parasitic fungus that inspired and helped formulate LSD. But please note: I am just mentioning this for informational purposes! If you happen to find to barley containing ergot, DO NOT ingest it in any form, as it can cause violent illness and even death.)

The Magic of Barley Water

Barley water in and of itself (even without hallucinogenic properties) is very magical stuff, especially when prepared with reverence and intention. It serves as a lovely offering or libation to the goddess Demeter, and it can be employed as a sacred beverage during ritual (in lieu of wine) or a grounding beverage after ritual (in lieu of ale or beer). What's more, it's delicious, and drinking it regularly has a ton of health benefits. It detoxifies the body, supports clear and glowing skin, helps heal bladder and kidney infections, clears mucus, soothes the throat, and reduces inflammation. It also has a cooling effect on your system, which comes in very handy while exercising or spending time in warmer climates. (I'd reach for it as a thirst-quencher before a sports drink any day!) Some studies even indicate that it might help prevent diabetes, bowel cancer, and high cholesterol.

Other ingredients commonly added to barley water are mint, honey, and lemon—all uplifting, energizing, and clarifying magical ingredients. In ancient Greece, the "mint" was most likely pennyroyal, but for safety's sake (and a pleasant flavor!), don't use pennyroyal, as it can be toxic. Spearmint, peppermint, or a similarly innocuous mint will do the trick.

Here's how you can make barley water at home.

Magical Barley Water Recipe

Ingredients:

1 cup pearl barley
2 lemons, scrubbed clean
1 bunch fresh mint
8 cups water
Organic honey, or another sweetener of your choice, to taste
(perhaps start with 3 tablespoons)

Begin by lighting a white candle and placing it on or near the stovetop. Call on the goddess Demeter and invoke her divine assistance by saying,

Goddess Demeter, I call on you.
Thank you for this barley, and all these ingredients.
Please bless them.
Please bless my efforts.
As I prepare this potion, please infuse it with your magical essence.
May all who partake of it be cleansed, refreshed, renewed,
*   inspired, and blessed.*
Great mother Goddess, as I prepare this kykeon, I honor you.
Great mother Goddess, from deep within my heart, for all your
*   abundance and bounty, I thank you.*
Blessed be.

Rinse the barley (some say this might not be necessary, but I just do it to be on the safe side) and place it in a usable cauldron or large cauldron-like pot. Add the water and bring it to a boil. Cover and reduce heat to low. Simmer for 45 to 60 minutes until the barley is soft enough to eat. While it's simmering, grate the lemon peels and juice the lemons. When you remove the cauldron from the heat, add the lemon zest (grated peels) and steep, covered, for an additional 20 minutes. Drain. Combine with sweetener and transfer to a pitcher or bottles to cool. Add the lemon juice. To serve, crush a small handful of mint in

a mortar and pestle, place it in a chalice or glass, and pour the barley water over the top. (Ice is optional.)

But wait! Don't discard the barley. First, take a small handful and go outside. Place it on the earth (perhaps at the base of a tree) as an offering to Gaia, Demeter's mother and the Earth Herself. Then save the rest of the barley to eat. You can add it to salads or soups, use it as you would rice or risotto, or prepare it with sweetener to eat as a hot breakfast cereal.

Magical Uses for Barley Water

Simply preparing barley water magically (as above) and drinking it regularly can boost health and to help fortify an everyday magical mindset. As previously mentioned, it can also be a perfect altar offering or libation to the goddess Demeter, as well as a ritual drink or post-ritual grounding beverage. And considering that barley water's ingredients lend themselves to magical intentions as diverse as prosperity, clarity, creativity, cleansing, grounding, vitality, and goddess energy—barley water can be employed in countless magical ways. Here are a few ideas to get you started.

Household Prosperity Ritual

On a Thursday during a waxing moon, brew a batch of magical barley water, as above. Place the candle in the center of the dining table and serve a glass of barley water to every member of your household. Before drinking, say:

> Great Goddess Demeter, Grain Goddess, and Earth Mother Gaia,
> We call on you and ask that you infuse us with your abundance
>   and sustenance.
> May our wealth multiply, our blessings expand, and our fortune
>   endlessly grow.
> In all ways may we prosper and thrive.
> Thank you.

As you drink, go around the table clockwise and take turns sharing things—big or small—for which you are grateful.

Goddess Alignment

Brew a batch of magical barley water on a Friday. As it simmers, direct your palms toward the cauldron and say, "Great Goddess, I call on you. Please infuse this potion with powerful feminine balance and strength. As I consume it, may it strengthen the health of my womb, my inner equilibrium, my beauty, and my feminine power. Thank you." Drink regularly.

Creativity Boost

While crushing the mint in your mortar and pestle for a glass of barley water, chant, "I now release the fresh, inspiring spirit of mint!" After preparing your beverage, but before you drink it, hold it in both hands and visualize it filled with very bright golden light with rainbow swirls and sparkles. Say, "Great Mother Goddess, Divine Creatrix, I call on you. As you breathe beauty and magic into all beings, may I breathe beauty and magic into the world through my creations. As I ingest this beverage, may I ingest your powers of infinite creativity. Thank you."

Grounding Tonic

While preparing the barley water, just before you put the barley in your cauldron, take a measuring cup containing the barley outside, spread a clean, undyed cloth (such as muslin) on the earth near the base of a tree, and place the measuring cup on top of it. Kneel and visualize the earth energy coming up from the soil to bless and consecrate the barley. Say, "Earth Mother Gaia, please recognize this barley as your child: as the fruit of your womb. Please consecrate it and activate it with your deeply grounding, nourishing, and stabilizing energy. Thank you."

Clarity Potion

Once the barley water is prepared, add two drops of apophyllite and one drop of fluorite essence. (These are gem elixirs that can be purchased from Alaskan Essences online or at metaphysical supply stores, or you can make them if you know how to do so safely.) Hold the pitcher or bottle in both hands and visualize it filled with blindingly bright white light. Say, "Great Goddess, I call upon your wisdom and your clarity. May I see and know the truth in all things. May I see and know just what to do. Thank you."

For Further Study:

Chevallier, Andrew. *Encyclopedia of Herbal Medicine*. New York: Dorling Kindersley, 1996.

Hoffman, Albert, Carl A.P. Ruck, and R. Gordon Wasson. *The Road to Eleusis: Unveiling the Secret of the Mysteries*. Berkeley: North Atlantic Books, 2008.

Homer. Trans. Hugh G. Evelyn-White. *Hymn to Demeter*. Cambridge, MA: Loeb Classical Library, 1914.

Illes, Judika. *The Element Encyclopedia of Witchcraft*. London: Harper Element, 2005.

Kerényi, Carl. Eleusis: *Archetypal Image of Mother and Daughter*. Princeton, NJ: Princeton University Press, 1967.

Brigid's Well
Kildare, Ireland

by Lisa Mc Sherry

Recently I had the pleasure of visiting Ireland, land of my ancestors. While there, I specifically visited a number of sacred places, looking to immerse myself in the land's rich history of spirituality. The one I was most looking forward to visiting was Brigid's Well.

There are a number of wells all over Ireland linked to St. Brigid of early Irish Christian history. Although the saint likely never lived, she was associated with agriculture, especially cows. Her feast day is February 1; this same day is also known as Imbolc and was originally associated with the Celtic fire goddess Brigid. Archeologists indicate that some of the wells dedicated to St. Brigid are Celtic in origin and were once sites of fertility rites or other kinds of Pagan rituals. After doing my research, I chose to visit the one located outside of Kildare because it wasn't as famous as other wells, and there is a local group—the Brigidine Order—who still tend Her flame.

Sacred wells are rarely human artifacts, but may have structural elements added to them (likely to provide better access to the well). Originally sacred to the earth goddess, many have been Christianized by the Catholic Church by associating them with female saints. The term "holy well," according to several online sources, refers to any water source of limited size (such as pools and natural springs, as opposed to lakes or rivers) that has some significance in the local folklore. This can be a particular name, a role in a local legend, healing qualities ascribed to the water due to an association with a guardian spirit or Christian saint, or a because a ceremony or ritual that uses the well site as a focal point. It has been said that all wells are sacred to the Goddess, as they are doorways to the Underworld and the womb of the Earth. People have visited these sacred wells for healing and divination, utilizing the emergence of living water as a tangible symbol of generation and purification. Interestingly enough, Christians [or Catholics?] visit these wells for the same purpose despite the co-option that has occurred. Often they don't even hide the original infrastructure around a well—they expand upon what already exists. The contrast can be striking.

Out from town, down a road, turning into a lane, I knew only that I was in the middle of Ireland's famous horse country. Tall hedges concealed stone walls that had been laid hundreds of years before, and just when I thought I might be lost, the lane ended at a small cul-de-sac. A brightly babbling brook flowed between the car park and the small park that contains Her well. Someone

had been doing some gardening: bright flowers bloomed in lovlingly weeded plots on either side of the wooden bridge over the brook. A tall stone column with a hollowed opening stands just inside and to the left. It is a fairly modern construction, and mostly dedicated to the Catholic Mary, with votive offerings, plastic flowers, and worn pictures sheltering inside the hollow. It feels remarkably like an altar. A sign nearby reads "Tobar Bríde: say the rosary at the station stones."

A modern well, complete with a life-sized bronze statue of Brigid is to the right, across the brook, which flows from a well covered by a stone arch. Her cross is carved into the capstone and painted white to strongly contrast with the dark stone. Water flows from two "shoes," which some have likened to breasts. The use of brick and hewn stone reveals its comparatively young age, as does the statue. St. Brigid holds a crosier, wears a cross, and holds a flame in her hand—once again, a mingling of her ancient lineage and her Christian reinterpretation. In the center of the park, a series of five stones follow the path of the underground stream and lead you to the original well, enclosed and protected by stone. An equal-armed stone cross sits above it—more closely resembling the astrological sign for earth than the Christian cross.

Behind the well, several trees were covered with "clootie rags"—strips of cloth, some braided or curled, and fetish objects, all clearly part of some ritual observance. (The name "clootie" comes from the word for cloth.) One tree was nearly covered in the rags, some brightly colored, others faded by time. I'd never heard of this practice before I went to Ireland, and when I asked a local about it, I was charmed by the answer.

"Oh yes, that's an old tradition. You take a bit o' cloth—it has to be good cloth, something natural, something you love—and you dip it in the well, and then tie it to a tree. But not just any tree! No, it's got to be a whitethorn [hawthorn], or maybe an ash tree. If your spirit is true, Brigid'll take your pain away."

The hawthorn tree (sceach gheal in Irish) plays an important role in Celtic mythology. Thomas the Rhymer met the Fairie Queen by one, and of course there is the famous tree planted on Glastonbury Tor by Joseph of Arimathea (uncle of Virgin Mary). Legends and lore tell us that the Fey often make their homes in hawthorn trees, and more than one field we passed had a wide swath of grass untouched around a lone tree in its center. It is tremendous to realize that this practice—one clearly from pre-Christian times—continues to this day.

There are several benches here, inviting one to sit and be still, enjoying the fresh air, the sounds of birds, and the slight scent of flowers and grass. In a blatant melding of old and new, one is invited to pray the Five Virtues of Brigid at each of the standing stones while walking round them clockwise seven times. The virtues vary a bit, but the ones I resonated best with are:

Stone #1: Brigid of the land
Stone #2: Brigid as peacemaker
Stone #3: Brigid as hearth-keeper (keeps the fire lit)
Stone #4: Brigid as healer
Stone #5: Brigid as contemplative

Brigid's Well is a place of great peace. In a land with a living history, where poets and Druids both turn to their connection with the land to express their spirituality, it is awe-inspiring to stand in a place sacred to the Goddess that is still actively used. When I reached down, a bit precariously, to drink from the well, I realized that I had joined a long line of my ancestors. We all had dipped into the same waters; we all whispered our supplications, our prayers, our gratitude. Like those before me, I left the Brigid's Well renewed by the power of the land.

Ireland's Sacred Wells

There are many sacred wells in Ireland, here is a list by county, according to *Ireland for Visitors* to get you started on your own sacred tour:

Clare County: St. Brigid's Well, Liscannor; Magh Adhair, Quin; Eye Well, Burren; Tooth Well, Burren; Margaret's Well, Ennis; St. Augustine's Well, Kilshanny.

Cork County: St. Olan's Well, Aghbullogue; Tobrid Well, Millstreet, Ballinspittle, Inchigeela; Sunday's Well and Mary's Well, Walshestown; St. Finbar's Well, Gougane Barra.

Kerry County: Well of the Wethers, Ardfert; St. Dahlin's, Ballyheige; St. John's Well, Dingle; St. Erc's Well, Listowel; St. Eoin's Well, Listowel; St. Michael's Well, Ballymore West; Lady Well, Ballyheige.

Kildare County: Earl's Well, Kildare; St. Brigid's Well, Kildare; Father Moore's Well, Kildare.

Meath County: Tobar Patraic, Ardmulchan; St. John's Well, Warrenstown; Tara (Neamnach, Toberfin, and Leacht), Castlebye.

Roscommon County: Tober Oglalla, Tulsk; St. Lassair's Well, Lough Meelagh; St. Attracta's Well, Monasteraden.

Sligo County: Tobernault, Sligo; St. Brigid's Well, Cliffony; Tullaghan Well, Tullaghan; St. Patrick's Well, Dromard; St. Patrick's Well, Aughris; The Bog, The Culleens.

Conjuring Up a Good Night's Sleep

by Monica Crosson

Sleep on sleep on another hour
I would not break so calm a sleep
To wake to sunshine and to show'r
To smile or weep...

This is the first stanza of Edgar Allan Poe's Poem entitled "To_____," a haunting poem that first appeared in the *Baltimore Saturday Visiter* on May 11, 1833. It was addressed to an anonymous woman and signed "Tamerlane." It is essentially a lullaby.

As a child, these were the words that sent me blissfully into dreamland. I remember being tucked under heavy blankets as a soft breeze played with the lace curtains through my open window and my mother's soft voice as she delivered the ethereal words of Poe. My goal was to stay awake to hear that fateful last line:

...But, O, thy spirit, calm, serene, must wake to weep.

I never did.

Sometimes I long for those days when I fought to stay awake long enough to hear a few stanzas of a poem. But alas, it's the small demons that keep me stirring, sometimes long into the wee hours of morning. They go by such names as "late mortgage," "youngest needs braces," "brakes need replacing," and "parent/teacher conference that went awry."

But being a practical yet creative witch, I have done my research, gathered my supplies, and put together a few techniques that have been successful for me. Remember, if you have chronic insomnia that lasts more than a week, consult your physician. These charms, spells, and brews are intended to help ease occasional sleeplessness.

Herbal Sleep and Dream Pillows

Dream/sleep pillows have been in use to induce peaceful sleep, enhance dreams, encourage dream memory, and protect against nightmares for centuries. No matter the reason, herbal pillows are beneficial for anyone.

To prepare an herbal pillow, select a piece of fabric, preferably cotton or another natural fiber. This is a nice way to use leftover fabric scraps. Wash and dry the fabric. Don't use a scented detergent or fabric softener—it will take away from your herbal mix. Now, cut it into whatever shape you wish. Of course, squares and rectangles are the easiest, but go ahead and get a little creative. Moon and star shapes are fun and relatively easy. If you're doing this for a child, have them draw a simple pattern, or if you're an adept seamstress, try a more complicated drawing that you can replicate. Making pillows is a great way to turn artwork into something special.

Next, create a blend of sleep- or dream-inducing botanicals from the lists below or craft your own mixture with fragrant herbs that you find especially calming or relaxing to use in dream magick. With the right sides of the fabric together, stitch along the edges, leaving a ¼-inch seam allowance and making sure to

leave an open space along one side. Once finished stitching, flip the pillow out through the open space and fill with your herbal blend. Finish the pillow by hand stitching the open area shut. You can embellish it with embroidered moons, spirals, or runes. Sew buttons or add lace—you decide. Remember, be creative.

Sleep and dream pillows can be tucked or pinned inside or under your pillow or placed next to pillows where they will release their fragrance throughout the night.

Here is a charm to say as sew your last few stitches:

Restful sleep come to me,
Release me from anxiety.
As I stitch, this spell is done,
As I will it, let it harm none.

Sleep Pillows

Sleep pillows are great for anyone who has difficulty falling asleep. For a blend that supports a deep, peaceful sleep, blend any of the following:

Balsam fir needles: Relaxing, soothing.

Catnip: Relaxing, helps bring deep sleep.

Chamomile: Calming, relaxing, and keeps bad dreams away.

Cinquefoil: A restful sleep or to dream of a new lover.

Hops: Relaxing and peacefulness.

Lavender: Soothing, relaxing, induces sleep, and relieves headaches.

Lemon balm: Eases stress, anxiousness and nervous feelings. Good for insomnia and relieves headaches.

Linden: Promotes sleep.

Rose petals: Brings warmth and love to a sleep or dream mix.

Rosemary: Encourages a deep, restful sleep and keeps away bad dreams.

Thyme: Ensures pleasant sleep, drives away nightmares.

Marjoram: Calms restlessness and nervousness.

Below are three combinations that have worked well for me in particular situations.

Stress Tamer: Takes the edge off when stress has you in its grip.
½ cup hops
½ cup mugwort
⅛ cup sweet marjoram

Out Like a Light: If you're looking for a deep, restful sleep, this is the mix for you.
½ cup lavender flowers
¼ cup hops
¼ cup mugwort

Blues Blend: The blues got you down? Try this blend to ease melancholy.
½ cup sweet marjoram
¼ cup rose petals
¼ cup mint
1–2 whole cloves

Dream Pillows

Whether you want to enhance your dreams or protect against nightmares, blend any of the following:

Anise: To prevent nightmares and to ensure pleasant dreams.

Bay: To induce dreams of a prophetic nature.

Catnip: Relaxing, induces sleep, used in dream pillows to dream of love.

Cedar: Used to dream of love.

Chamomile: Calming, relaxing, and said to keep bad dreams away.

Cinquefoil: To assure restful sleep or to dream of a new lover.

Clove: Brings warmth and an exotic feeling to dreams.

Hops: Relaxing, brings peacefulness.

Jasmine: For restful sleep and pleasant dreams.

Lavender: Soothing, relaxing, eases headaches, and induces sleep.

Marigold: Induces dreams of a prophetic nature and protection against black magick through dreams.

Mistletoe: Prevent nightmares and insomnia.

Morning glory: To safeguard your sleep against nightmares.

Mugwort: Induces dreams of a prophetic nature, enhances lucid dreaming, and helps with remembering of dreams.

Peppermint: "Compels one toward sleep," induces dreams of a prophetic nature enhances clarity and vividness in dreams.

Rose: Brings warmth and love; may be used to evoke romantic dreams.

Rosemary: To prevent nightmares and to bring deep sleep.

Sage: Helps makes dreams come true.

Sweet woodruff: Protection from nightmares.

Thyme: Drives away nightmares and ensures a restful sleep.

Valerian: To promote a peaceful atmosphere.

Vervain: To prevent nightmares.

Wooly betony: Keeps negative influences at bay. Prevents nightmares from interfering with your sleep.

Yarrow: Induces prophetic dreams.

Below are combinations that have worked well for me in three dreamtime situations.

Nightmare Be-Gone: This is a mix I made for my daughter when she was having bad dreams. She designed and sewed her own pillow in the shape of a ghost with big, black button eyes.

¼ cup rose petals

¼ cup rosemary

⅛ cup lavender flowers

⅛ cup hops

A Little Romance: If you want to stir dreams of a sensual nature, try this mix.

1 cup rose petals
2–3 whole cloves
¼ cup peppermint
¼ cup catnip

Dream Remembrance Mix: This mix encourages dream recall while also providing a restful sleep.

1 cup mugwort
¼ cup lavender

Tea Time

Besides being consumed as medicine, tea has been used to dye fabrics and fiber, create aromatic and healing baths, and flavor foods, soups, and stews since prehistoric times.

Sacred medicinal tea has also been used for thousands of years by shamans and other magickal practitioners as a way of connecting to divinity and receiving spiritual guidance. In our more recent history, tea has been consumed, not only for its medicinal qualities, but just for the sheer pleasure of it. The two recipes I have included support sleep and induce sweet dreams, as well as taste wonderful.

While your tea steeps, try this charm.

Anxious thoughts
You tried your best,
But now it's time for
My mind to rest.
By the power of herb, root, and leaf,
Time for me to have some peace.

Now sit in a favorite chair with some relaxing music and enjoy.

Nighty-Night Tea

2 tablespoons hops
1 teaspoon lavender, rosemary, thyme, and mugwort
1 tablespoon chamomile
1 pinch of valerian root

Take a teaspoon of the mixture and pour 1 cup of hot water. Cover and let steep five minutes and then strain. Makes 8 servings. Store in airtight container for later use.

Sweet Dreams Tea

1 tablespoon dried lemon balm
2 teaspoons dried peppermint
1 teaspoon fennel seeds
1 teaspoon dricd rose petals
1 teaspoon dried lavender flowers
2 slices dried licorice root

Place herbs and spices into a mortar and crush with a pestle until roughly combined. Take one teaspoon of mixture and place it in a mug. Pour about one cup of boiling water over the herbs and steep for five minutes. Makes approximately eight servings. Store in an airtight container for later use.

If you just don't have time to make your own blends, there are some great tea blends available online. My favorites are from Honey Bee Holistics, a shop that uses local and organic ingredients. They have a great tea that combines chamomile, lavender, and lemon balm.

Bedroom Reclaiming Spell

It's a busy world for the modern practitioner. With the demands of work and family, it's hard to make time for ourselves. To make time, we usually end up sacrificing our sleep. One hundred years ago, the average person slept 9½ hours per night. By the 1960s, it had dropped to 8 hours per night. Now, the average person only gets about 7 hours (or less) per night.

Sleep and dreaming were sacred to the ancients. The Greeks would visit temples to perform various religious rites that included sleep, hoping to have a dream that assured their good health.

With so many of us misusing our bedrooms as offices or entertainment centers, it's no wonder it's hard for us to "shut down" when we try to sleep. Playing a video game or finishing up some work on computer before bed may keep you awake long after you turn the computer off. Our bedrooms need to be designated as a place of rest, and it's time to reclaim them as scared space.

For this spell you will need:
One blue (healing, sleep) or white (all purpose) tealight
A small bundle of lavender
A white feather or small cast swan (symbol of the Goddess)
Moonstone (restful sleep)

> **Timing:** Waxing or Full Moon/Monday
> **Goddess:** Caer Ibormeith, Celtic Goddess of sleep and dreams

Before you begin, take the time to give your room a thorough cleansing. Wash all of your linens, and if possible, dry them outside on a line. Dust top to bottom and finish up by washing the windows and the floors. Now that it is clean, it's time to treat this room as a sacred place. Remove the television and/or computer and replace them with a few favorite books—or possibly a dream journal. Bring in fresh flowers, candles, incense, or anything else that comforts you and lets your senses know this is a space for rest.

On your nightstand or dresser arrange your altar. Make sure to place your tealight in a fire-safe container. Cast your circle. Now light your candle and say:

Swan Goddess of sleep and dreams,
My blankets wilt and anxious shadows creep,
Keeping me from a good night's sleep.
Send me your song of restful slumber,
And as it's sung—my anxiousness sundered.
I have reclaimed this room, the spell is spun,
As I will it, shall it harm none.

Close your circle and let your candle burn out on its own. Keep your altar set up as reminder that your room is a place of calm and rest.

The Ritual of Bathing

There is nothing more relaxing than a long hot soak in a bath. In Roman times, bathing was a communal activity conducted in public facilities that were more reminiscent of our modern-day spas. They were places for social interaction—a kind of community center where people could discuss business or just gossip about the neighbors.

Bathing has also been used as a ritual tool. Royalty, religious leaders, and magickal practitioners have bathed in waters infused with oils and herbs or milk and honey as a form of purification—cleansing both mind and spirit—for thousands of years. Many Pagan traditions today recommend ritual bathing before any sabbat, esbat, or major spellworking.

I've included a simple ritual bath that you can do any time (including a bath salt recipe that will be sure to leave you feeling relaxed and ready for a good night's sleep).

Goodnight Moon

1 cup Epsom salt
2 cups sea salt
½ cup baking soda
10 drops lavender essential oil
2 parts chamomile flowers
1 part lemon balm
1 part catnip

Pour all ingredients into a large bowl and lightly mix with your hands. As you mix, infuse your bath salts and herbs with

The power of this herbs

Wash peace over me

As I will so mote it be

positive energy. Keep stored in an airtight jar until ready for use. Makes enough for two to three uses.

On the night of your bath, gather as many candles as you like and place them safely around your bathroom. This is also the time to set up a stereo if you would like to listen to some relaxing music. Burning incense is also a nice idea; I would recommend frankincense for its healing properties related to relieving conflicts and stresses within the body. It is known to bring about a state of peace and calm.

Fill the tub with water as hot as you can stand. While the tub fills, fill a muslin drawstring bag with some of your bath salt mixture. Knot the drawstring three times, saying:

The power of these herbs (first knot)
Wash peace over me (second knot)
As I will, so mote it be (third knot)

Place the muslin bag in your bath. Light all your candles and turn on the music. Maybe sprinkle a few chamomile flowers directly into the tub. It's not only relaxing, but the flowers leave your skin with a soft glow. Turn out the lights.

As you immerse yourself in the bath, feel all the tension and stress leave your body. Focus on this. Imagine all that negativity draining out of every pore. The bath is relaxing and leaves you clean—body, mind, and spirit. As you get out, imagine your anxiety draining with the bath water. Dry off as usual and then spoil yourself with your favorite luxurious body lotion or oil.

Good Night

Well, I think it's time for bed. Now that you have relaxed in the tub and enjoyed a cup of tea, it's time to cozy up under crisp, clean sheets. Take in the scent of your newly reclaimed room, be it fresh flowers or incense.

The candlelight dances and flickers across your walls and the silence envelops you with downy wings. Let the silence and candlelight work their magick as you read a few pages from a favorite book or record your thoughts in a journal.

Are you feeling drowsy now? Time to extinguish your candles and lay your head on your pillow—don't forget the dream pillow you made. Now is the time for its magick to take effect. What dreams will you weave tonight? I hope they're lovely. Now sleep…

Tarot's Crystal Allies

by Lunaea Weatherstone

Tarot is a tool that brings understanding and insight, helps clarify intentions, and suggests solutions. Doing a tarot reading opens a window of wisdom through which you can contemplate your next actions. But what happens when you put the cards back in their box and head out into the world? How can you take that reading and make its message more tangible? One way is with the use of crystal allies.

From ancient times, humans have associated certain minerals with magical, spiritual, or symbolic power. The lore of gems alone fills many volumes, ranging from crown jewels to religious icons to tales of curses that follow a stone from owner to owner. But it's not just precious gems that hold this ancient planetary power. All stones and crystals have energies that assist on the physical and etheric planes.

The art of working with crystals and stones involves a combination of study and intuition. Crystal work is similar to working with tarot cards and uses the same skills: sensitivity to nuance, understanding of symbolism in color and structure, and willingness to trust the flashes of insight that come without second-guessing yourself. Combining tarot and crystals forms a talismanic alliance. Each tarot card can be associated with a stone that holds its essential energy, or in the case of negative cards, a stone whose energy works to protect or heal. Connecting tarot cards with stones allows you to learn more about each of them, as their messages and helpful energies are magnified. This article offers some suggestions to get you started.

Generally, there are two ways to work with the tarot: you either choose the cards randomly, face down, or you choose the cards consciously, face up, finding the ones that speak to your situation and illustrate its essential nature. The difference between these two methods might be summarized as you either know what's going on (conscious choice) or you don't know (divination). Crystal allies can assist you with both.

Conscious Choice

Choosing a card consciously can be an affirmation, a meditation, or an ingredient in magical spellwork. Let's look at examples of each of these and how you can include a crystal ally to enhance the work.

Affirmation

Affirmations are simple sentences that enhance positive thinking. They are phrased in the present tense whether they are currently happening or not. If you want to affirm good health, for example, you could say "I enjoy perfect health" even if you are ill at the time. If you are lack self-confidence when meeting new people, you could affirm that "I make new friends easily." Notice that affirmations always use positive language without mentioning the actual problem. Don't say "I no longer have crushing debt," but rather "I have all the money I need to meet my needs." The classic way to use affirmations is to write them down and place them where you will see them often, such as taped to your bathroom mirror or your desktop computer. By repeating the affirmation, you

make it part of your belief system, which gives the universe the opening it needs to make it a reality for you.

Let's use that last affirmation as an example of creating a tarot talisman to amplify its energy. "I have all the money I need to meet my needs" can be represented by the Empress, among whose qualities is the overflowing of material wealth and well-being. Like a loving mother, the Empress wants all wonderful things to come to you. A good crystal ally to hold this affirmation in your daily life is moss agate. A translucent stone with inclusions that look like moss, ferns, and other foliage, moss agate has earthy energy that draws riches to you and grounds you in stability and protection. It is also a stone of birthing, allowing a new flow of abundance to move through your life. Wearing or carrying moss agate takes the blessings of the Empress with you wherever you go.

Meditation

Choosing a tarot card and meditating on its symbols can be illuminating. Whether you use a familiar deck and find deeper meaning in its imagery or explore an unfamiliar deck and enter its world with fresh eyes, gazing at a tarot card offers a gateway through which you can pass into a new realm. When you practice this meditation using a crystal ally, you integrate the mystical with the tangible. Let's use the Star card for our example. In the Smith-Waite image, a maiden kneels beside the pool of universal conscious-ness and pours the waters of life into the pool and onto the earth, from which point the water flows outward in many directions. Above her head blaze eight stars symbolizing cosmic energy. As you meditate on this image, the qualities of the Star fill you and expand your consciousness: hope, inspiration, spiritual enlightenment.

These starry qualities are matched and magnified by the energy of celestite. This luminous blue stone reminds you that you are part of divine creation. You are made of stardust and connected to all that is. Hold a piece of celes-tite to your third eye as you meditate on the Star to fur-

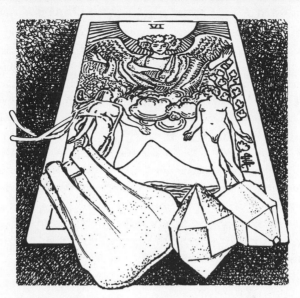

ther open your awareness of your own cosmic purpose. The stone will continue to hold that awareness for you to draw upon in times of doubt.

Spellwork

Practitioners of magic have long used stones to hold the energy of their intentions. Combining a stone's intrinsic energy with the symbolism of tarot helps bind your spell and boost its potency. Let's say you are doing a love spell to draw your soul mate to you. (As an ethical magician, of course you would never do a spell aimed at any particular person.) The Lovers card symbolizes blessed and eternal love between two people who are meant to be together, which makes it perfect as a focus for your intention. The Smith-Waite card shows a man and a woman (Adam and Eve), but other decks show same-sex couples or gender-ambiguous couples. Some decks simply depict the concept of love itself without specifying gender at all. Choose the card that best represents your desire.

After you've set up your spellworking space in the way you prefer, lay the Lovers card face up in the center and

Tarot Card	Crystal Ally	Talismanic Energy
The Fool	Aventurine	Optimism, serendipity lightheartedness
The Magician	Fluorite octahedron (double pyramid)	Unites earth and spirit; as above, so below
The High Priestess	Selenite	Intuition, wisdom, feminine mysteries
The Empress	Moss agate	Abundance, boundless love, protection
The Emperor	Tiger's eye	Leadership, positive use of power
The Hierophant	Labradorite	Spiritual authority and knowledge, ritual
The Lovers	Herkimer diamond	Union, soulmates, divine love
The Chariot	Carnelian	Success, mastery, taking control of your life
Strength	Garnet	Power from within, courage, vocation
The Hermit	Merlinite	Solitude, silence, pilgrimage
The Wheel of Fortune	Amber	Luck, good fortune, alignment with your path
Justice	Malachite	Good karma, ethics, fairness
The Hanged Man	Golden calcite	Open-mindedness, surrender, vision
Death	Obsidian	Release of grief, acceptance of loss
Temperance	Turquoise	Harmony, balance
The Devil	Moldavite	Ascent toward higher planes
The Tower	Tourmalinated quartz	Grounded transformation
The Star	Celestite	Hope, inspiration, spiritual enlightenment
The Moon	Jade	Lucid dreaming, imagination, vision quests
The Sun	Citrine	Lifts the heart into pure joy
Judgment	Aquamarine	Compassion, self-love, soul healing
The World	Amethyst	Brings integration to your fragmented self

place two Herkimer diamonds on top. Herkimer diamond isn't an actual diamond; it is a type of quartz that crystallizes in multiple terminations (points). Herkimers are usually quite small and brilliantly clear. Among their qualities is the energy of telepathic communication and soul union. Work your spell to draw the most perfect love match to you, asking the Herkimers to hold that energy for however long it takes for the spell to work. When you are done, place the two stones in a little bag and keep it with you or on your altar until such time as you meet your soul mate, when you can give one of the stones to that person to keep the Lovers energy between you clear and sparkling.

Divination (Random Choice)

Choosing tarot cards at random for divination means that the so-called negative cards can appear in your reading. The two most challenging cards are probably the Devil and the Tower. Like most responsible readers, I always look to the positive teaching of these cards rather than foreseeing doom and despair. But there is no doubt that these cards are daunting, and a likely first reaction is "uh-oh" when you flip them over. Using a crystal ally provides not only additional insight into the nature of the card but also a helpful talisman when dealing with its challenges and lessons.

The Devil represents a separation from the soul's higher energies, which may manifest as overattachment to worldly pursuits or material possessions. It can also represent addictions and harmful relationships or habits. What is needed from a crystal ally is a way to break the Devil's chains of bondage and set the spirit back on a more righteous path. One of the best stones for this is moldavite. Formed by meteoric activity, this pure green stone pulls the soul out of darkness and confusion, speeding it toward the light. Wearing or carrying moldavite helps you tap into messages from the higher realms, amplifying them to drown out unhealthy temptations and negative impulses.

The Tower card signifies abrupt and often unexpected change, which can be upsetting even if the change is positive. When what you thought was settled and sure suddenly comes tumbling down, a crystal ally can help you find your center of stability again. One of the best stones for this is tourmalinated quartz. This is clear quartz that contains threads of black tourmaline, often in what looks like a chaotic explosion. Black tourmaline is a stone that facilitates great transformation while establishing a strong energetic connection to the depths of the earth. This grounding energy is like a lightning rod that roots the powerful forces of the Tower card. The quartz crystal that holds the tourmaline adds the energies of protection, purification, and soul healing.

The chart on page 332 offers suggestions for crystal allies for the Major Arcana cards. (All of the stones listed should be easy to find at your local rock shop or online. On eBay there are many reputable rock sellers with good specimens at reasonable prices.) You can continue your exploration by connecting the Minor Arcana cards with crystal allies as well: What stone would best embody the creative fire of the Queen of Wands? Or comfort after the disappointment symbolized by the Five of Cups? By experimenting with their talismanic energies you can discover the many blessings offered by the tarot and its crystal allies.